MINING AMERICA

MINING AMERICA

The Industry and the
Environment, 1800–1980

Duane A. Smith

University Press of Colorado

TD
195
.M5
S6
1993

Published by the University Press of Colorado
P.O. Box 849
Niwot, Colorado 80544

The University Press of Colorado is a cooperative publishing enterprise supported, in part, by Adams State College, Colorado State University, Fort Lewis College, Mesa State College, Metropolitan State College of Denver, University of Colorado, University of Northern Colorado, University of Southern Colorado, and Western State College of Colorado.

Library of Congress Cataloging-in-Publication Data

Smith, Duane A.
    Mining America: the industry and the environment, 1800–1980 / Duane A. Smith.
      p. cm.
    Originally published: Lawrence, Kan.: University Press of Kansas, c1987, in series: Development of western resources.
    Includes bibliographical references and index.
    ISBN 0-87081-306-4 (pbk.)
    1. Mineral industries — Environmental aspects — United States — History. 2. Mineral industries — United States — Public opinion. 3. Public opinion — United States. 4. Mineral industries — Social aspects — United States. I. Title.
TD195.M5S6 1993
363.73'1 — dc20   93-13337
                                             CIP

10 9 8 7 6 5 4 3 2 1

For Gary Hart

CONTENTS

List of Illustrations   ix

Preface   xi

Prologue   1

1 Booming, Digging, and Dumping   5

2 "We Were Giants"   25

3 "Going to Cover Marysville Up"   42

4 "Mining Destroys and Devastates"   54

5 The Rustling Breeze of Change   67

6 "We Only Want a Square Deal"   81

7 Reprieve!   105

8 "A Tradition That Endured Far Too Long"   123

9 Environmental Whirlwind   136

10 A Vision, a Hope for the Future   149

Epilogue: The 1980s   163

Notes   171

Bibliography   189

Index   205

ILLUSTRATIONS

Hydraulic mining in California in the nineteenth century   7

Placer miners in Colorado in the 1860s   10

The impact of mining—Colorado's 10th Legion   20
Lode, 1864/65

Mining sites in the United States in the nineteenth   22
century (map)

Complete mining operation, Snowstorm Mine, Idaho   39

Hydraulic mining in Georgia, 1915   73

Butte's Berkeley Pit copper mine   76

Open-pit mining in Minnesota, 1915   87

Boston and Colorado Smelter, Black Hawk, Colorado   94

Smelter pollution in the Ducktown, Tennessee, district   97

Atlantic Copper Mill, Houghton, Michigan   100

Mining sites in the United States in the twentieth   106
century (map)

Placer mining in the 1930s: Boggs Branch Gold Mine,   120
Georgia

Coal mining in Pennsylvania in the 1970s   127

Tailings pond near Ophir Pass, Colorado   130

Dung from dredges, Colorado   138

Mine near South Pass, Wyoming   138

The heritage of placer mining—Clear Creek, Colorado   139

Relics and stream pollution from an old coal mine,   139
Northumberland County, Pennsylvania

The Urad reclamation project   166

Star Coal reclamation project, Iowa   167

Fishermen and grazing cattle on a reclaimed   167
strip-mining site

PREFACE

During the national debate over the environment in the 1960s, Indiana's Senator Vance Hartke called mining "a runaway technology, whose only law is profit, [that] has for years poisoned our air, ravaged our soil, stripped our forests bare, and corrupted our water sources." By and large, the mining industry has projected a less-than-favorable image in recent years.

The blame lies partly with long-established mining tradition, epitomized by the attitude of an early twentieth-century dredge superintendent from Breckenridge, Colorado, who tersely said, "Industry is always to be preferred to scenic beauty." An altered perception of mining has also contributed to its tarnished image. The public today does not see a mine as T. A. Rickard saw the Bunker Hill in Idaho, "more than a hole in the ground; it is an expression of hope, initiative, energy, and accomplishment; it is the fine flower of industrial achievement." Mining admits that it has contributed to environmental damage, but it should not be forced to shoulder the blame alone. As the comic strip's astute philosopher Pogo observed some years back, "We have met the enemy and he is us."

Arthur A. Ekirch hit the mark in his *Man and Nature in America*: "Man *and* nature is the basic fundamental fact of history. The relationship is mutual and necessary." However, my intent is not to approach the subject from Ekirch's broad point of view but to survey only one segment of the larger whole.

The theme of this study is the evolution of mining's attitudes toward the environment, the way that many of these attitudes have matured, and why some of them have remained stagnant over the past two centuries. The focus is on the why, not the what, of events; the objective is to give an inside view by letting mining speak for itself. Not all available examples could be included; instead, an attempt was made to present a judicious selection to illustrate trends and attitudes. It may be argued that western mining predominates in the chapters on the nineteenth century. So, in fact, it did attract most of that century's public interest and create most of its national impact. This in no way invalidates the conclusions that are drawn for the entire industry, both east and west.

One must try to understand these people and their attitudes according to the standards of their own time. By accepting the past on its own terms, as well as ours, we may gain a clearer perspective, not only of yesterday, but also of today and perhaps tomorrow.

Some readers may be disappointed that this is not an environmental history. It is not intended to be. This is mining's story, its reaction to the environment and to environmental criticism. It is hoped that readers will gain an understanding of both the practical and the philosophical sides of the industry and, through mining, acquire a better understanding of themselves and their ancestors. As trite as it may sound, the buck *does* stop with the public. How much are we willing to pay, to sacrifice, and to accept in order to protect the environment? The industry can do only so much. It can hardly be expected to lead the movement when the signals it receives from across the country are so mixed, as they have been for half a century. The pendulum sways between the dedicated environmentalist and the person who says, "We cannot be picayunish about environmental matters."

Historian Michael Malone has recently written that the mining man is a prototype of the nineteenth-century frontier capitalist, one of those who literally built the West at whatever cost. The same can be said of his contemporary eastern counterpart. Both gloried in the concept of America as the land of abundance and exploited the seemingly limitless sources of wealth over which they gained control. Throughout the national experience, America's bounty has been emphasized; this has truly been a land of abundance, and we have been a people of plenty. Our national success, as David Potter so aptly wrote in 1954, is based on the effective conversion of these resources through economic organization, technological advancement, and human endeavor. Only recently has there been broad-based concern for the environment and how it affects our cherished economic goals and the means to reach them.

The mining industry, one of the foundation stones on which America was built, includes not just that aforementioned dredge-boat superintendent; it also involves the land, which "has an emotional tie to Americans," the people, who find that "yesterday's pollution may be tomorrow's tourist attraction," and the individuals who seek dividends and the good life that mining's profits and production can provide. If there is going to be an understanding of mining's positions and its current environmental problems, it will have to grow out of past experience. The history of mining is not irretrievable; relatively speaking, the events of that history happened only yesterday and involved people no different from ourselves.

In the beginning there was the land, and the land was beautiful. Today there are "romantic" mining ruins, ghost-town sites, the steady progress of the strip miner, and a corporation-dominated industry. The land, the water, and the air have suffered. At long last, however, a large segment of Americans seems to care. Pogo has been proven right; it is always easier to point the finger of blame at someone else.

I owe a deep debt of gratitude to many people who assisted me along the way. Cooperative staffs of archives and libraries from the Library of Congress on the East Coast to the Huntington Library on the West Coast provided repeated examples of professional service and personal kindness. Friends such as Rodman Paul, Bill Gillette, Clark Spence, Allan Bird, Jon Raese, Ron Brown, Stan Dempsey, Tom Hendricks, Gene Gressley, Glen Crandall, Lyle Dorsett, John Clark, Terry Fitzsimmons, Maxine Benson, Bill Jones, and Norman Rue assisted in many ways. Janette Crandall and Catherine Conrad typed chapters, sometimes several editions' worth. A tip of the hard hat and round of thanks also to the staff of the University Press of Kansas for their generous and professional assistance. My daughter Laralee donated time to her father, and my wife, Gay, once more, was editor, critic, typist, and loving support in those "down" moments that every author endures.

This book is dedicated to a friend who also has an interest in the past, a concern for the present, and a dream for the future—Gary Hart.

PROLOGUE

A man born at the beginning of the War of 1812, had he lived his biblically allotted three score years and ten, could have participated in, witnessed, or read about the greater share of mining developments in the nineteenth century. When he reached his late teens, the thrill of gold discoveries in Georgia and North Carolina would have provided a glimpse of what would come, and in his early twenties, coal was coming to be accepted as a fuel. With much less fanfare, Pennsylvania came of age as a mining state. At about the same time, lead deposits in Illinois, Wisconsin, and Missouri attracted attention, although Missouri had a century's headstart on the other two, thanks to earlier Spanish and French efforts. Michigan's copper rush was under way when this hypothetical man reached his thirties, and the United States was moving toward the industrial age.

Up to this time, events had moved at a fairly leisurely pace, the excitement generally remained at a moderate level and local in scope, and the numbers of people involved stayed relatively small. A few brief months in 1848/49 changed everything; our mythical American had reached the age of thirty-six when the news of gold discoveries in California reached the Midwest and the East Coast. A national stirring exploded into a world-wide frenzy as one hundred thousand forty-niners dashed for pots of gold in the mother-lode country. The whole mining saga—prospecting, development, laws, camps, boom and bust—was compressed into months, sometimes weeks. Out of this tumult emerged the first mining-created state, California. After a brief period of calm, America plunged ahead. The year 1859 ushered the Comstock silver and the Pike's Peak gold rushes into American life and folklore, creating two more great western mining states, Nevada and Colorado. Almost forgotten amidst all the noise and activity were the iron mines opened in the Lake Superior region. Coal development gained momentum with the coming of railroading and the corresponding growth of American industry; iron and coal, however, did not inflame the human passion as did gold and silver.

Now in his fifties, the hypothetical American could follow one mining rush after another during the 1860s and 1870s, tempted by the lure of new bonanzas throughout the West. The newspapers abounded with rumors. In an extraordinary number of cases, the

1

rumors proved to be fact, and miners would uncover deposits that lasted a season or two, a decade or more, and sometimes indefinitely. Perhaps our observer wished to stay put somewhere east of the Mississippi River; if so, he could still have participated vicariously in the mining fever by risking a portion of his savings in mining stocks. If western stocks looked too speculative, investment opportunities beckoned in Pennsylvania coal, Michigan copper, or Missouri lead. In any case, the end result would likely be the same. The odds of making a sudden fortune were long; the chance of breaking even or less were very good. Had our friend fallen victim, in the prime of life, to the enticing call of western mining, new rushes would have called him every year to come and try his luck.

Upon reaching three score and ten, the hoary veteran would have seen mining emerge as a primary American industry, one that had become the capstone of a bustling economy and that was approaching the threshold of world significance. Thanks to mining, states on both sides of the Mississippi River had attracted jobs, businesses, promotion, and investment, as well as transportation—economic and urban development that would otherwise have come more slowly or not at all. Thanks also to mining, lands that had been wilderness or foreign territory in 1812 now were, or soon would be, states: Idaho, Montana, Colorado, Nevada, and California. Michigan, Wisconsin, and Missouri received an impetus for settlement.

The now aged citizen had witnessed a full lifetime of mining, and more was yet to unfold—copper in Montana and Utah, iron in Minnesota's Mesabi Range, gold in Alaska, more silver and gold in Nevada, and that big one, Cripple Creek gold in Colorado. Mining—the rushes, the sudden wealth, the adventure, the camps, just the difference in life styles—repeatedly warranted Americans' attention during the last half of the century. Not bad for an industry that, in 1812, was surviving more on the legend of the Spanish to the south and southwest and a few family operations scattered about the East and the Midwest than on any promise of national importance.

Mining not only produced wealth, power, and fame for the United States; it also attracted world-wide attention and investment to this underdeveloped nation, one that was sorely in need of a financial transfusion. Without mining—from coal to iron to gold—the United States could not have emerged as a world power by the turn of the century, nor could it have successfully launched its international career of the twentieth century. The Carnegies and Rockefellers, giants of the age, would have faced a hard go of it without the labor and sweat of thousands of now-nameless men digging in the bowels of the earth, blasting and hauling mineral out of dark caverns far underground in now-forgotten mines and mining districts scattered throughout the country.

All this development did not take place without disturbance—environmental, personal, economic, political, and social. Mining left behind gutted mountains, dredged-out streams, despoiled vegetation, open pits, polluted creeks, barren hillsides and meadows, a littered landscape, abandoned camps, and burned-out miners and the entrepreneurs who came to mine the miners. All for what? For the wealth of gold and silver, for the industrial power of copper, lead, and iron, and for the energy from coal—those would have been the resounding answers of our nineteenth-century friend, as he pointed proudly to the America around him.

If the siren call of profit or greed had been the sole reason and justification for all this exertion, this exploitation of natural resources, this scrambling over hill and stream, there would be little reason to continue this story. There is more to the saga than that, although it cannot be denied that the profit motive dominated thinking in the mining world of the nineteenth century, as it had before and will continue to do.

During these years, much occurred that subsequently shaped the mining industry and, to a degree, America; and prevailing attitudes of that time had a lasting impact on the industry. Neither society nor mining exists in a socioeconomic vacuum; they are interrelated and interacting.

While our nineteenth-century gentleman was concentrating on profits and mining developments, he was ignoring the significant impact that these were having on the environment. The initial focus of this study will be on that one issue; later it will broaden to include the conservation movement. The word *environment* would not have been recognized a century ago. To our friend and his generation that concept would have translated into land, water, and air, simple terms that could be readily understood. No question about it, mining (defined to include the auxiliary smelting industry) produced an impact on the land, water, and air of that day. To what effect, I will examine; this will be an analysis of the rationale that justified so much activity.

By 1900, attitudes, methods, and policies had become firmly fixed and would influence mining for several generations to come. Small segments of the press, the public, and the courts were beginning to challenge the industry's cavalier attitude toward the people, towns, land, and water that were involved in its operations, although such challenges seemed more like isolated incidents than like waves of the future.

A hundred years have passed since the wanderings of our nineteenth-century representative came to an end in some unknown graveyard. If he could somehow return, he would be amazed by the changes that have overtaken mining and, most important, by its industrial attitudes, values, and reactions to environmental questions. At the same time, he would also nod knowingly about things that seem to have changed not at all or very little. That is the concern of the last half of this study: the continuing influence of the nineteenth century and the adjustments wrought by new pressures, new concerns.

Mining cannot claim environmental sainthood for its actions over the past two centuries, but neither should it be smeared as a covetous, black-hearted, greedy sinner. The story is not that simple. We can learn much about ourselves from what took place in former years. Those actions should not be judged by standards other than those current at the time; it is not fair or historically accurate to evaluate 1820 or 1882 or 1914 solely by today's aspirations and values.

So now we bid farewell to our guide; he has served us well in tracing the route that we are going to examine in detail. When a real-life contemporary of his, Mary Hallock Foote, the wife of a mining engineer, wrote to her sister-in-law Mary Hague in May 1896, she quoted an obscure couplet by the Scottish poet George MacDonald as part of the description of her home, which was located near Grass Valley, California. Unintentionally, its words focused on the conflict that was even then welling up within mining:

> The Lightning and thunder
> They go and they come;
> But the Stars and the Stillness
> Are always at home.[1]

CHAPTER ONE

Booming, Digging, and Dumping

Today's visitor who approaches the site of a nineteenth-century mining district can usually identify it by the scars remaining from yesterday's frenzy. Some debris might also mark the location, although scrap drives, souvenir seekers, and looters have done a good job of removing what was once considered expendable. Not infrequently a stream or two, still polluted after all these years, runs past tumble-down buildings. These are the surviving visible shadows of mining that linger from the last century. A hundred years ago, the much more recognizable substance of these shadows seemed awesome to those who watched the extraordinary progress. The land existed then solely to yield its bountiful mineral blessings to onrushing Americans who had the grit and determination (and, one might add, luck) to find them.

Henry Rowe Schoolcraft, visiting the Missouri lead mines (about 60 miles southwest of St. Louis, near Potosi) in 1818, described a countryside, torn up by mining and the "constant itch for discovery, . . . winding along among pits, heaps of gravel, and spars, and other rubbish constantly accumulating at the times, where scarcely ground enough has been left undisturbed for the safe passage of the traveller, who is constantly kept in peril by unseen excavations, and falling-in pits." Two decades later, the Englishman George Featherstonhaugh toured the same Missouri districts and observed that not much had changed: "The diggings are so numerous in every direction, and the country is so wasted, that the cattle running at large frequently fall into holes."[1]

Hundreds of miles west, at about the same time, Josiah Gregg, looking over placer operations south of Santa Fe, noted: "In some places the hills and valleys are literally cut up like a honey-comb."[2] Spanish miners, who created the mess that Gregg observed, proved to be highly adept at placer mining—the extraction of free gold from its deposit in hillside, desert floor, or stream bed. Their use of the pan and the more efficient sluice to separate the heavier gold from its lighter neighbors differed little from later American methods.

The gold-mining region around Dahlonega, Georgia, drew this observation from geologist Featherstonhaugh: "All the valleys being dug up and washed gravel thrown into heaps, their beauty was

entirely destroyed, and the scene resembled a series of brickyards."
Finally, Featherstonhaugh, surveying Jamestown, North Carolina,
pictured the scene as "turned topsy-turvey by the gold diggers, who
had utterly ruined the beautiful valley for agricultural purposes."
These environmental atrocities came long before nineteenth-century
mining and technology hit full stride. The methods that created them
were the rule, not the exception, having been endorsed as the
quickest route to wealth. An 1821 report on a Pennsylvania coal mine
assured would-be purchasers that despite the mine's lying on the top
of a mountain covered with twelve feet of loose dirt, it could easily be
worked because the dirt could "be removed by cattle with scrapers,
and thrown into the valley below so as never to impede the work."[3] If
the new owners had taken the advice, they might have created one of
the first strip mines in America.

In the years following the excitement of the 1849 gold rush and
with the general development of large-scale industrial mining, visitors and miners alike left abundant testimony to mining's impact on
the land. Montana miner Henry Clark wrote his brother about
working his hillside claim near Virginia City: "Water brot in ditch and
the whole bank washed down into boxes." There it was carried out of
the way, and the pay dirt was washed over riffles. In all, concluded
this one-time Iowa farmer, "this is the prettiest mining that I ever
done." Time-consuming panning and sluicing offered limited re-
wards for the hard work involved. American ingenuity and technology, augmented by Mexican and European experience, quickly
developed more efficient, faster, and more profitable ways to uncover
the ore. The output increased accordingly, no more so than with
hydraulic mining, which is done by shooting water under high
pressure through a nozzle against a bank of gold-bearing earth.
Wrote one startled viewer:

> The effect of this continuous stream of water coming with such force
> must be seen to be appreciated; wherever it struck it tore away earth,
> gravel and boulders. . . . Hydraulic, or even sluice mining is not an
> aesthetic pursuit; the regions where it is practised may be, before the
> miner's advent, like the garden of the Lord for beauty; but after his work
> is completed, they bear no resemblance to anything, except the chaos
> which greeted the eye of the seer at the dawn of the Mosaic record of the
> rehabilitation of the earth for the use of man. . . . It is impossible to
> conceive of anything more desolate, more utterly forbidding, than a
> region which has been subjected to this hydraulic mining treatment.

Linus Brockett could not have described the effects more accurately,
his Victorian bombast aside. Hydraulic mining never was defined as

California miners developed hydraulic mining to the state of the art in the nineteenth century. The search for gold pushed all other considerations aside (courtesy Western History Department, Denver Public Library).

an ''aesthetic pursuit.'' It rearranged everything it came into contact with: land surface, vegetation, streams, and the ''whole vista.''[4]

Even the influential mining reporter Rossiter Raymond, more perceptive of environmental matters than most of his generation, supported ''booming,'' a real ecological horror, in his 1872 federal mining report as commissioner of mining statistics:

> During the past season the process of ''booming'' has been inaugurated in Summit County [Colorado]. This consists in collecting water in a proper reservoir, of large capacity, and discharging a great volume of it at once, thereby removing an amount of gravel impracticable by any other means. Notwithstanding the great volume of water used, and the amount of gravel kept in motion in the flume in a state of thick mud, the results seem favorable as regards the collection of gold. Large areas of

ground can be worked by this method, which cannot be mined profitably by other ways. Ground which, by ordinary hydraulic process, pays $3 per day to the hand, can be made to yield $25 a day. The extensive application of "booming" to many of the gulches of Summit County cannot fail to raise the gold-yield of the county.[5]

Booming (Californians called it "flooding"), hydraulicking, and, later, dredging proved to be the most destructive methods of their day, with strip mining gaining rapidly during the last years of the century.

Hard-rock or deep mining was more common throughout the country, as miners burrowed into the mountainsides in search of coal, gold, silver, lead, copper, or whatever mineral struck their fancy at the moment. Its methods also produced multiple impacts, the most noticeable of which were water seepage, mine dumps, and scarred landscapes. Artist and writer Mary Hallock Foote followed her mining engineer husband Arthur into various mining districts. After examining California's New Almaden quicksilver mine, she concluded that if the work continued with the same vigor, the mountain in question might someday be nothing but emptiness—"a huge nutshell, emptied of its kernel." Coming west in 1866 on an inspection tour for the army's quartermaster department, James Rusling took time to visit several mining areas. Of the Central City, Colorado, district he said the ranges had been prospected "until they seemed honey-combed or like pepper-boxes, so ragged and torn were they with the process. He [the miner] digs and tunnels pretty much as he wills—under roads, beneath houses, below towns—and all things, more or less are made subservient to his will."[6] In that last statement Rusling scored a bull's-eye on why such activities were permitted: they were "subservient," a topic to be explored in the ensuing chapters.

John Muir, after visiting Nevada and California mining districts, left with an ambivalent attitude, displaying both grudging respect and critical awareness, which was surprising in a young man who had already come to appreciate the western landscape. He described Nevada's White Pine District as a place where miners covered the ground like grasshoppers, seemingly determined by their very violence to turn every stone to silver. This violent disruption left behind only ruins to testify to the tremendous energy expended. Muir, who was not particularly impressed with Nevada, described it: "Mining discoveries and progress, retrogression and decay, seem to have been crowded more closely against each other here than in any other portion of the globe." California miners, he believed, had been less destructive, probably because they had recovered from "the first attacks of mining fever'' while ''crawling laboriously'' across the plains. In his conclusion, Muir saw hope for the future: a ''vast amount of real work is being done, and the ratio between growth and decay is constantly becoming finer.''[7]

Muir's observations about California would be challenged, and he himself would modify his 1870s attitude about mining's romance and contributions. All the impacts that he described could be seen wherever miners and prospectors tramped and dug, more so in the West than elsewhere, because here mining opened and settled the land all at once under the public's eye and the journalist's pen. The panning, digging, dumping, and moving were industrial compo-nents essential to the everyday work of recovering ore.

The unintentional impact proved to be hardly less disruptive, as settlement came to the wilderness. Sometimes an accident caused grief, as described by a discouraged California miner, Charles Harvey, when he wrote to his parents in September 1850. He and his partners had worked for weeks building a dam to store water to work their company's claims. They turned the Yuba River out of its bed, only to fail to find enough gold to make ''day wages.'' Then their dam, which ''had risen the water over six feet and had backed the water up several miles,'' gave way and destroyed their work of months, as well as that of others whose claims were inundated before the crest of the flood passed.[8] That calamity ruined Harvey's season, changed the course of the river, and washed sediment down to the valley below.

What was seen by Muir, Foote, and the others displayed only the tip of a huge mining iceberg; like its cold counterpart, most of mining's destructive potential lay hidden and uncomprehended at the time. One could observe a mining dump easily enough, along with scarred hillsides and dug-out stream beds. Less obvious were the more subtle repercussions of mining's advance.

Murky stream water was apparent to even the most casual observer, who was less likely to perceive the ramifications of those foreign particles that engulfed once-sparkling streams. Stream pollu-tion came from two basic sources, either the direct fouling of the water from tailings or waste, or the draining of water from mines. Both mines and mills received the blame, and justly so.

Comments on the problem became numerous. Riding along the Blue River in Colorado's high country beyond Breckenridge, news-paper editor and writer Samuel Bowles lamented that the Blue was no longer blue. It was, instead, a mud color, thanks to the local placer mining. And a Michigan visitor was shocked by the situation at Central City: ''The water had been rendered unfit for use by the

With pick and pan, shovel and sluice (shown here), miners attacked the land in search of gold. These placer miners are working in Gilpin County, Colorado, sometime in the 1860s (courtesy Western History Department, Denver Public Library).

numerous mines and gulches along its course. At Central City the water supply, once abundant and pure, is now utterly destroyed by the mining interests." Alexander McClure concurred when he viewed the muddy water of Montana's Alder Gulch, and he went on to note that where clear water flowed, it was "densely peopled with the finny tribe."[9]

When Mark Twain worked briefly at a stamp mill near Aurora, Nevada, he observed streams of dirty water steadily flowing from the pans to be "carried off in broad wooden troughs to the ravine." Where they went, he did not speculate. Neither did a writer who visited the lead district of Galena, Illinois. Water, he said, was the greatest problem the miner faced; fortunately, it could be pumped out of the mines. Not always a costly inconvenience, water proved useful in washing the ore, the residue in this case going down some unnamed Illinois stream. Coal mines in Pennsylvania also faced problems with water and solved them by draining it away from the workings to some other place. Where it went did not concern the owners. Forty years after Georgia's gold excitement, its rivers still ran "chocolate-tinted" from milling and mining.[10] Water, scarce in some districts, a problem in many more, was handled much as any other obstacle—immediate needs superseded any long-range impact.

Miners occasionally comprehended the damage they perpetrated. The experienced mining reporter J. Ross Browne decided that the "deleterious" quality of the water in Virginia City, Nevada, after it filtered through mineral and mine, helped cause the prevailing sickness.[11] Drinking water engendered far more concern than did any other issue and created a cruel dichotomy: pure water and perhaps no mining, or poor water and a thriving economy.

Leadville, Colorado, with its population of 15,000, confronted a health crisis during the late 1870s; two of the three assumed causes were too much lead in the drinking water and the smelter smoke, which contained "arsenic, bismuth, lead and other poisons."[12] The smoke problem could be seen and smelled, if not completely understood. Smelting and milling did affect the environment; their industrial effluents fell on all employees of the industry and on those who lived near the plants.

Ducktown, in a copper-mining region of southeastern Tennessee, became infamous for roasting its ores. Carl Henrich, who visited there in 1896, bluntly stated that no civilized community ought to be afflicted with the continuous dissemination of scores of tons of sulfurous acid gas. Butte, Montana, which will be examined in more detail later, also gained notoriety for its smoky atmosphere. Mining engineer John Mackenzie remarked that the air was so loaded with sulfurous smoke during the mid 1880s that people could hardly find their way on the streets at times. He left in 1886 to seek purer air because the smoke made his throat so sore. Furnaces that worked mercury ore in California were forced to offer higher wages to induce men into employment. "Sulphurous acids, arsenic, vapors of mercury, etc., make a horrible atmosphere, which tells fearfully on the health of the workmen," commented Professor William Brewer, who toured the quicksilver mines in 1861. J. Ross Browne smelled the same "noxious odor," which had a very "pernicious effect upon the nervous system." Persons of "delicate, nervous organization" were peculiarly subject to being injuriously affected by mercury fumes, Browne concluded.[13] Perhaps this category excluded most of the men who gambled their health for higher wages.

Whether early or late in the century, smelting went on with little attention being given to the control of smoke emission. Schoolcraft watched the cheap, simple Missouri method of smelting lead in open air "log furnaces" to burn the sulfur off, followed by several washings of the lead ashes, then resmelting. The Boston and Colorado Smelter, nearly sixty years later, roasted heaps of ore for six weeks, driving off smoke containing "considerable arsenic."[14]

This roasting did not enhance Black Hawk, Colorado, and the surrounding countryside, and its effects were readily perceived by travelers into the valley, as these three reactions illustrate:

> The road enters a gulch filled with sulphurous vapors, highly suggestive of the infernal regions. [A tourist publication]
>
> What a glorious time pilgrims had in struggling with these sulphurous fumes, as the lumbering heavy coach dragged its way at a snail's pace up the steep grade, past huge piles of roasting pyrites! . . . this entertainment was forced upon all men and beasts.
>
> Immense smelting works fill the atmosphere with coal dust and darkness. One mill at our right is sending forth volumes of blackness from *seventeen* huge smoke stacks.[15]

Black Hawk earned a reputation for cough-compelling odors, as did its counterparts elsewhere.

Despite denials of the toxic quality of these fumes, they killed vegetation and animals, endangered human health, and clouded the scenery. One-time California miner Charles Harvey, who was residing in Denver in 1879, wrote his family about a visit to the Argo works, then the pride of Denver and one of the most advanced in the country:

> [It is] the largest works of the kind it is said in the world. They finish ore there ready to be sent right to the mint to be coined or sold as the June metal. The smoke from their furnaces darkens the sky in that direction at all times, and with a wind drifts the smoke the way the wind blows so that it is a mist of cloud moving along and it seems to me that about all the clouds we have here come from that smoke.[16]

Mining and smelting, along with this whole generation of Americans, consumed cords of wood. The trees came down indiscriminately. In the East the large expanse of forests and the faster utilization of coal kept expenses lower and concern minimal, but this was not true in the West. Here freight costs slowed the introduction of coal and often raised the cost of mining, as scarce wood had to be transported for miles before reaching its destination. Forests were denuded in the relentless search for more wood. No place displayed this consequence better than Nevada's booming Comstock in the 1860s and 1870s.

William Wright, better known to his contemporaries as Dan De Quille, wrote: "The Comstock lode may truthfully be said to be the tomb of the forests of the Sierras. Millions on millions of feet of lumber are annually buried in the mines, nevermore to be resurrected." Though no one knows for sure exactly how much was used for timbering and fuel, one calculation was 600 million feet of timber and more than 2 million cords of wood. Other estimates range to even higher figures, a prodigious amount, no matter how measured. An idea of the extent of devastation can be better comprehended by imagining how many homes might have been built had this lumber gone into construction; Elliot Lord estimated thirty thousand two-story frame houses. Fortunately, few other districts matched the Comstock's consumption.[17]

While most people were shaking their heads in wonder and calling this ravaging of the forests an example of American hard work and initiative, De Quille was speaking out against it. He and a few others grasped that this kind of progress took its toll. First, Mount Davidson, which towered over the Comstock mines, was trimmed of its sparse growth; even the stumps were dug up for firewood. Nearby hills and mountains fell to the saw soon afterward. De Quille feared that the Sierra Nevada range, adjacent to the Comstock, would be "utterly denuded of trees of every kind." He noticed that the first spell of hot weather swept nearly all the snow from the mountains, sending it into the valley in one great flood. Pines had previously sheltered the snow, allowing a more gradual melting and guaranteeing a good volume of water throughout the summer and fall months. Finally, this perceptive newspaperman predicted that the loss of trees and snow fields would increase the summer heat, where once these natural phenomena had cooled the breezes.[18]

This degree of concern was atypical. Quite the opposite attitude prevailed—forests that hindered mining should be removed. Fires, whether intentional or caused by carelessness, consumed forested mining districts throughout the country. Westerners saw them as a way to foster prospecting. That philosophy prompted the exasperated and furious Rossiter Raymond to explode: "Tracks of prospectors can be everywhere seen by blackened trunks and lifeless, desolate-looking hillsides." In his 1870 mining report, he lashed out: "I desire to call attention particularly to one of the worst abuses attendant upon the settlement of the mining regions and other portions of the West. I allude to the wanton destruction of timber." He went on to decry overcutting, uneconomical use, and the plain waste of timber in the name of mining. Where would it all end? Raymond concluded that "the answer of denuded hillsides, of the dismal wastes upon the mountain slopes, with their millions of charred trunks and ghostly whitened branches, is terribly suggestive."[19]

Roads needed to be built to reach the mines, freight the ore, and haul the wood. Some of them exemplified the marvels of engineering; most of them also offered breath-taking vistas for travelers; and all dug relentlessly into the land. Except for the weather, perhaps, no other topic was more discussed—and cussed—than the condition of the roads. Unlike the weather, though, something could be done about this problem, and great effort went into building roads, some of which remain the favorite paths of jeep drivers and hikers today.

With little regard for the land, except to be sure that the grades were not too steep, the road builders crossed deserts, valleys, mountainsides, and meadows without restraint. Vegetation was stripped away, obstacles were dug or blasted out and thrown aside, and streams were bridged or forded. That it might take decades or a century to heal these scars caused no concern; that erosion resulted was of little interest, unless it obstructed travel; that these rivulets might become man-made rivers during the spring runoff or after summer showers generated no anxiety, aside from the possible deterrent to travelers. These defacements, combined with the drainage and pumping from the mines and with the lowering or changing of the water table, affected the long-range ecological balance of the district. Those little roads, harmless enough in conception and certainly imperative, precipitated both immediate and long-term impacts. So did the railroad, as it slashed and cut its way to the profitable mining camps and mines.

Meanwhile, the miners continued to sully their own occupation through carelessness. Schoolcraft observed this phenomenon early in the century in Missouri. The roads through the lead mines generally were good, he believed, but after heavy and continuous rains the ground softened. The wagons loaded with lead were then "particularly injurious," cutting up the road and gullying it. Miners near Dahlonega, Georgia, in 1879, were no more considerate. They built dams to divert water and ditches to carry it to their property.[20] The fact that a ditch crossed a road raised no fuss, except when some vehicle passed over it and an angry miner had to make repairs to his conveyance.

Water ditches were another outgrowth of mining, particularly of placer and hydraulic operations. Raymond estimated that by 1870, Californians had dug over six thousand miles of water courses for mining purposes. These courses cut into hillsides, were subject to leakage and collapse, thus causing damage to the land, and brought changes in stream flow and loss of water through evaporation. Essential to local mining, they had been built at great effort and at a cost that Raymond judged to be over $15 million.[21]

If all these things affected the land, they also touched the animals, birds, and fish. For reasons that ranged from attempts to circumvent the time and trouble of fishing by dropping a stick of dynamite into the water and then selecting the best from among the stunned and dead fish (this appalled many people and was generally frowned upon) to the introduction of pollution and the change of the water flow, streams in mining regions no longer supported the fish population that they once had contained, and some were already dead to any form of life. Irving Howbert noted, for example, that trout inhabited all streams in the Hamilton, Colorado, area except where placer mining had either killed them or driven them to clearer streams. Smelter smoke either stilled the song or drove away many of the mountain birds. Mines and hunters who supplied the meat markets stalked game animals, and everything, it turned out, became fair game, even chipmunks. Miner Benjamin Marsh wrote to his wife that he had been trapping chipmunks near Silverton, Colorado. "They were about to take our grub and I took them." Deer, elk, and other large animals more readily fell victim to the gun or to the destruction of their habitat until they nearly disappeared. T. A. Rickard (he never seems to have used his given name, Thomas), taking a sentimental journey back to the Colorado San Juans, where he cut his teeth as mining superintendent for the Enterprise mine at Rico, commented that the once-abundant game were gone from the area.[22] This observation, made just after the turn of the century and hardly a decade after he had worked there, showed the speed of mining's impact.

At the same time, the garbage that littered mines and camps tempted smaller animals to rummage for meals (Marsh's problem at Silverton), creating a nuisance and a health hazard. A mining community without rats and mice would have been rare indeed. These disruptions changed the natural balance of animals for years to come.

Neither mining nor the people who were involved in it invented refuse. Americans of their generation and before marked the advance of the frontier with litter, from the Atlantic to the Pacific; these new entrepreneurs simply brought with them to mining their already entrenched habits. So they continued to scatter debris, and mining left a trail across the continent and north to Alaska.

Several examples will illustrate the extent of the desecration on the landscape. A visitor to Auraria, Georgia, in the late 1870s noticed that broken dams and ruined bridges bore witness to the excitement of a previous generation. In California during the 1850s, the discerning New Englander Dame Shirley (pseudonym of Louise Amelia Clappe) drew an unforgettable picture of mining's remains. Looking out of her cabin window at Indian Bar, north of Marysville on the

Feather River, in November, 1852, she saw only a large gravel pile, which, by standing on tiptoe, she could barely peer over. The effort allowed her, she wrote, to observe a "hundred other large piles of gravel— . . . excavations of fearful deepness, innumerable tents, calico hovels, shingle palaces." Indian Bar looked like a town dump that had been brought into town, "thickly peppered with empty bottles, oyster cans, sardine boxes, and brandied fruit jars, the harsher outlines of which are softened off by the thinnest possible coating of radiant snow."[23] Dame Shirley reported her observations in a somewhat offhand manner, seeming not to be particularly upset by them.

The view from her cabin illustrated that generation's prodigal attitude toward nature and toward man-made resources. It was estimated that two of every three coal arks that were sent down the Susquehanna River in Pennsylvania prior to the 1820s failed to reach their destination; they either sank in the rapids or fell victim to some other accident. Quicksilver was lost in Nevada mills at a rate that De Quille could only conclude was "very great." The spills not only cost money; they also poisoned everything with which they came into contact. The mills always lost a certain percentage of the ore they treated; it went out with the tailings and down the streams. Visiting Colorado in May, 1865, the future smelter entrepreneur Nathaniel Hill was shocked at the waste, writing that the territory needed a method of treating ores so that "at least" 50 percent of the gold could be saved. This particular problem usually peaked when a new district was opened or where one or more processes were being tested to find the one that would work. Mine owners could not afford to tolerate this type of waste for very long.[24]

Miners themselves wasted their ore. Low-grade ore, which they could not treat profitably, went out on the dump. J. Ross Browne, commenting about this procedure at Bodie, California, said that most of the wealth was lost, since there was always more low-grade than high-grade ore. While visiting Colorado in 1871, the midwesterner John Tice was dismayed over the way in which the individual extracted paying quantities of ore at the least possible expense, "regardless of how much he wastes." In a muckraking attack on the kings of the Comstock bonanza and on speculators in mining stock, an admittedly biased reporter pulled no punches in summarizing mining's waste: "The waste of energy, physical and mental, and of capital gained in other pursuits, has palsied the public pulse and strewn the cost with human wrecks." Not content with branding the whole industry as wasteful, this unknown writer went on to say, "The flash that dazzled with its glare was brief in its brilliancy, leaving after it darkness and obsolation.''[25] Carried away in his syntax but on target with his sentiments, this writer accurately described the appalling waste. Later miners redeemed their forebears in some respects by reworking old dumps with better processes, which allowed a profit on low-grade ore. The same happened with mill and smelter tailings piles.

Even with the experiences of a century of mining upon which to profit, prospectors and miners had not learned. The rush to Alaska and the Klondike, in 1897 and later, ended the frontier period of mining. Comments from participants showed that what happened there proved to be little different from what had happened in Georgia, California, or Colorado during an earlier era.

Digging in the tundra was hard work and foul smelling, complained Joseph Grinnell, who mined near Nome. Those obstacles, however, did not thwart him or his friends as they scrambled for gold. A miner at Council City described how the tundra was torn and hacked off, leveled, and ditched, while the creek was diverted into sluice boxes and the tailings were washed out over the land. Machinery, tents, waste, and boxes lay scattered for miles on the beaches of Nome, by-products of the rush.[26] North to Alaska the miners carried with them the same habits, the same full-speed-ahead determination, and the same attitudes of disdain toward the land and the water that supported them.

One thing the miners carried with them to Alaska—and everywhere else by the turn of the century—was improved industrial technology. The nineteenth century thrived on such progress. Shovel-and-pan placer mining evolved into clanging dredge buckets in only a few years in Alaska, which contrasts with the several generations that the process took earlier in California. By 1900 the "jackass" prospector and the hand-driven tunnel seemed as outdated as the commercial sailing ship. Mining had become highly industrialized by then, with integrated production, processing, transportation, and, in some cases, even a distribution system under one corporation. The "hard-rock stiff" found himself in a new world, one in which the cost to the environment and to humans meant little when weighed against the total benefits to be derived.

Advanced technology obviously could force a greater impact on the environment. A dredge could tear up a valley faster and more completely than a hundred or so placer miners, panning and sluicing, could do it. A strip mine threatened a more devastating environmental nightmare than did its cousin, the hard-rock mine. The technology that allowed the low-grade, large-volume mine to operate successfully also created a huge dump at the mine site and an unsightly pile of tailings at the mill. So high was the price of progress destined to be.

The immediate impact of mining proved not always to be visual nor long-term. Although mining-created noise no longer can be heard crashing down the canyons, thundering over hillsides, and echoing across valleys, it used to produce a sizable volume of aural pollution. Dame Shirley complained at Rich Bar, also on the Feather River, about the din from the flume and the machinery, which "keeps up the most dismal moaning and shrieking all the livelong night—painfully suggestive of a suffering child." Of Virginia City, Nevada, Mark Twain wrote, "Often we felt our chairs jar, and heard the faint boom of a blast down in the bowels of the earth under the office."[27] Blasting on or near the surface produced even more vibrations and resounding racket. Hoists straining, pumps laboring, steam engines whistling, anvils clanging, men shouting—these were the thousand sounds of mining, the clamor produced by American industry at full throttle. Wagons rumbling up and down the mountain trails, burros and mules braying their music, and the commotion of people going about their daily tasks—all added to the hubbub.

If that din failed to catch one's attention, the clank of the stamp mill as it crushed the ore surely would have. To some it was the exciting sound of progress: "The music of its twelve stamps was first heard by happy ears," happy because every district yearned for its own mill. Without one, mining beyond the placer stage faced expensive handicaps. Its music, however, generated noise pollution of the loudest decibels. De Quille thought the roar of Niagara Falls was a faint murmur compared to the "deafening noise of sixty stamps" in full operation. Throughout the mill itself, raucous sounds made conversation almost impossible. Before going on to fortune with his railroad cars, George M. Pullman tried mining in Colorado's Central City region. He attempted to describe the sounds:

> I imagine it would be somewhat astonishing to a person that had never heard of the existence of gold in these mountains who might be traveling through and come suddenly into this vicinity *some dark night* where his ears would be greeted with the whistles from a hundred *Steam Engines* and the noise of all the machinery attached. I think he would be apt to consider himself in close proximity to the *infernal regions*.[28]

It should not be surprising, considering the cavalier attitude that mining men held toward the environment, that such a philosophy often carried directly over into their treatment of their miners. They stubbornly refused to recognize the industrial hazards to the safety and health of their workers, much as their contemporaries had failed to do in the Pittsburgh steel mills or in the New York City garment district. Profits ruled, and technological improvements were judged against that standard, with no regard to personal dangers.

As the nineteenth century slipped by, this particular problem increased in proportion to the growing dominance of corporation control and technological improvements. When a miner was someone whom the owner worked alongside of and knew personally, there was a one-on-one relationship; when the miner became merely a day laborer on a shift, and one that was fairly easy to replace, their relationship became an entirely different matter. So, too, the introduction of the machine drill (which was not called a widow maker out of love for it) improved the capability for more daily tonnage; it also compounded the already high risks of hard-rock mining with a cloud of razor-sharp dust particles. Inadequate safety precautions, combined with ignorance and carelessness, converted the technological breakthrough of electricity into one of the more dangerous mining innovations. Thus it went, year after year, as mining modernized.[29]

The callousness of industrialists and their superintendents permeated their work and business ethic. For the moment, though, little disturbed their complacency. They concluded that progress and profit justified the costs, both environmental and human. After examining the mining industry, the *Mining and Scientific Press* for October 7, 1862, was moved to say, "Our progress has been wonderful, but we, ourselves, cannot believe or surmise what mighty strides we will make in a few years to come." This progress was shown in mines, mills, roads, railroads, and camps. Along with the neighboring mines, each community also put its imprint on the environment, polluting and littering in the name of "fabulous, unparalleled" progress and riches. Mining camps and towns came in a variety of sites and sizes. The 1870 census takers, for illustration, reported these population figures: Hiko, Nevada, 54; Rich Bar, California, 200; Dahlonega, Georgia, 471; Virginia City, Montana, 867; Central City, Colorado, 2,360; Mineral Point, Wisconsin, 3,275; and Pottsville, Pennsylvania, 12,384.

In the transitory life of these communities, too few people concerned themselves with permanence and with making a lasting home; hence, it was all the easier to go about one's own business without worrying about the consequences. As a result, the camps added to the environmental destruction, although most of their impact lies beyond the scope of this study.

Mining life was transitory. Scores of abandoned districts, hundreds of ghost towns, and thousands of failed or gutted mines testify

A classic view of the impact of mining—denuded hillsides, litter, roads running hither and yon. This is Colorado's 10th Legion Lode, near Empire, in 1864/65 (courtesy 1st Federal Savings, Denver).

to this. Observing the Mineral Point, Wisconsin, lead district in 1837, Featherstonhaugh concluded,

> With but few exceptions, the diggings for metal were quite superficial; such a thing as a steam-engine, to drain a shaft or hoist out the "mineral," as it was called, was unknown here; so that, as soon as the superficial diggings were exhausted, the population was always prepared to flock to another quarter. . . . Men do not always seem to select situations in that country with a view to live tranquilly and happily, but to try to find ready money by digging for it, or to live upon others; the moment they find there is no likelihood of success, they go to another place.[30]

His conclusion would have fit nearly every nineteenth-century mining rush. To be sure, the few Homestake-type mines (Lead, South Dakota) that are still operating after a century and the communities that continue to struggle for existence substantiate a more permanent nature; but they display more the exception than the rule.

This transience was obvious, even at the apex of nineteenth-century mining activity. The frontier ebbed and flowed, leaving behind relics of waste, extravagance, and lost dreams. People back then were just as fascinated by the past as they are today, and in some cases, they were equally as appalled by the squandering of materials, effort, and, especially, money. Traveling between Georgetown and Idaho Springs, Colorado, in 1869, a newspaper reporter for the *Colorado Miner* sharply criticized those "costly monuments" of previous mining: "These 'compliments to the dead' will not be found to resemble marble, nor nothing grand and imperishable, but rather will they be found after the pattern of ruined and *ruinous* mills, surrounded by old rusty machinery, and decked with scattered fortunes." Erected "years ago" (probably five at the most) by men who had no more idea of what was needed "than the man in the moon has of what is going on in the Georgetown policy court room," these relics represented, to reporters and others, an indifference that hurt the district's efforts to raise outside funds.[31]

In that same year (1869), a Yale professor of agriculture, William Brewer, while on a Colorado mountain-climbing expedition, happened to visit Buckskin Joe, which was barely seven years old. The "old town" intrigued him:

Such places have a sort of fascination for me—the old signboards in the streets, the roofless houses, the grass growing in the old hearthstones and flowers nestling in the nooks of mudded walls—or broken chimneys, the multitudes of empty fruit cans, sardine boxes, etc., lying in the streets, bits of old saddles, rusty prospecting pans, old shovels, the stamps from mills—in fact, all the varied implements of a city rusting and rotting neglected.

Brewer concluded that one often heard of the West's rapid growth, rarely of "these declines, which are more common than public men dare tell of."[32]

A decade later in Nevada, John Muir pictured similar desolation, the remains of mining that had moved on to more promising discoveries:

Wander where you may throughout the length and breadth of this mountain-barred wilderness, you everywhere come upon these dead mining towns, with their tall chimney-stacks, standing forlorn amid broken walls and furnaces, and machinery half buried in sand, the very names of many of them already forgotten amid the excitement of later discoveries, and now known only through tradition—tradition ten years old.[33]

This, then, was the mining frontier, its urban offspring, and its industrial descendant, each of which affected the land, the water, and the air around it and colored the attitudes and actions of the people who arrived to make their fortunes and fame. Many of these people moved on, but some lived out their allotted years involved in the mining industry in some way. For them, the impermanence evolved

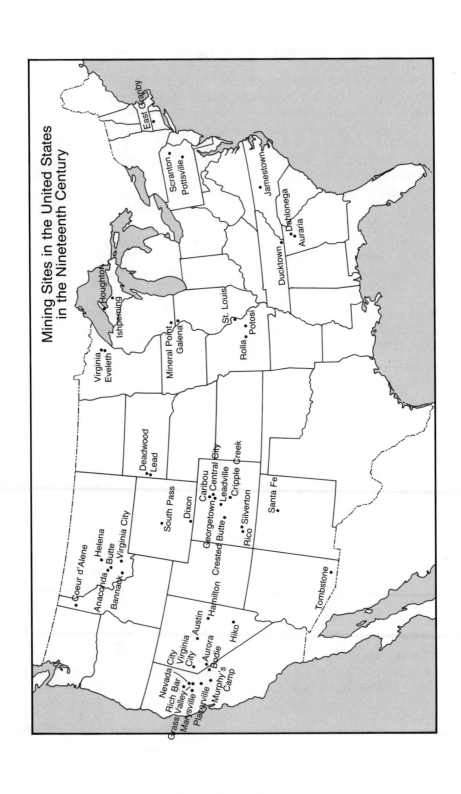

Mining Sites in the United States
in the Nineteenth Century

East Granby

Scranton
Pottsville

Jamestown

Dahlonega
Auraria

Ducktown

Houghton
Ishpeming

Virginia
Eveleth

Mineral Point
Galena

St. Louis

Rolla
Potosi

Deadwood
Lead

Caribou
Central City

Georgetown
Leadville

Cripple Creek

Cresteed Butte

Rico
Silverton

Santa Fe

South Pass

Dixon

Coeur d'Alene

Helena
Anaconda
Butte
Virginia City

Bannack

Hamilton

Austin

Virginia
City

Aurora
Bodie

Hiko

Murphy's
Camp

Tombstone

Nevada City

Rich Bar
Grass Valley
Marysville
Placerville

into a way of life, which was filled with failure and occasionally crowned by success.

One wonders whether they comprehended the impact that they had on the environment. Some—like Dame Shirley, Rossiter Raymond, and Dan De Quille—obviously did. Yet even they, who simply reported what they felt or saw, often lacked a deep concern or a total awareness of the implications. Mining fit into a larger picture, the settlement of the land and the development of American industry. Because of its position, the few who spoke against its depredations seemed to be out of step with reality, with progress, with American development—prophets without followers and little honored by their own generation.

An indication of the lack of concern for the environment became evident in the mining-district and state laws that evolved. No attempt was made to curb the free development of one's opportunities for the sake of the environment; protecting the rights of others who were threatened by pollution was the only criterion. Minnesota's mining law of 1867 was typical. It dealt with such traditional topics as organizing mining districts, the size of claims, and the abandonment of claims. From New York to Alaska, nineteenth-century mining laws remained silent on environmental issues. The 1869 and 1870 Pennsylvania and the 1874 Ohio laws on coal mining, for instance, made no mention of what could be termed environmental matters. Both provided for a mine inspector, whose duties included responsibilities for inspecting mines and mine machinery and for reporting on accidents, but not pollution. Idaho's legislature created the office of inspector of mines in 1895, which covered such duties as collecting statistics and making annual reports. The Colorado constitutional convention in 1875/76 organized the Committee on Mines and Mining, eight of whose nine members came from mining counties. Their deliberations produced sections on mining ventilation, the prohibition of child labor, and the creation of a commissioner of mines. The only discussion that touched on environmental issues involved a statement that the general assembly "may" make mine-drainage regulations. In spite of Butte's infamous smelter smoke, Montana's Constitutional Convention discussed the matter only in relation to making the city the state capital. Some states, such as Georgia and Virginia, developed no "mining legislation of a general kind."

The same pattern emerges in an examination of western laws for mining districts. Little evidence suggests that miners worried about water, timber, land, or air beyond their immediate needs or concerns. The Sugar Loaf District in Boulder County, Colorado, offers an example of one that did. As early as April, 1860, a person who set a fire, either through negligence or deliberation, was guilty of a misdemeanor. Needless to say, enforcement of the law failed to equal its intent.[34]

Here, in the most rudimentary type of democracy in the mining industry, was the perfect chance for some group to speak out about its concerns. If someone did boldly sally forth, his neighbors either voted him down for heresy or did not worry about enforcement and continued their freewheeling methods of making a fortune from nature's abundance.

The nineteenth-century mining industry, from Alaska to Mexico and from California to Georgia, dug and dumped, consumed and wasted, and polluted and altered the environment. From its captains to the lowliest coal miner, the industry was characterized by a general lack of concern for what was taking place around it, either from the short- or the long-range perspective. It acted in a prodigal fashion, almost as if it proclaimed for itself the blessing of divine right.

The justification that underlay its actions developed right along with the industry, and some of its roots went back for generations. Assuming that mining men took time to seek some justification—a risky assumption at best—actions still spoke more loudly than words in their world.

CHAPTER TWO

"We Were Giants"

The action and the impact proved to be easy enough for visitor and mining man alike to see; rarely did either of them stop to consider, beyond progress and profit, why the environment—land, water, and air—received such shabby treatment. Nor was this attitude unusual in the nineteenth century; not many American farmers, miners, or town builders gave consideration to the environment if a dollar could be made.

Mining's onslaught, railroading's rush to everywhere, and lumbering's freewheeling cutting all turned previously useless commodities into valuable resources, not unlike the dream of the alchemist in the Middle Ages who sought to turn lead into gold. Greed dominated both eras.

In the minds of many, greed and action, mixed with a generous portion of American mechanical ingenuity, provided all the justification required for exploitation. They needed only to glance at the increasingly impressive production statistics that were featured in weighty government tomes to indulge in self-congratulation. Coal tonnage jumped from 40 million in 1870 to 270 million thirty years later. Gold production in 1848, the first year of the California rush, was 484,000 troy ounces; by 1900 it had reached 3,800,000. Copper's spectacular increase topped both of these, from 8,000 tons in the 1860s to 367,000 in the 1900s.

Mining contributed mightily to accelerating American growth, to underwriting American industrialization, to shaping the American economy, and to creating modern America, a twentieth-century world power. As hardly insignificant side effects, the industry helped to open and settle the West, promoted urbanization, and fulfilled the American dream of opportunity and a better life for hundreds of thousands of people.

This was one dream that the miners underground shared with the men aboveground and with the distant stockholders; the opportunity to make money motivated all of them. No other justification prompted mental exertion among the multitudes. Those who chose to go beyond production, profit, and nationalism collected a conglomeration of fact, fancy, reality, and legend and bequeathed it to future generations. This heritage would both shape an industry and survive the trials of the next century.

The actions of both the mine owners and the miners seemed logical to them—they were simply doing the same things that they and nearly everyone else around them had always done. There seemed no reason to tamper with accepted practice. American ingenuity and hard work would pull them through should any trouble arise. They surely did not consider themselves a product of the past, even though miners had behaved similarly for centuries.

The heritage that they handed to their generation was as old as mining itself. Pliny the Elder, writing in his *Natural History* about A.D. 75, could have been describing a hydraulic operation of eighteen centuries later when he pictured the violent stream of water used for mining purposes: "Thus is the shattered mountain washed away." In discussing a gold-mining operation, which involved undermining a hill, Pliny wrote:

> Then all at once . . . the mountain cleaveth in sunder, and making a long chink, falleth down with such a noise and crack as is beyond the conceit of man's understanding, with so mighty a puff and blast of wind besides, as it is incredible. Whereat these miners and pioneers are nothing troubled . . . they stand with joy to behold the ruin of Nature's works, which they have forced.[1]

Pliny thought he knew why men would labor in that fashion: "There is nothing more stubborn in existence—except indeed the greed for gold, which is the most stubborn of all things . . . they stand with joy to behold the ruin of Nature's works." That statement speaks volumes about attitudes from Roman times to modern days.

As mining took on new significance in the mercantile world of the sixteenth and seventeenth centuries, critics made their appearance. English poets rose to defend Mother Earth against the depredations of mining. In the 1590s Edmund Spenser, in his masterpiece, *The Faerie Queene,* wrote about the two great sins against earth— avarice and lust—and about despoilment by greed. Seventy years later, John Milton hammered away at a similar theme in book 1 of *Paradise Lost.* Men, he lamented, "rifled the bowels of their mother Earth, For treasures better hid." The metaphysical John Donne vigorously supported the position of these two great English poets.[2] In the end, all of them lost this round; mining came to be viewed as a means of improving the human condition and of stimulating commercial activity. The battle had been joined; the war would be waged between those who blamed mining for a multitude of sins, from greed to violence, and those who saw it as the key to the future.

An angry priest, unhappy with mining's repercussions on the Indians, characterized the Spanish, who carried Rome's mining tradition to the New World, as men "who out of greed for silver and gold would enter Hell itself to get them." The English who settled along the east coast of North America brought mining traditions that were rooted in Rome and in their own long experience. *The Compleat Collier*, published in 1708, had as one of its themes "All things obey money," which plainly included anything environmental. The way the colonials translated this maxim was illustrated by Samuel Hermelin, a Swedish visitor to America in the last year of the Revolutionary War, 1783. This knowledgeable gentleman visited New Jersey coal and iron mines and found the miners handling a water problem by simply draining it somewhere else, to what effect no one, including Hermelin, seemed to care. He also noted that forests owned by mine owners had been extensively cut and that, as a consequence, "leasing" was out of favor because of its exploitation of timber and minerals. "Little timber or coal" could be bought unless the ground also was purchased; anything else left the owner holding an empty bag.[3]

As the mining industry bestowed these devil-may-care traditions, it also developed counterbalancing ideological defenses for its actions. In his classic sixteenth-century *De re metallica*, Georgius Agricola sounded themes that would echo down through the decades. Without metal mining, he believed, life would regress and "men would pass a horrible and wretched existence in the midst of wild beasts." Miners, he claimed, dug "almost exclusively in mountains otherwise unproductive" and in "valleys invested in gloom," doing in either situation "slight damage to fields or none at all." According to Agricola, mining improved the land; where woods and glades were cut down, new fields soon produced rich crops that more than repaid the losses to inhabitants from the increased costs of timber. "Birds without number," beasts, and fish could be purchased elsewhere with the profits made from mining, Agricola theorized, to replace their predecessors who disappeared before the onslaught of mining.[4]

From Agricola to T. A. Rickard, the late-nineteenth- and twentieth-century champion of mining, there runs a consistent theme. Rickard described the miner as "not only the pioneer, but he left marks to show his way; he blazed the trail for civilization." Mining, the "herald of empire and the pioneer of industry," had found a worthy new spokesman.[5] Although the ideas were old, the enthusiasm was as fresh as the most recent mining rush. Exploitive methods and the justification for them found precedents that had been established long before the nineteenth century and that continued to be repeated throughout it. Greed, which had been mentioned so frequently in the earlier texts, was translated to "fever"—gold fever, silver fever, and other fevers, depending on the metal involved. The obsession justified a multitude of sins, regardless of time and place. Traveling through North Carolina in 1829, William Graham wrote a friend: "I have heard scarce anything since my arrival, except gold. Nothing before has ever so completely engrossed the attention of all classes of the community in this section."[6] It was gold fever in California and silver fever in Nevada, with many repetitions elsewhere. For some people, coal, copper, and other base metals aroused only slightly less emotion and attention than the previous metals.

Henry H. Clark, residing in Virginia City, Montana, in 1864, explained why he had migrated west: I had to "leave my family in such a situation and it was the hardest thing I ever did but everyone did not know my circumstances. . . . I had little or nothing left and thought this was the best chance for me to get another start and I could not give it up. It's a hard tussle but I shall get something before I come home if I am able." He had caught the fever and stubbornly determined to stay, as had Mark Twain in the better-known Virginia City, Nevada: "By and by I was smitten with silver fever. Plainly this was the road to fortune. . . . Go where you would, you heard nothing else, from morning till far into the night." Determination to stay, the "best chance," the "road to fortune"—mining exerted a strong attraction. Just thinking about those attractions allowed Richard Hughes to pass pleasantly the long hours on a Union Pacific immigrant train to Cheyenne, the jumping-off spot for the Black Hills: "Had our minds not been busy with possibilities of the near future, we might have found the journey monotonous." Nathaniel Hill resigned himself to being separated from family and friends in hopes he could make fifteen to twenty thousand dollars by going to Colorado. Mark Twain summarized the prevailing attitude of a whole century of miners, "I would have been more or less than human if I had not gone mad like the rest. . . . I succumbed and grew as frenzied as the craziest."[7]

All-consuming excitement, greed, and "fever" caused men and women to throw off restraints, to tolerate severe privations, and to ignore everything except the drive for wealth. Their single-mindedness boded ill for the environment. The participants themselves and the onlookers aptly testified to this in a variety of ways. That attitude affected life in the mining communities and in the mines, and it touched everyone who came into contact with it.

Anything that cooled this fever had to be eliminated, if at all possible, or compromised, if all else failed. This meant, in practical terms, that concerns for land and water were overridden by mining. Contaminated air likewise generated no remedial action unless community health was seriously threatened.

Mining men looked upon exploitation as their natural right, just as they had in Pliny's day. They took pride in their own achievements and in those of their industry, a pride that was heightened by the accomplishments of miners in general, if not of each individual. The Pottsville, Pennsylvania, *Miners' Journal,* for February 11, 1843, expressed plainly what coal meant to that community: "The whole welfare of this region depends upon the prosperity and success of the coal operator. It is then evident to all that whatever affects his interest likewise injures the storekeeper, mechanic, miner and laborer." Intoxicating words, these, to the ears of miners and owners alike. Coal reigned as king here; copper, somewhere else; and silver in yet another place. All together they had built America. In Murphy's Camp, which had deteriorated badly since the days of the California gold rush, an old miner talked to John Muir. He apologized for being a "bummer" now, "compared with what we used to be in the grand old days. We were giants then, and you can look around here and see our tracks." Those tracks were everywhere, the heritage of a free-wheeling generation.[8]

No one better exemplified the hallowed tradition of nineteenth-century American individualism than did the miner. J. Ross Browne wrote of the Bannack, Montana, placers that "each operation is carried on by itself."[9] The prospector and the miner migrated at will and did what they pleased; that was their definition of individualism. The *Mining and Scientific Press* (December 7, 1860) rose to lyricism when it spoke of the "star of 'manifest destiny'" lighting their way. Mining had become part of America's destiny, only a step removed from serving as the handmaiden of God's mystical plan. It was questionable whether a hard-rock miner in Galena, Illinois, or a sourdough in Alaska thought in those terms; nevertheless, each subscribed to that concept of individualism in his right to search, mine, and sell. Though unlikely or unable to express it, all of them found it exhilarating to be a part of something larger than life.

Montana's William Clark, a mining man himself, spoke at the nation's centennial exposition in Philadelphia in October, 1876. He explained to his audience, most of whom probably had never seen a mining operation or known many miners, that "as a class miners are an industrious, generous and large-souled people, guided by the warmest sympathies. The sanguine temperament largely prevails, and although often pursuing a phantom, the pursuit is animated by an earnest, hopeful and self-reliant ambition.'' If his listeners believed Clark, they saw the miner as he wanted to be seen. A mining engineer pictured the miner similarly in 1897 and went on to say that he should be ''honest as the day is long, quick to see the meaning of any new facts, and . . . in short, a man in every sense of the word.''[10]

As he soared into flights of oratory, Clark used the generic term ''miner'' to describe all individuals active in the industry. Even in the nineteenth century, groups that existed within mining had differing aspirations and complicated relationships involving a variety of subjects. The Pottsville coal miner would be easily distinguishable in dress, social status, political influence, and economic worth from the owner of a Pottsville coal mine. The same would hold true for the Virginia City, Nevada, miner and the owner/stockholder. Less obvious would be the differences found in the transitory Murphy's Camp; placer districts symbolized poor man's diggings, with correspondingly much less social, occupational, or economic status.

The prospector trudges through the story as the most ''individual'' of this individualistic generation. Beyond his original discovery, however, he had little impact or influence. Small in numbers and as flighty as the spring wind, prospectors furnished the raw materials of which legends are made, but they forsook the influence to shape an industry.

As mining became more technical and corporation-dominated, the prospector and the individual miner became even less important in the overall picture. This industrial evolution also negated the once proudly proclaimed opportunity and equality of the mining frontier. Status and business power now carried more weight and influence. These changes surfaced most clearly in the conflict over union recognition and in struggles between workers and management over safety, health, and wages. During the last decades of the century it was usually easy to discern the owner, the mining engineer, the miner, the mill man, and the mill worker; each supported a different employer/employee viewpoint and customarily lived a different style of life.

The changes that took place with the evolution of mining in the nineteenth century have raised questions, particularly in the last twenty-five years, about making sweeping generalizations regarding miners' views. When it came to the environment and mining's significance to America, however, this generation—from the hardrock stiff, digging in the drift, to the greedy small operator, to the large company, spouting laissez-faire rhetoric—spoke almost in unison. The industry stood preeminent: ''All things obey money.''

Mining ruled supreme, untouchable. That concept permeated nineteenth-century mining: Pottsville proclaimed the glories of coal; a Marysville, California, editor asserted that "gold must be had, or business flags"; at its height of wealth and fame, Leadville proudly affirmed, "To no other king than Carbonate are we expected to bow." Even New Hampshire, not far famed for its mineral wealth, joined the parade, stating that it had "a remarkable variety of minerals, containing a greater number of metals than any other state in the Union." Nowhere was this theme more clearly expressed than at the 1882 National Mining and Industrial Exposition in Denver. For the pioneer and the investor, no surer highway to fortune existed. "There is a reason for this, and an honest reason, too. It is because everything has been made subordinate to mining for precious metals. That prompted the early settlement and induced the following immigration to a great extent."[11] Rusling had made the same point more than a decade before, stressing the word *subservient*. Everything subservient, subordinate to mining. This fundamental attitude profoundly shaped the thinking of the industry and its spokesmen.

Another attribute of mining was that it appeared to have an unlimited future. As one of the best known mining men of his day, Horace Tabor, emphatically stated in 1890: "There are going to be many valuable mines found yet in Colorado that are sleeping today; there is no question about that." Colorado, Georgia, Wisconsin— wherever one looked, this confidence in the infinity of mineral resources served as bedrock for the industry. Mining engineer Frederick Corning could write with unbounded enthusiasm about the vastness of minerals in this rich, prosperous country.[12] Others reiterated the theme. Let anyone challenge this basic tenet and the industry immediately leaped to its defense. Pacific Coast reserves were not giving out, declared the *Mining and Scientific Press* in 1860; quite the contrary, "[We] perceive that its minerals are inexhaustible for ages to come."

Assuming that the reserves were inexhaustible, why the need to conserve? Somewhere over the next mountain or in the neighboring valley there would be another bonanza. That rationale had boosted several centuries of American farmers in their relentless march westward. Several generations of miners could do likewise.

The industry's voice, speaking through mining journals and newspapers, testified exuberantly to its virtues and importance. New York's *Mining Magazine*, in April 1854, called for common sense and economy in mining matters, "and then only, can we look forward to finding the mineral character of our country, assuming and maintaining that high and proud position which her true and actual mineral wealth so justly entitles it to claim." The need for some reforms was granted, but after that, it was ever onward and upward. Thirty years later, Las Vegas, New Mexico's *Mining World* for May 1, 1884, announced, "The mining industry is happily in the position where it can honestly and earnestly challenge critical examination and searching inquiry without fear of an unfavorable verdict." The *Mining and Scientific Press* for November 15, 1890, affirmed that mining had accomplished a "good deal," but what lay ahead looked more exciting: "We know what is past but can only guess as to what lies before us."

Understandably, mining saw itself in a highly favorable light that fit into the contemporary American business image and work ethic. Lest mining appear to be glamorous, one should never lose sight of the fact that it involved long, strenuous labor, as George Parsons found out in Tombstone, Arizona: "Hard hard work. I used to think the laboring man's a hard life at the best, but their work is child's play alongside this."[13] For that hard work, all miners expected a day's wages at the very minimum; at best, a fortune. They tolerated nothing that stood in the way of their quest, which meant that mountain, desert, deer, and the Indian must yield to them.

But what did others, those outside of mining, think of it? People in general, whether investors or rank and file, had to be increasingly aware of it as the century progressed. Interest and enthusiasm mounted with each new rich discovery of gold and silver. Outsiders, too, expected something from mining, preferably profits, but certainly a saga of adventure and excitement that would create a diversion from the tedium of their daily lives. They visited, watched, read, and invested; and these tenderfeet saw fact and fancy intertwined as reality. Nonminers exerted an important influence on the course of the development of the industry and molded the industry's perception of itself.

In some ways the impressions of outsiders proved to be even more glamorous, more positive, than those that emerged from the industry itself. Over the years, such words as *pluck, enterprise, endurance,* and *courage* flowed from writers' pens and joined phrases such as "heroes of the pan and spade" to characterize the miners. James Rusling splendidly depicted those whom he saw in Central City, Colorado: "The men carried keen, clear-cut, energetic faces, that well explained the enterprise and *elan* of this audacious town." Old-time prospectors and hard-bitten miners might have had trouble recognizing themselves under the deluge of flattering phrases. They would have agreed more readily with Dame Shirley when she noted,

"Really, everybody ought to go to the mines just to see how little it takes to make people comfortable in the world."[14]

Reality had to climb a steep hill to counteract the legends that attached themselves to mining. Particularly was this true in the East and the Midwest, where distances measured in days separated the western miners from their eastern brethren. The cultural and social gap was no less wide. This remoteness made it hard to sift fact from fiction and allowed the image of a larger-than-life individual, the successful mining man (e.g., Horace Tabor), to grow. Only a legendary step behind came some of those "rugged" individuals, the prospectors and the hard-rock miners. The coal miner, the mundane companion of the hard-rock miner, was largely ignored; in any case, he could be readily observed in Pennsylvania and nearby states. He was seen as a mere day laborer, struggling in a dangerous, difficult job.

Overglamorization arose from distorted perceptions. When combined with the materialistic contributions of mining, these perceptions were parlayed into an attractive proposition and became the seeds of legend, the justification for environmental exploitation. A few examples will suffice.

William Keating said about mining in 1821: "The art of mining is one of the most important branches of public economy . . . one of the noblest and most interesting pursuits to which the attention of man can be called." Fifty years and a civil war later, the former Confederate General John D. Imboden insisted that mining would restore war-ravished Virginia: "We are upon the eve of a new era of great wealth and prosperity." It might, he reasoned, be a valuable counterbalance to the concentration of sectional power; the old rebel would not concede a thing to those Yankees! Coal mining, an earlier writer believed, ameliorated frontier conditions and brought conveniences and development in their stead. To reinforce that idea, one of the "views" in the book portrayed a virgin countryside in the foreground and a thriving mine in the background; the dullest reader could grasp the symbolic contrast. An Illinois newspaper editor agreed with the concept, despite the country's being in the throes of civil war, when thoughts might have been presumed to be at the battlefront, rather than on mining. He found time, however, to ponder how coal mining would transform his town into a manufacturing point, invite capital, and develop a business village "into a city of no mere importance."[15]

Supporting this mélange of blessings that were sure to come stood the keystone conviction that mining and the success of America marched inseparably, hand in hand, and that the industry bestowed only bounties. Cursed indeed was the state or district that did not have mineral deposits.

For stockholders, no greater good could be served than a declaration of dividends; for no other reason did they invest in mining. The investors, who might never come any closer to a mine than their mailbox, wielded power that the industry had to reckon with. They provided financial support, often desperately needed by the industry, in return for the expectation of profit. Consequently, the two collaborated with that one goal in mind. Investors, having read of millions of dollars worth of ore being hauled from the earth, fully expected their share of the wealth.

Instructions to a new mining superintendent, Pope Yeatman, in Missouri typify what was expected by employers: maintain a constant supply of ore, treat the ore successfully, and "ensure the best economy in our work." Nowhere did there appear a hint of concern about the impact of mining beyond those profits. Across the Mississippi River in Illinois, John Rockwell, an absentee owner, wrote numerous letters to his superintendents, stressing such topics as the coal market, the grade of coal, and the price—all in the name of turning a profit. In Nevada, letters from the president of the Comstock's Savage Mining Company showed evidence of abundant interest in mill runs, the condition of the roads, the weather, and other mines, but none whatsoever in environmental issues. Manager George Daly wrote from Leadville that he would soon have the mine running "smoothly, profitably and economically." Daly's three words, accompanied by dividends, delighted the stockholders. In Upper Michigan the superintendent of the Tamarack and Osceola mines found his company stewing about the price of copper, docking for its lake boats, smelting, and labor conditions.[16] Mining records teem with examples such as these.

The industry willingly played upon the primary profit theme from the first contact with the investor. Mining-company prospectuses were laced with phrases such as "given results seldom equalled and never excelled" and "contains the richest lodes." A report on a mine usually expanded on that theme, either implicitly or explicitly. An examination of the Walton mine in Virginia produced this summation: the property could be profitably worked provided that the company practiced sound economy and furnished competent management and good machinery. This statement allowed no contradiction, but in the rush for riches, some of its components (economy and competence) were forgotten or ignored. When a company ultimately incorporated, its purpose was simply stated: to own, work, and sell ore and mines. Investors anticipated reassuring words like these: "The San Antonio Mines are developing richer, more, and easily reducible metals than I ever anticipated they would."[17]

Attuned to the siren call of profit, the miner, the mine owner, and the stockholder walked the same road. In their obsession with earnings, stockholders wielded an influence that reached into every mining district in the United States and helped to shape the industry's course in the nineteenth century. Never before had it been truer that "all things obey money."

The industry could not avoid reinforcing the demands for profit that were weighing on it, at no time more manifestly than during the Comstock's two great bonanza epochs. Commenting on this circumstance, Eliot Lord pointed the finger: "The shareholders spent their monthly quotas, well pleased, and did not call for increased profits through a reduction of expenses, but through an augmented production of bullion." A. D. Hodges concurred that stockholders were eager for sudden fortunes and cared little how much metal was wasted by rapid treatment, ". . . if only dividends could be increased temporarily."[18]

The respected mining man Clarence King spoke for his generation when he described this "fever":

> But it may be said, as a rule that capital invested in precious-metals mines in this country has always secured quick returns, if any. This is necessitated by the demands of investors, who are seldom satisfied, when interested in precious-metal mining, with the plodding methods which perhaps in the long run would be more profitable, and on which they could rely in any other branch of industry.

The mining engineer could hardly be blamed, he reasoned, because "on the one side he is pressed by the stockholder, clamorous for speedy profits, and on the other hand he realizes that the chances of a long period of bonanza are slight."[19] This tension between managers and investors prevailed throughout American industry; nothing about it was unique to mining.

Without doubt, the intense pressure justified a multitude of sins, which might, of course, have been committed anyway. This justification does not, however, deny the reality and the persuasiveness of the investors' demands, and they must carry their share of responsibility for much of the environmental devastation. The investing public, directly or indirectly, made demands and had its own expectations of what mining should do for it and why.

On the other hand, the investor could become a convenient scapegoat for unscrupulous behavior on the part of the mining industry. Mining, meanwhile, was expected to utilize the most effective methods available to it in order to turn a profit. Over the years, this translated into hydraulic-mining, dredging, and surface-stripping operations. Each process could be relied upon to move more placer gravel than could a pan, a rocker, or a sluice. Strip mining and open pits caught the imagination of several segments of the industry. The anthracite coal fields of Pennsylvania were using steam shovels for stripping by 1881, and Indiana claimed to have had them operating four years earlier. When Minnesota's great Mesabi Range opened in the early 1890s, open pit mining furnished the answer to what would be the most practical method.[20]

To anyone who questioned these methods, the industry offered ready answers. Each could handle vast tonnages with more economy, thereby allowing the successful mining of lower-grade ore and coal. The initial investment was less, and there was no expensive plant to depreciate with age. Fewer damage suits arose from accidents, because the men were able to work in daylight. Finally, the hand of tradition should not restrain the operator—he had to be free to modernize and mechanize as the opportunity arose. Hard-rock mining also refitted itself with power drills and other innovations; their impact on the environment, however, was limited to the ability to work more ore, only accelerating what was already taking place. Investors and management applauded any evidence of ingenuity, dismissing the side effects as inconsequential when weighed against progress and profits.

In the eyes of its practitioners, American mining had assumed world leadership of the industry by the 1880s. Although there may have been a few aspects in which it still needed to catch up with European standards, the tide of supremacy was definitely running in the direction of the United States. No one seemed to be more enthusiastic about this development than Clarence King, who sang the praises of the industry in 1885.

King saw a multitude of things that were worthy of praise. The originality and the ingenuity of the methods adopted, particularly hydraulic mining ("a completely new departure"), earned his tribute. The "rapidity of execution," with the consequent saving of time and interest, was a striking industrial feature, though King admitted it was often pushed too far. In his opinion the blame for rapaciousness lay with the investors, not with the industry. Because of their quest for quick returns, mining investors "always preferred" to take a greater chance rather than the smaller, safer investment. The American genius for bold engineering enterprise was nowhere better displayed than in mining. The extensive tunnel enterprises, flumes, ditches, deep shafts, and "daring feats" of railroad engineering all testified to it, as did the actual conduct of mining operations on a large scale.[21]

Impressive as these feats were, they would never have been accomplished had one other ingredient of American mining not prominently asserted itself: the "intelligence and versatility of our skilled mine operatives." King did not build his argument on mere chauvinism; even Europeans, who were not always impressed by Americans' achievements, stood in awe of the accomplishments of their counterparts in mining engineering. As King correctly observed, both United States engineers and American practices were being exported instead of imported, reversing the previous trend. American mining stood at the pinnacle of international acclaim; why change it?

King's remarks defined the mining traits that Americans considered to be most significant. Nowhere was there any mention of environmental concern. King did include some of mining's sins— recklessness, waste, the frequent disregard of foreign experience, and the aforementioned desire for quick returns—each of which could severely damage the environment.

He hedged on the issue of foreign experience; England and continental Europe differed too much from the United States to afford a close comparison. After hypothetically describing the German engineers' careful and economical opening of the Comstock, King concluded that their "system [was] more economical but less suited to the time and locality." Impatient American stockholders would not have been tempted by this type of mining. Fast and flashy discoveries of great bonanzas attracted them: "There is always a point beyond which saving costs more than it is worth." American mining encountered problems of distance, the high cost of living, harsh climates, lofty altitudes, few people, and no near markets for the by-products of smelting, obstacles that were unknown in England or Europe. King reasoned correctly—conditions did differ too much for the direct application of foreign methods to American mining and environment.[22] In their speculative haste for wealth, Americans were not ready to accept foreign methods that emphasized economy. King could not have summarized more succinctly the prevailing attitude when he said that saving cost more than it was worth. That idea struck a responsive chord and rationalized a prodigal extravagance that has not been equaled in American mining.

More education did not create more awareness. Professionally trained mining engineers, as opposed to their "school of hard knocks" compatriots, became more credible and were more often consulted as the century passed the three-quarters' mark. Improved environmental consciousness, however, did not accompany them. The magnitude of the problem becomes apparent when one realizes that neither college-trained nor field-experienced engineers understood the impact of mining. Most Americans who sought professional education at first traveled to Europe; European standards and methods shaped American programs as they developed. Rossiter Raymond, in his capacity as United States commissioner of mining statistics, had occasion in his 1869 report to discuss the European education of mining engineers. Three of the leading schools of mines—Freiburg, Paris, and the Prussian Royal—offered no courses that even remotely touched on conservation or environmental matters. The Prussian Royal School of Mines spoke for all of them when it stated that its purpose was to provide students with "the opportunity to obtain the necessary professional knowledge" to manage mining, metallurgical, or "saline works."[23]

Shortly after 1900, one of the best and most experienced mining engineers of his generation, James D. Hague, outlined what he considered to be the essentials for a mining engineer; they included being learned in the law, up-to-date, and concerned with "practical" methods for the exploration, development, and treatment of ore.[24] Hague should not be faulted for not advocating environmental studies, nor should Raymond or the professors in mining schools. They, like the miner in the field, did not comprehend the issue. Nothing called their attention to it. Professional journals of the day rarely included articles on the subject. At the very peak of nineteenth-century mining in the United States, a generation of professionally trained and self-trained mining engineers, superintendents, and mine managers unthinkingly ignored the environment. Their example would influence several generations to come.

King failed to mention the transitory nature of mining—a common mistake. That fact, however, played a role in the miners' perception of their "home." The Mineral Points and the Buckskin Joes of the previous chapter had their counterparts everywhere, and James Fergus, out in Bannack "City," Montana, tried to explain their influence: "Bannack was not supposed to be a settlement, but simply a mining camp where everyone was trying to get what he could, then go home. Consequently the majority were simply trying to attend to their own business and to let that of others alone." A few years later and a few miles down the road, James Miller visited Alder Gulch (Virginia City, Mont.), where placer mining already had come and departed: "Immense piles of dirt and corresponding holes, all the result of the toil for gold, looking as if thrown up in some wallowing 'sports' which had taken place. All is deserted and still, but speaking

The complete mining operation at the Snowstorm Mine, boarding house, tram, and mill, Mullan, Idaho. Wherever miners dug, cut, and lived, they marked the land and left behind their legacy of litter (courtesy University of Idaho, Barnard-Stockbridge Collection, Moscow).

with voices louder than ever could be made by the miners were they there." Similar observations were made by others, from Dame Shirley's likening the effect of mining to a "fairy's wand," to James Hague's picturing the mining West as a "fast country." Mining promised much, which each new boom had to fulfill, lest prospectors abandon it in a rush over the hill to the next valley in search of their bonanza. In the all-consuming passion of getting there, no one worried about the impact on the land and on the creeks that he left behind.[25]

Two more facts strengthened the hold that mining had on America and supported the methods that the industry used while it was exploiting the country's natural resources. Mining was part of this country's pioneer heritage. Since the days of the Coronado expedition and the Jamestown settlers, gold and silver had lured people to the frontier. Especially during the last quarter of the nineteenth century the western frontier had captivated the public's imagination, strengthening the mystique of this unique facet of the

American experience. Mining as part of this—Deadwood, Leadville, Tombstone, Virginia City, Cripple Creek, magic names all—caught the public's fancy in more than dollars-and-cents terms. With the romantic pioneers came the methods to extract the minerals. For example, strip mining marched west with the pioneer miners from Pennsylvania, Kentucky, Alabama, Illinois, Kansas, and beyond. It was all part of America's growing up.[26]

Those dollars and cents were important also, and the contribution that mining made to the national wealth could not be denied. Mineral production of $587,230,662 in 1889 demonstrated that the industry precipitated a monetary windfall that commanded attention.[27] No one wanted to imagine where the United States would have been without that wealth, sitting, as the country was, on the threshold of industrial and world power.

For reasons of tradition, current technology, self-image, and outside pressures, the emphasis of the mining industry zeroed in on profit; all else, from laborers to the land, suffered because of it. The self-esteem of the mining industry remained high, despite some well-publicized setbacks because of overexpectation, poor management, and rampant speculation. Members of the general public obviously looked upon the industry with favor, particularly those who received dividends from it, as well as the much larger group that expected them momentarily.

Mining was a business, one of the best of its day in which to make a small fortune without a great deal of effort on the part of the investor. As such, anything that stood in the way of profit was viewed with a jaundiced eye. Environmental concerns, had they surfaced strongly, would have been scuttled by the startled opposition, once the cost factor and the inconvenience had been weighed. When a mining district moved away from its bonanza days and mining grew more expensive, it was harder to turn a profit, and all else became subservient to that end. The destiny of mining was hitched to the hard-driving team of profit and dividends.

Circumstances conspired to implant in the collective industrial mind, and the mind of the individual as well, the idea that the future could be ignored. Efforts to meet the needs of the day were all-absorbing. How deeply this attitude became ingrained will be examined later.

As strong as is the case for a nonenvironmentally oriented mining philosophy in the nineteenth century, further evidence will develop a fuller understanding of the reasons for its evolution and why it has stood the test of time. In the next chapter, governmental and legal attitudes come under examination, and the mining man is called upon to testify about his attitude toward environmental questions. The industry must be given a full opportunity to present its views in order to comprehend what was transmitted to subsequent generations.

CHAPTER THREE

"Going to Cover Marysville Up"

In an age preoccupied with the development and utilization of the country's abundant natural resources, the environment was taken for granted. *Poole's Index to Periodical Literature* from 1802 to 1906 lists only four articles dealing with the impact of mining on the environment; all four dealt with hydraulic mining. Thus, from the miner to the mining-camp resident to the general public, the theme ran deep. It took a perceptive and courageous individual to "buck the tiger."

Yet to assume that miners and mining men lacked an appreciation for the land over which they prospected and into which they dug would be erroneous. Those who admired it, however, rarely expressed their admiration. Enough observations were recorded, though, to gain an idea of their awe and appreciation of nature's handiwork. Riding across Colorado's newly opening San Juan mining region in August, 1879, the veteran Nevada mining man and United States Senator John P. Jones surveyed it in wonder. He wrote his wife, Georgina:

> The country we have passed over and the scenery spreading out on every hand all day has been magnificent and grand beyond my powers of description, far surpassing anything I ever saw in the Sierras.
>
> This place must be the backbone of the world. So rugged a country, such tremendous mountains, such awful trails I never saw.[1]

Newcomer Nathaniel P. Hill, after admitting that he was not inclined to go into ecstasies over such things as scenery, promptly described the Colorado Rockies near Central City as "grand and sublime beyond description." While its namesake was directing streams of water at the countryside and eroding the natural beauty, the *Hydraulic Press* of North San Juan, California, found space in 1858 to recommend that its readers take a trip into the mountains. Breathe the pure air, the editor advised. Clear the lungs of city dust, invigorate the system, see the stately pine, "whose music shall enliven the careworn," and think of something besides wealth, the "curse of mankind." Emerson and Thoreau would have saluted this particular mining-camp writer of 1858 for recognizing and promoting nature's benefits. Thirty-four years later, *Mining Age* extolled the Spring Creek district, otherwise unidentified, as the loveliest location for a mining camp, with smooth, gently sloping foothills, thickly clothed with luxuriant grasses and plentiful timber. A "beautiful stream of sparkling ice-cold water" bubbled through a district that was "strewn with myriad wild flowers."[2]

As he accidentally destroyed nature's beauty with a careless fire, would-be miner Mark Twain could still appreciate the majesty of the scene: "Every feature of the spectacle was repeated in the glowing mirror of the lake [Tahoe]! Both pictures were sublime, both were beautiful."[3] This was the same Mark Twain who was caught up in the frenzy and fever of the Nevada silver excitement in the previous chapter. Twain demonstrated the ambivalence of his generation between Tahoe's wild beauty and the delightful prospect of striking it rich. The zeal for money and mechanization swept up nearly all in its path, and Twain and his contemporaries, in and out of mining, shifted back and forth. Understandably, they sometimes appeared to be hypocrites.

Spellbinding, awesome, grand, magnificent—these words were used to portray the land by individuals who respected what they perceived. They held in esteem the land they trod, and they readily discerned its grandeur. Few miners could bridge the gap between simple appreciation and the ability to grasp the transcendent qualities of nature and the mountains. The *Hydraulic Press* did so, along with a handful of others who looked beyond the rampant materialism of mine and camp.

No one lectured more eloquently on the subject than did Professor Amasa McCoy, who explained how mountain mining redeemed men. In imaginative flights of rhetoric he told his Chicago listeners that living in the mountains decreased "profane swearing" and irreverence and lifted conversation to a self-respectful, manly, and considerate level, "even high-minded, generous and noble." Mountain mining refined and elevated the character, "so that a bad man is made less bad, and a good man is made better."[4] One may legitimately question how all this could be accomplished; fortunately, those Chicagoans had little or no firsthand knowledge upon which to judge the professor's observations. The important point was that on his trip west, McCoy sensed something special about the impact that nature had on the miners.

These individuals—all of whom were involved with mining in one way or another—proclaimed that the environment meant something to them. To most of the industry, however, discovery, development, and dividends meant much more. The more typical response was to ignore the topic of the environment entirely, or to mention it only in passing. Examples are as numerous as the mining districts themselves.

Keating's *Considerations upon the Art of Mining,* which appeared in 1821, delved into the many facets of mining, but environmental impact was not one of them. Neither Eli Bowen's examination of Pennsylvania coal regions in 1848 nor Eric Hedburg's look at Missouri and Arkansas zinc mines at the close of the century mentioned the subject. The Pittsburgh and Boston Company's 1866 report on its Michigan copper mine, which discussed the operation's involvement with the environment, from wood cutting to washing the slime, gave no evidence of awareness beyond the business of mining. Finally, the Monitor Gold Mining Company, working in the Yukon Territory, operated on a "grand scale," with no apparent concern for anything besides "insignificant" returns.

Correspondence and reports of the mining companies generally disregard the topic, or mention it only offhandedly, in a business-as-usual manner. The same can be said for the mining engineers whom these companies hired to direct their enterprises. The attitudes of the miners themselves, while harder to generalize simply because they chose not to record their thoughts or failed to preserve them, follow the same pattern. Charles Harvey, Joseph Horskey, and Daniel Conner, for instance, mined in California, Colorado, Montana, and Arizona without taking any notice of environmental matters.[5]

Just as concerned mining men were atypical, so were concerned citizens in the mining communities. Alfred Doten migrated from California to Nevada and from mining to the newspaper business, leaving behind a remarkable set of journals that describe himself and the world around him from 1849 to 1903. Doten was involved in more aspects of mining than were most people of his generation, but his voluminous notes contain no observations about the environment. No mention of the subject is found in the writings of miner's wife Anne Ellis, nor in those of Estelline Bennett, who grew up in Deadwood, South Dakota. James Chisholm, who went to South Pass, Wyoming, in 1868 to participate in the excitement of mining, ignores the issue.[6]

The same holds true for the industry's publications, such as the *Engineering and Mining Journal,* the *Mining and Scientific Press,* and the *Coal Trade Journal.* Rare exceptions are descriptions of such things as California's hydraulic fight and Butte's smoke-pollution case. The classic mining studies published in the latter part of the century— James D. Hague et al., *Mining Industry* (1870); Joseph Curtis, *Silver-Lead Deposits of Eureka, Nevada* (1884); Samuel Emmons and George F. Becker, *Statistics and Technology of the Precious Metals* (1885); and

Emmons, *Geology and Mining Industry of Leadville, Colorado* (1886)—display little sensitivity to the environment. The many articles in the *Transactions of the American Institute of Mining Engineers* from 1890 to 1903 follow the same pattern.

What investors liked to read about the environment is evident in the prospectus of the Atlantic and Pacific Gold and Silver Mining Company's Nevada mine. The mine was located within walking distance of the foot of the mountain, near accessible lumber sources, with available water. It sat high enough to "give good tunnel privilege," but not so high that it could not be connected by a good road to the valley. If the ore should prove rich and rampant, the cup of blessings would overflow.

Timber, too, free for the taking, added to the blessings. Regarding the waste of timber, Rossiter Raymond had this to say: "Timber is plenty; it belongs to the United States, and the pioneer 'has as good a right to it as anyone else.' " "As good a right" excused a multitude of transgressions. This attitude underlay part of the American heritage, a foundation of the American dream since the days of the first explorers and settlers. That natural resources might be exhausted or that the land might be permanently damaged seemed incomprehensible and inconsistent with experience. Always new land and new opportunities beckoned to the west.

A few people dared to insist that this lack of concern, this waste, was a benefit. Consider the case of Butte's smelter smoke and its alleged blessings for smoke-choked residents. James Hague received a letter from F. E. Sargeant, who said that "La Grippe" (flu) was raging in Butte, though in a much milder form: "It is the opinion of physicians that the sulphur smoke which permeates everywhere has a discouraging effect upon the microbe and causes it to relax its grip." William Clark staked further claims at the state constitutional convention when he discussed the possibility of Butte's becoming the capital: "I say it would be a great deal better for other cities in the territory if they had more smoke and less diphtheria and other diseases. It has been believed by all the physicians of Butte that the smoke that sometimes prevails there is a disinfectant, and destroys the microbes that constitute the germs of disease . . . it would be a great advantage for other cities, as I have said, to have a little more smoke and business activity and less disease." Not finished, Clark unfurled his *pièce de résistance:* the ladies were "very fond" of Butte "because there is just enough arsenic there to give them a beautiful complexion and that is the reason the ladies of Butte are renowned wherever they go for their beautiful complexions."[7]

No one wanted to dispute those kinds of benefits. Butte triumphed—a smoky elixir of life and beauty. John Waldorf, who grew up in Virginia City, Nevada, remembered the great dumps as play areas and the old ponds as wonderful places for swimming: "All small boys know that the weather gets warm long before the water does."[8] For the young the mines, the camps, and the surrounding territory abounded with childhood delights, albeit dangerous ones. The more littered the sites, the better. Not everyone savored pleasant memories of the remnants of mining. The state of Connecticut purchased the Simsbury copper mine at East Granby and used it as a prison for fifty-four years. For part of that time the prisoners worked as miners. Utilization of abandoned mines in that way was unusual.

A downstream claim could bestow a blessing in disguise, contended Rossiter Raymond, because in many cases it filled every year with gold-bearing gravel, washed in at no expense from the claims and mines above. "This class of mining property now [1873] proves the safest for investment." Arizona's Crown King Company persuasively pointed out to prospective investors that benefits would accrue to them because the previous owners' dump washed down into the valley below the mine. It could be reworked at $800,000 profit![9]

The apex of that kind of reasoning came when contentions were made that tearing apart the environment made mining easier and more profitable. No company stated this idea more boldly than the Cataract and Wide West Hydraulic Gravel Mining Company of Calaveras County, California. Like the Crown King, Cataract's prospectus appealed to the reader's greed. The company planned to rework the old placers around Murphy's Camp, which had been "terrific rich," and to open the "ancient gravels" of long-gone rivers. Previous miners had done the "spade work": "The hills have been cut and scalped and every gorge and gulch and broad valley have been fairly torn to pieces and disemboweled, expressing a fierce and desperate energy hard to understand."[10] This desperate energy had been understood by the forty-niners, and they had paved the way for the hydraulic company to try its hand. It could hardly do any more damage to the land.

Eliot Lord stated the prevailing attitude best when he wrote about the Comstock and its wasteful milling practices. To have asked for evidence of competence for millmen, he said, "would have abridged the privilege of American citizens to waste the mineral resources of the public land without hindrance."[11]

The federal government aided and abetted its citizens and its would-be citizens in these wasteful practices. Washington generously gave away or sold for a minimal price the mineral lands, timber, and water rights. In regard to minerals, no explicit and coherent policies were formulated. When Congress finally enacted mining laws in 1866 and 1872, the understandable intent was to promote private exploitation of the mineral wealth of the public lands. A recent scholar of mining law concluded that the 1872 law was based on a single premise, one dating back to Roman times: mineral exploration and development hold preference over all other uses of the land, because they represent the highest economic use.[12] In this great era of laissez faire, finders were indeed keepers. The anonymous English writer who described coal mining in 1708 would have nodded knowingly— "all things obey money."

Uncle Sam proved to be just as generous in other ways. In 1878 a legislative act allowed miners and others to cut timber on public lands, even though Commissioner of the General Land Office J. A. Williamson had written to Secretary of the Interior Carl Schurz about his concern for preserving young timber and for preventing the denuding of mountainsides.[13] The federal government encouraged mining in so many direct and indirect ways that the miner cannot be blamed for assuming that Washington would support him in his actions. The bold policy that *Mining Magazine* advocated way back in December, 1854—namely, that "mining interests must be protected and sustained"—had been affirmed by the United States Government.

Within limits, state governments did their best to support the industry. With the exception of Texas, they did not have land to give away. They encouraged mining by taxing little or not at all and by promoting local mines and districts. The miner virtually had free rein to operate as he pleased. Considering the inherent dangers of mining, it is surprising that regulatory laws came late, if at all, and were often rendered useless because of lax enforcement. Environmental questions were almost totally ignored. A study of Wisconsin, for example, found only one statute (1893) that prohibited the pollution of streams with "saw dust, lime or other deleterious substances."[14] Mining, in certain states, and business and industry, in general, carried big political sticks during those years.

The judicial branch of government, both state and federal, supported mining's interests no less than did the legislative. The industry could generally count on an extremely conservative, business-oriented judiciary before which to plead its case. Ignoring, for the moment, the classic legal struggle in California, mining did well in the courts. During the two decades before the Civil War, the ideologies of laissez faire and rugged individualism gained momentum in American law. As a legal scholar recently wrote, "Dominion over land began to be regarded as an absolute right to engage in any conduct on one's property regardless of its economic value."[15] Courts made no attempt to strike a balance between the harm done by and the utility of a particular course of action; they held to the idea that economic development could best be promoted by giving the individual property owner free rein to develop his land. These trends proved to be tailor-made for mining and for other active and powerful elements in American society.

One of the most noteworthy victories for mining came in Pennsylvania in 1886 in the case of *The Pennsylvania Coal Company* v. *Sanderson and Wife*. The plaintiffs, J. Gardiner Sanderson and Eliza Sanderson, sued to recover damages when the mining company's operations polluted Meadow Brook, which flowed through their property in Scranton. The case, which was originally filed in 1878, reached the Pennsylvania Supreme Court seven years later for a final decision. On the surface the question seemed a simple one; its implications, however, ran deep and threatened to undermine the profits of one of the state's major industries. The suit directly challenged mining and the business-is-king attitude of that generation.

The company's lawyers opened the defense with a sarcastic slash that emphasized several points: "If, in our case, we cannot use our land for the natural purpose of mining coal because our neighbor cannot keep his tame fish in his pond, the same rule should apply to him. He should not be allowed to maintain a fish-pond so near our mine that we cannot use it." Then they went on to the salient issues. The right of mines to drain into rivers had always been recognized in Pennsylvania, they argued. The discharge of water was absolutely necessary for working the mine, and the water was discharged without "negligence or malice" in the same condition in which it entered, without pollution "by use." The company claimed that it was making a "natural, proper and lawful use of our own land" and that no direct damage had resulted to the Sandersons.

The defense lawyers argued that without coal mining, Scranton never would have existed, and the right to mine coal "is not a nuisance: the exercise of that right is so far from being a nuisance that it has always been the policy of our state to encourage it." They pointed out that mining, just as other businesses and trades, had its own particular customs and usages, and "if the natural courses for drainage are affected by the natural drainage of these mines, the consequence is inevitable and must be submitted." In order to develop the resources of the country and freely to prosecute lawful business, "the trifling inconveniences to particular persons must sometimes give way to the necessities of a great community."[16]

There, boldly stated for all to read, was mining's predominant right to use the land and the natural resources. Mining, as a legitimate business, could not be prevented from utilizing resources in accordance with its industrial practices, and no blame could be assigned to it for incidental side effects. The justices of the Pennsylvania Supreme Court concurred with those arguments in a clear and forceful decision (a later scholar was moved to call it "infamous"). They agreed that coal mining constituted a "perfectly lawful business," that the right to mine coal was not a nuisance in itself, and that the right to work mines "is a right of property, which when duly exercised, begets no responsibility." The Sandersons were doomed. They had, the court reasoned, purchased property in a mining region in a city born of mining, and they knew that all mountain streams were "affected by mine water or were liable to be. Having enjoyed the advantages which coal mining confers, I see no great hardship, nor any violence to equity, in their also accepting the inconvenience necessarily resulting from the business." The justices declared that

damages resulting to another, from the natural and lawful use of his land by the owner thereof are, in the absence of malice or negligence *damnum absque injuria.*

The trifling inconvenience to particular persons must sometimes give way to the necessities of a great community. Especially is this true where the leading industrial interest of the state is involved, the prosperity of which affects every household in the Commonwealth.[17]

The mining industry could not have wished for a more positive affirmation or justification of its actions. The fact that the justices went on to point out that the case "may arise in which a stream from such pollution may become a nuisance, and that the public interests, as involved in the general health and well being of the community, may require the abatement of the nuisance" did not inhibit the victory celebration. California and Pennsylvania provide the most complete series of cases involving tailings and debris. During the nineteenth century the political power and interests of the miner gained ascendancy over those of the farmer and the domestic user.

Mine drainage presented another problem, but by the time Daniel Barringer and John S. Adams wrote their weighty tome *The Law of Mines and Mining in the United States* (1900), the question of "natural pollution" had been won by the industry: water with impregnated substances "may be conducted into the streams which form the natural drainage ȯf the land in which the mine is situated.''[18] The burden of proof did not lie with the industry; the plaintiffs inherited that onerous task.

For placer operations, nothing was more important than water. As would be expected, a territory founded on a gold rush, such as Colorado, moved quickly to regulate tailings and water that flooded a lower, downstream neighbor. Not everyone shared Raymond's sanguine opinion that material washed from above enhanced the downstream claim. A November 1861 statute, reiterated in an 1877 general law, stated: it ''shall be the duty of every miner to take care of his own tailings, upon his own property, or become responsible for all damages that may arise therefrom.'' Tailings flowing over someone else's property threatened the success of that person's operation, as did tailings or waste material that turned essential water to the consistency of mud. Courts in Nevada, Colorado, and California all handled cases involving these sensitive matters.[19]

Water law favorable to the miners grew naturally out of problems like these. The English common-law riparian doctrine of reasonable use was quickly challenged in California. That state's supreme court had laid the basis for the doctrine of prior appropriation—first in time, first in right—as early as 1855 in the case of *Irwin* v. *Phillips*.[20] During the 1850s, mining had reached a stage in its development where order had to be created. The riparian doctrine, which favored owners of the land through which the stream ran, failed to meet the needs of placer mining; it needed to be replaced. With the doctrine of prior appropriation, the California court was simply following the customs of the miners, who had struggled with water questions since 1848. How great an impact this law would have could not have been anticipated at the time.

The mining industry emerged the overall winner in the legal contests challenging its use of land and water. When necessary, it retreated behind a defense based upon the vital nature of the business, accepted practices, natural developments, failure to establish legal cause, and one catch-all category, ''act of God.'' A successful legal challenge to mining demanded an extremely strong case, determined lawyers, and a bucket of luck to overcome the industry's historical advantages.

Mining had one ultimate argument to vindicate its actions. G. W. Baker, in his sharply critical examination of milling in Gilpin County, Colorado, in 1870 claimed that he had heard it too many times: ''It is the best we can do, it cannot be avoided.'' Baker scorned these lame excuses that produced gross waste—''the very waters give a gleeful laugh as they bear away treasures stolen from the rock.''[21] If all else failed, miners shook their heads in dismay, excused their efforts as having "tried their best," and dismissed the criticism. Baker was right—this weak excuse constituted a last resort.

With legislative and judicial blessings and with tradition, economic significance, technological advances, public acceptance, self-image, and the general profit-motivated business orientation of the day weighing in its favor, mining plunged full speed ahead in the nineteenth century. No environmental hand held the brake. Mining men evolved a rationale for their actions that satisfied them and became a cornerstone of the industry. So confident were they of the rightness of their actions that justification of policies and practices seemed unnecessary. The challenge, when it finally came, was a shock and could not be viewed as anything but a temporary aberration. Even when the federal government started setting aside forest reservations in the early 1890s, mining hardly grumbled initially about losing its rights. This, they felt, would pass. To challenge so boldly (miners would have called it foolhardily) took courage, particularly in the mining regions, where active, vocal, self-interested, and sometimes irrational support of the industry predominated. A willingness to stand unflinchingly in the face of criticism was a prerequisite to bearding the lion.

The attitudes and ideas presented in chapters 2 and 3 do not exhaust the available supply. Repetition, however, would hardly serve the industry's cause. Suffice it to say that mining and its participants felt secure in what they were doing and why. They instilled these attitudes in the younger men moving into the field, who, in turn, perpetuated them as the older generation retired or died.

The mining industry was dealing from a strong position when it reached the point that it could make this statement with impunity: "to tear [the land] to pieces; where the banks are low and the gravel tenacious, the hydraulic is, by the testimony of most practical miners, the most advantageous." Nowhere was this attitude better expressed than in a note in the *Mining and Scientific Press* in 1877. Some miners reportedly claimed that "they are going to cover Marysville [California] up." The editor, for one, saw more truth than fiction in the statement.[22]

During the late nineteenth century the mining industry rode a crest of popularity and success that defied its previous American experience. Kings of all they surveyed, miners went to work unfettered by environmental concerns or policy. Although Marysville was not literally buried by the tailings that washed down the Feather and Yuba rivers, the implication was clear: nothing would stand in the way of mining.

If mining had stood alone in its cavalier disregard for the bounties of nature that allowed it to flourish or in its failure to comprehend its impact on the environment, then it would have faced public censure, even in the nineteenth century. Mining did not stand alone. It differed only in degree from other constituents of American industry. The steel industry, the oil fields, and manufacturing also produced waste and pollution. Lumbering attacked the forests with a ferocity that matched mining's onslaught on mineral deposits. American railroads ribboned the country with the same disregard for the environment as mining, except where profits could be made by selling land grants. Refuse was scattered everywhere, and lives were wasted, victims of industrial ignorance and arrogance, in Pittsburgh and Chicago as well as in Leadville and Butte.

In the post–Civil War years, business and industry became enthroned in the temple of American success. For a generation they could hardly do wrong. Business permeated most aspects of American life, from cradle to grave, if the *Golden Manual or the Royal Road to Success* was to be believed. This 1890 volume told how to deal with all aspects of life, from etiquette to marriage, health, and culture. The longest section was reserved for "business rules and forms."[23] What was good for business was good for everybody. In this intoxicating atmosphere, nonmining industrialists and businessmen also became arrogant, unconcerned, and prodigal toward the environment. Mining mirrored what went on elsewhere; its attitudes were those of its contemporaries. The end justified the means. That end might be defined effusively as a stronger and wealthier America—or more mundanely as a statement of profit or loss.

The future oil millionaire John D. Rockefeller defined the goal: "I'm bound to be rich! *Bound to be rich*!" He overachieved, while others failed; nevertheless, the opportunity lay in wait for anyone to seize. Sounding every bit like a mining man, Andrew Carnegie stated his basic business practice: "Run our works full; we *must* run them at any price." One of his favorite maxims for business—"Put all your eggs in one basket, and then watch that basket"—served equally well as an aphorism for mining. All of them could be interchanged—the people, the ideas, the dreams, the determination, the actions. These men and these industries were kindred spirits in an age that esteemed them for their accomplishments. In 1889 the economist David Wells wrote, "An almost total revolution has taken place, and is yet in progress, in every branch and in every relation of the world's industrial and commercial system."[24] Certainly mining had never before witnessed the same magnitude of development or the influx of inventions to improve its performance. For mining and the other industries, this exalted status served as a fitting tribute to the efforts of the past several generations. The future blazed brighter yet.

Very little stood in the way of mining's future. Few individuals challenged this industrial monolith, which espoused the cause of individualism and collectively justified its existence in star-spangled terms. The environment was captive to industry, and that heritage was bequeathed to the next century.

CHAPTER FOUR

"Mining Destroys and Devastates"

The overwhelming consensus described in the previous chapters did not stifle a few voices that were raised in condemnation of mining for its sins against the environment. Some of those voices emerged from within mining; others were closely associated with it. Although they suffered repeated discouragements, they did not labor in vain. A smattering of followers slowly gathered, and by the nineties the industry itself had begun to take an interest in what it had always considered the basest of heresies.

Like mining itself, this awareness evolved during the century, far more slowly, however, than did the mechanical improvements and inventions that so threatened the environment. Criticisms about the impact of mining go back as far as the years immediately following the War of 1812. By the time of the Spanish-American War, eighty years later, a new generation of Americans had begun to pay more heed to them.

The prophet Jeremiah warned the people of Judah, "The summer is over and we are not saved." In a like manner, the respected mining man J. Ross Browne bluntly admonished his contemporaries in 1868: "No country in the world can show such wasteful systems of mining as prevail in ours."[1] Would the industry be saved, or more to the point, did it want to be?

First had to come the perception that something had gone wrong. That perception came much more quickly when profits were endangered. Mining could clearly comprehend the loss and waste of precious metals in milling and smelting. Under those circumstances, the practice of conservation (which was defined from the mine owner's view as saving resources to enhance profits) and the improvement of methods seemed only logical. The industry could easily perceive its direct visual impact on the land also. The *Engineering and Mining Journal* admitted in its April 15, 1876, issue:

> The operations of the miner are always attended with more or less damage to the land. Even in ordinary deep mining, the buildings, machinery, roads, dumps, drainage-waters, cavings of the surface, etc., are serious disfigurements, if not positive injuries. But the destruction effected by sluicing and hydraulic mining is far greater. (P. 365)

Those two factors—financial considerations and visual impact—
sired this budding consciousness about environmental conservation.
Both came into play when concern mounted over the wasting of
forest resources. Rossiter Raymond was not the only one to speak
out. John Tice, for one, strongly concurred with him. After visiting
Caribou, Colorado, near the site where a forest fire had raged, he
lamented the waste, which might have furnished several generations
with ample supplies of lumber and fuel: "For what? Merely to clear
away the fallen leaves so as to expose the naked rocks to the
observation of the prospector. This wantonness has no parallel except
the folly of killing the goose that laid the golden egg."[2]

Laws against this kind of wanton destruction existed on the
books, Tice noted, and he hoped that the guilty parties would reap
the "full penalty." The waste of timber did not come as a new
concern to Raymond and Tice. Twenty years earlier, Josiah Whitney
was admonishing that care should always be taken to ensure a good
supply of this "indispensable material." At the same time, he praised
Germany for setting aside large tracts of forest land, from which a
certain percentage of trees was cut every year to ensure a constant
supply. This enlightened policy can be contrasted to the American
"cut-and-run" system, which prompted Demas Barnes to caution in
1866 that at its present rate of use, Austin, Nevada, would soon be
importing wood from 200 miles away.[3]

Warnings such as these proved timely and were spoken from a
sincere conviction of their importance. Unfortunately, their advocates
did not proffer solutions, as Raymond admitted, except to turn public
lands over to private enterprise. Miners did not understand that their
own self-interest dictated conservation; they remained stubborn
victims of their own individualism. When the price of a cord of wood
soared to unanticipated heights or when shortages stared them in the
face, consumers would conserve for a short time. When the crisis
passed, however, business returned to normal. Nothing could dimin-
ish the sight of all those millions of trees standing on public land, just
waiting to be cut and used. Refusing to regulate themselves, miners
became angry when the federal government finally stepped in to do
so.

This change in policy came about during the administration of
President Benjamin Harrison and his secretary of the interior, John
W. Noble. They listened to the demands of forest conservationists,
scientific groups, and ordinary Americans that the abuse and waste of
lands and forests be stopped. For over a decade, protests had been
directed to Washington; on the eve of Congress's adjournment in
1891, the president had been granted power to set aside forest

reservations. Harrison immediately created six reservations and, by the end of his administration, over 13 million acres of timber reserves. Grover Cleveland, hampered by financial problems resulting from the 1890s depression, was less active in creating more forest reserves, but in the last months of his tenure in 1897, he set aside thirteen.

The small victory for forest conservationists did little to smooth the tortuous path that still had to be traveled before their final victory. The new forest reserves received only paper protection; in practice, exploitation went on as usual. Also disconcerting was the lack of a clear definition of purpose for these reserves. John Muir simply hoped to protect the forests in their undeveloped condition. Others sought a more utilitarian approach—the management of timberland for the benefit of various interests. A victory by either group would require a new approach by Washington. The mining industry, among others, watched with amazement and disgust this change in government philosophy, wishing to continue its business as usual with no interference, light or heavy. It did not like the way the wind was starting to blow off the Potomac.

Gifford Pinchot, who was soon to become *persona non grata* to the mining industry, wrote an article in 1898 to explain why forest reserves had been set aside and how this policy would benefit mining. He believed, somewhat naïvely, that mining men should wholeheartedly support the idea. In his opinion, their hostility to it arose from the government's mishandling of the announcement and from the prevailing attitude that "all men keep out [of the forests]."[4] The real intent, according to Pinchot, was something very different: the management of forest reserves and the fullest, continuous development of all resources.

The fullest development, according to Pinchot, included access for actual settlers, the construction of wagon roads, and the development of water resources. Owners of valid mining sites would be permitted to work their claims and to cut and remove timber for their own use. These regulations, he argued, would particularly help those who had to "deal with low grade ores." Pinchot concluded: "It will be used, but the differences between use and waste in our western forests is something which can be fully appreciated only by men who have seen the thing for themselves."

Western mining men, unconvinced, would lead the fight against the national-forest concept in years to come. Fear of economic setbacks and loss of the "right" to use the public domain incited them. Small miners saw open land as their last defense against the growing dominance of mining corporations.[5] This growing estrangement between the corporations and small miners would play a larger role in the twentieth century; for the moment it seemed inconsequential.

One small conservation effort took place unwittingly when scavengers gathered planks, blocks, and bits of wood from mine dumps for cooking and heating. Both John Galloway and John Waldorf remembered the scramble on the Comstock, sometimes by swarms of people, to find choice pieces.[6] Thus, not everything was squandered; need, rather than lofty intentions, forced the reutilization of a tiny portion of the waste.

Pinchot's plans and the failure of mining to respond favorably focused attention on the divisiveness. Tradition, assumed rights, availability, dividends, need, and economy—invalid standards in the opinion of some—seemed to justify industry's right to use timber without regard for long-range impacts. The mining industry would never be converted voluntarily to prudent use unless it could be demonstrated that the change would be economical. More likely, it would be forced into reforming its methods, succumbing only to overwhelming pressure. This refusal meant that mining would pay the price of eventual public condemnation.

The question of water pollution proved to be different. The industry made some progress here, though limited to the narrow issue of the rights of fellow miners. From the simple bylaws of Colorado's California Mining District, which prohibited the dumping of tailings on another person's claim and assessed fines for failing to return water to a ditch, to the statutes in Barringer's 1900 *Law of Mines*, there ran a continuous line of increased complexity. Mining intended to take care of its own.[7]

In 1897, when T. A. Rickard complimented the Homestake and other mining companies for their recycling of limited water supplies, an awakening seemed to be taking place, utilitarian and self-serving though it was. The Homestake constructed two small dams below its stamp mill; their reservoirs served, during the winter low cycle, as reserve supplies once the mud settled out. Some companies also used drainage water from mines to supplement the natural supply, if it ran low.

Interestingly, the industry had already tentatively acknowledged its ecological impact. As early as 1818 in Missouri, Schoolcraft had observed botanical changes wrought by mining. He told how soil that was thrown out of the pits nurtured several plants that were not native to the area. Comprehension of the impact that mining was having on vegetation came slowly. A bibliography of articles about injuries caused to vegetation by furnace gases, the most obvious of impacts, listed the first article on that subject in 1843, the second in

1880, followed by two more during that decade, and then a flood of thirty-four during the 1890s. Most of these studies were published in England or other European countries and involved all types of industries, not just smelting. Europe pioneered, while America procrastinated. The enlightened mining engineer, however, could not help but be professionally aware of what was being attempted in order to curb the nuisance.[8]

A progressive attitude toward conservation was also evolving in the smelting industry. John Tice stated it simply: "The interests of society demand that there should be no waste." Mining men heartily concurred, their only question being how to attain that goal. Studies and experimentation eventually produced methods and equipment that cut the waste to a more acceptable percentage and were less harmful to profits, though these were not without their drawbacks. All of these reforms were forced by the demand for a profitable business. Smoke pollution did not receive the same impetus. Until finally forced into court, the industry made little headway against a problem that, as early as the 1860s, was recognized as being injurious to vegetation and to human health. Though dust chambers and flue-dust appliances trapped some airborne minerals, most wafted out of the smokestack. Something more needed to be done, but that something eluded the industry. Samuel Emmons condemned those who did nothing as being "unworthy of imitation."[9] Clean air would be a twentieth-century challenge, not a nineteenth-century accomplishment.

These small beginnings toward conservation and environmental awareness were narrowly circumscribed and were always weighed against their dollar benefits. The land and water rights of nonminers generated little concern. *Damnum absque injuria* (loss in the legal sense, but with no damages assessed against the person or company causing the harm) continued to be the guiding principle, as always.

A hodgepodge of other issues that arose from time to time aroused even less general interest than did the ones already mentioned. Several writers criticized coal mining for its squandering of that resource and for its indifference to the future. "As a consequence, we are wasting our valuable mineral treasures in a most shameful manner," wrote Andrew Roy, the state inspector of mines for Ohio. He went on to say that because mineral property "is cheap and abundant, the great object is to mine out the best coals in the cheapest manner possible, without regard to ultimate consequences."[10] The United States, he believed, compared unfavorably with Europe and Great Britain in the development of coal lands and in preventing the useless waste of coal.

Well stated and to the point, this idea had come before its time. Mining engineer Winfield Scott Keyes decried the inefficient early placer methods of Last Chance Gulch (Helena, Mont.), which lost gold (conservatively estimated at $1.5 million) in the tailings.[11] He, as well as others elsewhere, had begun to comprehend the cost of the ruthless exploitation during those early rushes. Still, given the excitement and the prevailing devil-may-care attitude, it would happen again and again.

Booming also earned sharp criticism, not, however, because of the environmental horror that it created, but, as California's state mineralogist, Henry Hanks, wrote, because "this mode of mining is very wasteful. The force of the flood is so sudden and powerful that the lighter particles of gold are washed away and lost."[12] Having proven to be only marginally sound economically, booming was replaced. The dredge, for instance, could handle gold much more efficiently. This classic example illustrates the thinking of the mining industry and explains why it abandoned a method that severely threatened the environment for one that was less damaging, an unpremeditated reform.

Mining engineer Frederick Corning was one of those individuals who were bold enough to point out that since a mine's mineral deposit was exhaustible, mining operations should be planned accordingly: "Graphically represented, a mine's life is something after the fashion of a crescendo with a corresponding decrescendo." He did not venture so far as to suggest that the mineral resources of the country might be finite; he argued only for the legitimate management of mines. Too many people scoffed at those suggestions in his generation. Corning went on to plead for the careful supervision of all departments of mining and for the judicious management of mines.[13] After a mine had failed or dividends had ceased, the stockholders began to see the wisdom of an approach that encouraged conservation.

The visual pollution of having unsightly mine dumps silhouetted along the skyline generated a few protests that would have gladdened Dame Shirley's heart. Dan De Quille, for instance, was pleased when a number of Virginia City dumps were leveled to use as fill. Writing in his mining textbook, Samuel Daddow complained about the immense amount of waste being constantly piled up around the coal mines—"vast, unsightly mounds, burying our mining villages, and sadly encroaching on the limits of our chief towns." As if that were not bad enough, every rain carried off a portion of that waste to rivers, streets, and cellars. "It will become a necessity in time to find some mode of disposing of it." More typically, the attention to unsightly waste resembled that of *Harper's Monthly* in 1857, when it offhandedly mentioned the "immense artificial hills" being created around the Pennsylvania coal fields.[14] These straws in the wind of enlightenment made little headway against the high tide of nineteenth-century mining—they offered little to appeal to the industry in general. Then, too, these criticisms repeatedly failed to provide or point to solutions. What practical marketable product could be made from a coal dump? Environmental issues by themselves did not encourage involvement. Profit-seeking reform obviously did not arise from the goodness of the reformer's heart or from some deep concern about the environment. The industry could be satisfied with this kind of response; some others could not be. They were the real Jeremiahs, willing to risk public damnation in order to warn their generation about its foolishness and extravagance.

The reform-minded Victorian Helen Hunt Jackson visited O-Be-Joyful Creek above Crested Butte, Colorado, one summer day. She saw little to be joyful about, even though she was surrounded by breath-taking natural beauty. A field of purple asters and a "foaming, plashing, sparkling" torrent only accentuated the disturbing contrast between men across the stream who were digging coal and prospectors who were working the water higher up. They did not seem to see, did not feel.

> There is a field of purple asters two miles west of Crested Butte that some people would rather possess for the rest of the summers of their lives than the coal bank opposite it,—a million times rather; and if a man would secure them a perpetual "claim" to the roadway and a narrow strip of the shore of O-Be-Joyful Creek, he might have all the gold and silver in the upper levels of its canyon, and welcome. There is no accounting for differences in values; no adjusting them either, unluckily. The men who are digging, coking, selling the coal opposite the aster field, do not see the asters; the prospectors hammering away high up above the foaming, plashing, sparkling torrent of the O-Be-Joyful water do not know where it is amber and where it is white, or care for it unless they need a drink. . . .
>
> There is one comfort: the "market" in which stock in aster fields and brooks is bought is always strong. Margins are safe, and dividends sure. Ten years from now, that coal bank may not pay, but I shall have my aster field.

Jackson, who from her travels and writing, knew mining life and attitudes better than most women of her day, philosophically concluded that there was no accounting for differences in values, "no adjusting them either, unluckily." In that statement she bared the prevailing attitude toward the environment. Miners' values differed from hers. Until they could both agree that the "market which stock is in aster fields and brooks" had as much intrinsic value as the market for coal and silver, there would be no reconciling those differences.[15]

Reconciliation would require innovations that were repugnant to the Victorian business mind. Even Helen Hunt Jackson would have thought twice about curbing the prevailing laissez-faire attitude by means of governmental regulation or some form of enforced voluntary agreement. Sentimentally, she believed in changing the heart, but whether that could be done in the materialistic mining world of the nineteenth century was open to a wide margin of doubt.

Jackson did not stand alone in her convictions. The English poet James Thomson traveled to Colorado on mining business in the early 1870s and spent some time in Central City. He, too, was captivated by the wild flowers, the magnificent vistas, and the "wonderfully pure, azure or deep burning blue" sky. Then he turned to what man had done:

> . . . prospectholes, primitive loghuts, mill-sheds, of which many are idle, fragments of machinery that proved useless from the first, heaps of stones and poor ores, and all sorts of rubbish. No one has ever cleaned up anything here [Central City]; . . . Men dig a shaft shallow or deep, and leave it gaping for anyone to tumble into. Trees are cut down and the stumps all left to make night-wandering safe and agreeable. The hills surrounding us have been flayed of their grass, and scalped of their timber; and they are scarred and gashed and ulcerated all over from past mining operations; so ferociously does little man scratch at the breasts of his great calm mother when he thinks that jewels are there hidden.

The sharp-penned writer and world traveler Isabella Bird pulled no punches when she railed against mining: "Agriculture restores and beautifies, mining destroys and devastates, turning the earth inside out, making it hideous, blighting every green thing, as it usually blights man's heart and soul."[16] Jackson, Thomson, and Bird all appreciated nature's beauty, and each saw and recorded the impact that mining had on the environment. Unfortunately, none advocated a way to accommodate the two—they simply reacted to what affected and angered them.

Mining's armor of prestige easily deflected criticisms such as these. As fruitless as the protests might seem, though, they carried within them the seeds of reform that would slowly mature within the industry and elsewhere. Jackson and the others stood only on the fringe of mining; agitation had to come from its core to signal that the reformation was at hand. Somehow, the heart had to generate as much emotion as did the silver dollar.

Rossiter Raymond wrestled with the problem and concurred with the idea of conservation. Forests, he wrote, might be replanted; fishing grounds, restocked; farmland, revived; "but coal, iron, copper, lead, petroleum, gold and silver will not come again within the history of the human race into the places from which they have been extracted." Then he came to the core of the matter: "A waste of them is a waste forever." Raymond's quandary lay with how to implement conservation measures, a problem that he, like his generation, did not see as pressing, because no immediate danger threatened the exhaustion of mineral resources.[17]

A handful of others already agreed with Helen Hunt Jackson. The editor of Rico, Colorado's *Dolores News* called upon his mining readers to save the trees; they were necessary "not only at the present, but for all future time." The significance of his statement lay with the fact that he not only advocated saving the trees but also had thought far enough ahead to the legacy that must be passed on. His concern cried out to be nurtured. Clarence King esteemed nature, as his *Mountaineering in the Sierra Nevada* amply testifies. This geologist and mining man well understood mining's impact on the land. King pointed to two factors that might help heal or ease those wounds: nature's reclamation of her own, and stability and permanence within the industry.[18] He did not explain precisely how these things would be accomplished, particularly the latter, probably because his thinking followed along business lines rather than environmental ones. King was correct in believing that permanence tended to create a climate for concern. When people had breathed the air, drunk the water, stumbled over the waste, and lived in the dust, dirt, and mud for a longer period of time, they would tolerate pollution and litter less readily.

In a less esoteric realm, strides were being taken in conservation. Eckley B. Coxe, who was active in the anthracite coal industry but was no early paragon of waste prevention, illustrated this change in tactics. With enthusiasm and his own money, Coxe chaired the committee of the American Institute of Mining Engineers to deal with the waste of anthracite. In meetings and reports, Coxe formulated plans to cut the loss of coal. By the 1890s his efforts earned this tribute: "In that field of true and immediate 'conservation,' [it] was more important than any subsequent achievement in the same direction."[19] Coxe's work exemplified both the practical and the profitable, a winning combination. If the mining industry had been able to reconcile the entire environmental issue in the same way, it would have been at the head of its class, rather than near the bottom.

Awareness needed to be followed by concern; and concern, by action—the search for a remedy. The industry had to crawl before it could walk, and in the nineteenth century it appeared at times to be unable even to move. One possible course of action was to take the polluter into court. The odds of success for an individual were long in this day of conservative, business-oriented judiciaries. Only rarely did one mining company sue another over stream pollution; seldom did a mining community charge a company with violating a water ordinance. The reason for this reluctance is easily understood. The very nature of the case—the demand for an injunction or for monetary relief—threatened mining's profitability and a community's well-being. A long-drawn-out, expensive suit hurt all of the participants. A sufficient number of mining cases dealing with important matters such as apex rights had already crowded the dockets and were discouraging the consideration of environmental matters. These circumstances demanded a good, hard second look at the consequences of lengthy litigation. Determining whom to sue when properties had been abandoned could also be a problem, as Silver Plume, Colorado, found out. When the spring runoff threatened to dislodge portions of deserted dumps on the mountainside above town, no one had remained who could be held accountable.

When the courts failed to provide relief, when laws were laxly enforced and warnings went unheeded, and when an industry remained largely unresponsive, what other environmental recourses remained? Private individuals could reclaim the scarred land and set an example. In the spring of 1867, James Rusling saw the "ragged hills" near Placerville, California, which had long been abandoned by the miner, being changed into vineyards and orchards. By the skillful use of irrigation, the wastelands were "rapidly being converted into productive farms."[20] Unfortunately, this small start was not imitated because of circumstances that included the cost and the lack of pressure for reclamation.

In those days when the doctrine of laissez faire prevailed, it was unthinkable, even un-American, for the mining industry to consider empowering an agency or an official to provide the regulation and the enforcement that it was unable to give itself. Rossiter Raymond gave the industry's rationale for opposing government interference in an 1884 sketch of the evolution of mining law. For governmental control, he wrote, there was no precedent in American legislation—the right of the landowner remained supreme. He agreed with Herbert Spencer that government was "conspicuously unfitted to do those things," such as controlling the economy and preventing the waste of mineral resources. Individual citizens and industries were in a much better position to know what was best. Aware that this philosophy could and did lead to waste, Raymond voiced some reservations about it: "We have, perhaps, gone too far in this direction. Better so than to have gone too far in the other." He darkly hinted of "encroachments" and of governmental blunders if regulation came to pass.[21]

The quandary that industrial leaders faced was clear in an 1876 address given by Abram S. Hewitt, president of the American Institute of Mining Engineers. Obviously agreeing with Raymond's later position, Hewitt said:

> Our people waste as much as they like and no one interferes. Admitting this is an evil, it still remains a matter of doubt how far, under the circumstances of our particular case, the supervision of authority could remedy it.
>
> . . . I am not disposed to say that for so great an end as the conservation of mineral wealth of the country it [government] may not properly enforce some measures of economy with as good right as it may forbid the reckless waste of timber or the slaughter of game out of season.[22]

What should be the limits of governmental regulation? Hewitt, like the others, found himself caught in a cruel dilemma—he recognized the problem, but he had no answer. Governmental interference was the last resort, a "poor substitute" for other efforts, which "in the atmosphere of freedom and intelligence, ought to be effective."

Hewitt did care about conservation, and he worried about waste. "We are, perhaps, in our material career as a nation, like the young man who has 'sown his wild oats,' and now by mature reflection and the lessons of experience, is likely to be better restrained than by the hand of parental authority." Perhaps he was grasping at the weak straw of self-regulation, but that does not negate his sensitivity to the issue. His listeners did not rally to the colors to launch a crusade; therein lay the tragedy of that generation.

One of Hewitt's contemporaries, J. Ross Browne, had dared to propose the unthinkable a few years earlier in his 1868 mining report. Prefacing his main concern with the statement that "no country in the world can show such wasteful systems of mining as prevail in ours," he went on to make this suggestion: "The question arises whether it is not the duty of government to prevent, as far as may be consistent with individual rights, this waste of a common heritage, in which not only ourselves but our posterity are interested." Before the astonished reader had time to digest this heresy, Browne concluded that a miner retained the right to the produce of his labor, "but has he a right to deprive others of the benefits to be derived from the treasures of the earth, placed there for a common good?"[23] Strong, biting words were these, particularly when weighed against the attitudes of his generation. A champion of conservation, an environmental prophet, had emerged.

Browne lost the opportunity to translate his idealism into action, and his words were forgotten, relegated to the waste can of governmental reports. Tragically, his sentiments failed to inspire others to follow his lead; Browne had not even lightly shaken the temple of mining, let alone had he threatened to topple it. The times and the prevailing attitudes of the mining industry submerged his progressive opinions and overwhelmed him. J. Ross Browne would have found himself more at home in the 1960s than in the 1860s. The duty of government, in this earlier century, was not to regulate but to encourage development and to hand out unstintingly the natural resources and the public lands for private gain. Although mining could be wasteful, it could also build a stronger America, settle the West, and enrich Americans. Regard for the future or for the common heritage had every appearance of being heretical or, even worse, socialistic. So Browne's ideas died, having evolved far ahead of their time. He concluded, however, with a statement that would come back to haunt the industry: "Our children have an interest in them [the treasures of the earth] which we cannot with propriety disregard."[24]

All was not lost. By the 1890s, faint rays of environmental awareness (provided that it generated profit) had begun to lighten the industrial darkness. When the Gold Valley Placer Company, operating near Dixon, Wyoming, listed as one of the six essentials for successful placering "tailing ground that prevents trespass," then times were surely changing. Mining engineer Richard Stretch emphasized the same point when he wrote that the presence of ample dumping room should first be ascertained.[25] Some attention now had to be paid to the land and to how the company operated. No longer could a miner act only in his own best interest, without regard to anyone or anything else. Rip, rape, and run were perhaps becoming unfashionable.

When viewed against the traditional late-nineteenth-century position of the mining industry, the struggle to mitigate environmental damage appeared to be a one-sided, losing one. Logic, money, political power, local concerns, courts, and public awareness conspired to subjugate the proponents of reform.

Undaunted, the Jeremiahs of the era presented their case. They may have sensed the deep feelings that Americans held toward the land, feelings that were so eloquently stated by K. Ross Toole in *The Rape of the Great Plains:*

> Whatever he used of the land, or, however, in truth, he abused the land, he was not filled with the ultimate arrogance of believing that he had the power, to say nothing of the right, to use it all up. *He was no eater of carrion.*[26]

Perhaps simple optimism, which has so often been ascribed to Americans, kept them going. These prophets may have felt that they were hitting a sympathetic nerve within the American psyche or that they were fighting to educate, to warn, so that their ideas would live for another day to arouse another generation.

As impossible as their cause might have looked, as few in number as they may have been, and as inefficient as their efforts appeared to be, these people proposed an alternative to the practices and the philosophy of that day. Recognition and justification would come, but not during their lifetime. They never attained a unity of organization for their common cause or a public concern or alarm. They stood to be counted individually. Perhaps they sensed the changes that were coming when mining found itself confronted by two environmental issues that would not go away: the problem of debris in California and the controversy over smoke from smelters. The dawn of a victory was at hand.

CHAPTER FIVE

The Rustling Breeze of Change

California, the land of the forty-niner and of the first instant legend about American mining, attracted the initial major challenge to the industry. The attack focused on hydraulic mining, a horror to land and water. The results of its devastation must be seen to be appreciated. Shooting water under high pressure through a cannonlike nozzle made it possible to move mountains and to pollute streams with incredible ease. William Brewer observed, "I have seen works and effects that one would imagine it would take centuries to produce, instead of the dozen years that have elapsed since the work began."[1] Someone else compared the effects of hydraulicking to the aftermath of an earthquake.

Hydraulic mining grew from a need to work lower-grade gravel more quickly and in larger amounts than the pan or the sluice box was economically or physically capable of doing. Proud Californians liked to think they had invented the concept in 1852, but the idea dates back at least to Roman times. Regardless, in California it secured a profitable foothold and spread to other gold-mining areas throughout the country.

Almost from its beginnings, the industry was preparing a defense for hydraulicking, much earlier than for any other facet of mining. The industry obviously had qualms about and felt the need to justify what it was doing. As might be expected, the economy of operation was underscored, including the time and the tonnage involved, the costs of equipment and labor, and water's attribute of being "ever active and untiring." The industry praised the "venturous spirit" that led the miner to seek the "quick realization of his hopes for great wealth" through bold engineering feats. A mining man from Dahlonega, Georgia, announced that "the only way to work this property is by means of water"; government reporter John Hittell described hydraulic mining as the most "effectual method ever devised" for excavating large quantities of earth. Winfield Keyes pictured it as nature's method; the more closely it could be copied by man, "so much more completely can he separate the valuable particles from the valueless, and gather the rich booty stored up in gravel forming the placers." Keyes also believed that claims would produce for a longer time under this type of mining, which would be a definite advantage for the owner and for the investor. Stated or unstated, every defense implied that more profit could be made by hydraulicking. "That this property can be worked to a great profit by hydraulic process is beyond dispute, and that it cannot be worked profitably by any other mode, is in my opinion a settled fact." At least two publications promoted hydraulic mining as a tourist attraction, something that the visitor would wish to see, "the mountain removing to the sea."[2]

All of these arguments convinced the miners, who eagerly developed the hydraulic mines. Not everyone could be swayed so readily, however. The downstream farmers and townspeople, who saw their water sources being muddied and their lands being flooded and covered with debris (they called it slickens), found little joy in the mining industry's good fortune. These people condemned the depreciated land values, the ruined crops, and the debris-filled river-beds (especially in California). They viewed as nuisances the tailings that were strung along riverbanks, and they saw many miners as "irresponsible persons," against whom action to recover damages was a worthless endeavor. According to these people, the miners "absolutely" refused to discontinue their "wrongful and injurious acts."[3] The industry saw itself and its contributions to society in a much different light.

Because American hydraulicking originated in California and was carried on much more extensively there, that state became the battleground for these two conflicting opinions. Problems came quickly; by the late 1850s, tailings had obstructed the channels of some rivers and had flooded river bottoms, killing trees and other vegetation. At Marysville (which had not been covered up, despite threats to that effect), the floods in 1862 washed down debris that ruined agricultural lands. The annual winter floods gradually filled the Sacramento and Feather rivers, obstructing navigation and commerce. Marysville was forced to build higher levees to protect itself from the overflow. Adding to these damages were those from floods that were caused by collapsed reservoirs and other accidents in the mining regions. The downstream malcontents had a justifiable right to complain.

Nevada City, California's *Transcript* for January 22, 1875, asked: "What are the owners of the farms to do? It is evident mining can never be stopped. It is an industry the whole world desires to foster." Those few sentences concisely summarized the argument for mining: mining could not be stopped; the whole world needed it. Its opponents obviously disagreed. The 1860s brought the start of litigation, and in the 1870s, hydraulic miners regularly found themselves in court, usually defending against suits to force payment for damages or for improvements to stop the flooding and silting. In 1877, farmers in the Yuba River Valley (joined by some miners who were hoping to head off further trouble) published a pamphlet, encouraging companies to contribute to the cost of a levee. They believed a conciliatory response would do much to dispel animosity and to save money on vexatious litigation. Conciliation was not in the cards.[4]

Out of this growing dispute materialized the classic case of *Woodruff* v. *North Bloomfield, et al.* The mining industry now faced a legal challenge of unprecedented proportions. The industry's unspoken right to the ultimate use of the land and its resources rested on the outcome of this litigation.

This particular case, the most famous of several during the 1870s and 1880s, involved Edward Woodruff, the owner of farmland outside Marysville on the Feather River. That land had been partly covered by debris in the 1860s, and his town lot had been damaged by the 1875 flood. Woodruff sued North Bloomfield and other mining companies, requesting a permanent injunction against further operations. Supporting his plea was a state law, passed in April, 1855, to protect the owners of growing crops, buildings, and the like against damage resulting from mining. On the miners' side, several statutes placed agriculture at the mercy of mining.[5]

The farmers and the townspeople skillfully prepared and aggressively presented their case. Their basic argument developed as follows. Material that washed down river was covering the land and raising the riverbed, thus ruining fields, disrupting river commerce, and causing flooding. This was costing landholders, mechanics, and farmers money and lost time. Agriculture had as much right to use the land and stream flow as mining had, and agriculture's interests must be protected. The farmers and citizens had at hand the facts, the witnesses, and varied evidence to support their accusations; they, becoming every bit as emotional as the supporters of mining, charged that the profits from hydraulicking fattened pocketbooks in San Francisco and London, where only the benefits accrued, without the drawbacks. The plaintiffs claimed also that hydraulic mining did not increase local business and population. Sounding much like their twentieth-century descendants, they accused mining of utterly destroying the rivers for fish and as elements to be used by the general public, arguing that one of life's pleasures was a sparkling stream with opportunities for enjoying it.[6] The phrase "quality of life" was unknown as such, yet these Californians obviously had a good idea of what it meant to them. Mining would have to move cautiously or it would lose this fight.

The industry, forewarned by earlier disputes, stood ready to defend itself with its best legal arguments. It was, however, confronted by some overwhelmingly damaging evidence. A California legislative report in 1879 described the dumping of more than forty million cubic yards of material into the Feather River by hydraulic mining during that one year alone.

The mining industry countered by threatening that an injunction would cripple the industry "to which California owes her rapid rise and wonderful prosperity." To stop gold mining would subject California and the United States to direct economic loss and might cause damage to American credit abroad. Continuing their scare tactics, the defender of mining envisioned thousands of people being out of work, the demise of populous and thrifty towns, and the relegation of mining districts to their "original solitude and desolation."[7]

The mining industry quickly encountered a setback: the court rejected its claim that either Congress or the state had authorized the use of the river as a deposit for debris. In virtual desperation, the defendants asserted that because tailings had been discharged onto Woodruff's farmland for ten years, a "prescriptive right" to the land had been acquired. The plaintiffs scoffed at that assertion. Changing tactics, the defense argued that much more agricultural than mining land remained available; therefore, mining should hold sway where it could successfully operate. Furthermore, miners had been there first, long antedating the farmers (at least American farmers) in the Feather and Yuba rivers drainages; agricultural interests, when they arrived, of necessity, acted with their "eyes open," in full knowledge of the mining industry's rights. The defendants' final argument reverted to an old favorite: earlier mining had already disturbed and changed the land; hydraulicking was simply following in its footsteps.[8]

With the generalities out of the way, the defense of the mining industry dug into specifics. Marysville was situated below the high-water mark of the river and therefore was subject to overflow; moreover, river water had been unfit for use long before hydraulic mining had contributed its debris. Nor had the floods of 1875 and 1876 been related to hydraulic mining—they were "wholly attributable to other causes." Mining could not be held solely responsible for the filling up of the Sacramento and Feather rivers, something that had been occurring since "time immemorial." Occupation and settlement—farming, lumbering, railroads, ranching, mining—all accelerated the natural siltings: "Of course it is pure nonsense to assert that the filling in the beds of the Feather, and the Sacramento below its mouth, has taken place since these mines have been in operation, or has been caused by their operations.'' Neither had over forty thousand acres been damaged by debris and flooding, as charged; at most, it might be fifteen thousand. As for Woodruff, the defendants' lawyers charged that his farming property had been flooded and covered with debris before their clients ever had engaged in mining in the Yuba River watershed (the Yuba ran into the Feather, which joined the Sacramento). The lawyers protested further that the plaintiff had not sustained injuries and grievances and that much of the information included ''garbled and incomplete'' statements.[9] That catchall accusation covered almost every possible point of contention.

Switching to a positive stance, the defenders of hydraulicking drew a rosy picture. Company reservoirs helped to prevent flooding during the rainy period, and they allowed more water into the streams during the dry months. Then came the *pièce de résistance:* affidavits were presented to show that the sediment in the water actually enriched the soil and made it more productive. Nonenriched water had never bestowed such a blessing.

The hydraulic companies claimed that they had acted in good faith in building their dams and in working their projects and that to grant an injunction would have a disastrous effect with far-reaching consequences. Their argument closed with a prophetic fantasy about the ill effects of the proposed permanent injunction:

> The direct and immediate effect of it would be to paralyze one of the leading industries of this commonwealth; to deprive this State and the world at large of millions of dollars which the mining industry of California annually ''pours into the lap of commerce''; to render practically worthless all the hydraulic mining properties in the States . . . ; to drive from the state and keep away from it, a large amount of much needed capital; to make valueless the property of thousands of people in the mining regions, who are not themselves mine-owners at all, but who are dependent for their support upon the mining industry, and to drive them and their families out upon the world without employment or means of subsistence; to depopulate villages, towns and cities, and cause schoolhouses and churches to go to ruin and decay, and even to cause the disorganization of county government; in fine, to scatter widespread ruin and disaster over what is now one of the most populous, enterprising and prosperous sections of the State.[10]

The defense rested.

Mining journals and papers, meanwhile, had long since taken up the issue in articles, editorials, and letters. Many of the arguments, of course, were repeated. Some writers admitted that damage had been done and called for the question to be settled on a broad and permanent basis. For others, such as Louis Garnett, president of the El Dorado Water and Deep Gravel Mining Company, the debate meant only one thing: "It is absolute prohibition or nothing, and the former, I conceive, is simply out of the question." For those who agreed with Garnett's assessment, no verdict other than a complete victory for mining was tolerable. The *Mining and Scientific Press*, in January, 1877, had asked who was to blame—was it not all who mined, and how would damage be assessed? No one came forward to answer those legitimate questions. A year later, in March, 1878, the same journal pleaded editorially for forebearance and good sense on the part of "our people" and for recommended levees, fluming, and relief canals as remedies. Optimists lived on the assumption that a solution would be found—man's "ingenuity and energy" would save the day. Mining engineer Richard Stretch observed: "And the so called 'debris' question is one of vital importance to all hydraulic mines at the present time."[11]

On January 7, 1884, United States Circuit Court Judge Lorenzo Sawyer, coincidentally a forty-niner, rejected the defendants' claims and "perpetually enjoined and restrained" them from discharging or dumping into the Yuba or its tributaries.[12] Marysville and its environs rejoiced that evening. "Profound sorrow" shrouded the mining regions, where the news was received as "one would the death sentence." Henry C. Perkins, who had been superintendent of North Bloomfield since 1874, simply resigned; hydraulic mining in California was no longer profitable.

The times had changed, but mining had not changed with them. The industry no longer had the population or the economic and political power of the days of forty-nine (or even of the decade of the seventies) to impose its will. Miners no longer represented California's present and future. Mining lost out, too, because it had been made abundantly clear that hydraulicking was the villain in the flooding and silting of rivers. Agriculture could successfully make the challenge, because its economic impact had grown steadily.

Many of the defendants' arguments could not stand up to intense scrutiny. The Yuba and Feather valleys reaped no benefits comparable to the cited blessings to Egypt of the silt from the Nile River, thus destroying any valid comparison. Hydraulicking had not aided either navigation or stream flow. The economic facts of the late 1870s and the early 1880s failed to support the emotional outburst in which possible damages to the region and the state were outlined. Little by little, defenses of the mining industry were stripped away,

Hydraulic mining has made its mark on the environment, from the Atlantic to the Pacific, in small mines and large ones. Brier Patch Mine, Lumpkin County, Georgia, 1915 (courtesy Georgia Department of Archives and History, Atlanta).

until only selfish profit-over-all materialism remained. Mining had met its match, overwhelmed by the needs and demands of the agricultural community.

Further hurting the cause of mining as the court fight dragged on was the growing resentment of big corporations on the part of local miners, who objected to the control over their individual lives that the companies brought. Translated into other terms, this meant the hiring of Chinese miners and a lack of concern for the working miner by absentee owners. The people of the mining districts took offense at the wealth and power of these corporations. Unity, which is hard to come by at any time, was harder to maintain under the pressures of the day.

Unspoken throughout the judicial sparring lay concern for the environment, a concern that was defined as how it could be used to the best economic benefit. The views of the mining industry lost out, but no general reassessment of attitudes followed. Unaffected hard-rock mining predominated throughout most of the rest of the country, and confidence continued that a less objectionable way could be found to work profitably the low-grade placer deposits. Eugene Wilson, in his 1898 textbook *Hydraulic and Placer Mining,* proffered the unreconstructed view: hydraulicking would come back with new equipment and methods. He warned only that care be taken with the dump. No mention of conservation or the environment occurred on his pages.[13] Wilson also approved of dredges. Dredging was the direct descendant of hydraulic mining, because it handled successfully, as did its forerunner, the low-grade ores.

In a continuously declining, limited way, hydraulic mining was carried on for years, though never again in the manner that prevailed during California's heyday of the seventies. The state and the Anti-Debris Association kept a close watch on developments, and mining was forced to toe the mark as it had never done before. In spite of the magnitude of the defeat for one segment of the industry, mining failed to learn the fundamental lessons implicit in the fight over hydraulic mining. An angered public could successfully challenge the industry, and nothing disturbed that public more than a threat to its economic well-being. In the name of profit, concern for the environment rallied supporters. The unchallenged right of the mining industry to use the public domain for its own capitalist benefit could not continue indefinitely; those days were slipping away. And last, the methods of yesterday would not suffice for tomorrow; changes must come if the industry hoped to survive as a viable segment of America's economy. To incredulous spokesmen of mining that last statement was inconceivable, and they resisted it vigorously.

Just as hydraulic mining incited public ire in California, so did smoke from smelters inflame it. Infamous Butte, Montana, had no contemporary equal, yet Oakland, California, had confronted the problem earlier when it had grappled with the decision about whether to allow a smelter to be constructed in that community. A series of hearings from February 26 to March 5, 1872, permitted the industry and those who opposed the construction to state their views before the city council.

Opposition to the smelter centered upon the unhealthful, irritating, and offensive fumes, which would "poison our pure air" and render this "beautiful city an undesirable place to live." Examples were supplied to show the extensive damage that smelting works had contributed to the atmosphere, vegetation, and land in and near Swansea, Wales; Liverpool, England; and Freiburg, Germany. Residents of Oakland feared a similar fate, one that would threaten the health of the community and, they implied, would eventually reduce the values of land and real estate. They preferred to decline the honor of having a smelter for a neighbor under those circumstances.[14]

Taken aback by those kinds of accusations, the industry offered its rebuttal, but none too effectively or convincingly. The objections to smelting, a spokesman replied, were "purely and entirely imaginary." To buttress his unconvincing statement, he pointed to Nevada's experience with smelters, which he defined as "good" without going into specifics, while ignoring the dissimilarities between Oakland and mining towns in Nevada. The examples of Germany and Great Britain proved harder to dismiss, and the only rejoinder was a rhetorical question: If the smelters had proved so unhealthful, would not Great Britain have passed laws to control them? Going on the attack and foreshadowing Butte's claim of a few years later, the smelter people pointed with pride to the manufacturing and steel center of Pittsburgh, with all of its smoke and fumes, the "notorious healthiest city in Pennsylvania."[15] Promising confidently that great economic blessings would be showered upon Oakland with the advent of the smelter, the proponents closed their case.

On March 6 the city council pronounced that Oakland would welcome all smelting works, except those producing gases that would be injurious to the health of "her inhabitants." The smelting of lead and argentiferous ores fell into this category, and the council admonished that these would be tolerated only in localities where "placed in almost an isolated position."[16] The industry had suffered a minor setback, which was more embarrassing than fatal.

The smelter officials, caught somewhat off guard in Oakland, had failed to put forth a very strong case on their behalf. To be challenged, as they were, was almost unheard of at this time, and they simply were not prepared. Nevertheless, the battle lines had been drawn as the industry skirmished in this opening round of what would be a long fight.

Butte's controversy made the furor in Oakland seem like mere child's play. Unlike Butte, Oakland did not represent a mining town in a mining district that depended on the industry for its economic future. Butte's problem, therefore, was more complicated. The struggle here would be a protracted one, beginning during the 1880s in Butte and not ending in the nearby smelter town of Anaconda until well past the turn of the century. The first phase involved primarily the issue of public health and the general well-being of the community.

By 1889, Butte had accommodated six "of the most modern and potent" smelters in the world along the base of its hill of copper, as well as a population of ten thousand. "The thicker the fumes the greater our financial vitality, and Butteites feel best when the fumes are thickest," bragged the *Butte Miner*. Boasts about Butte's health

Few copper mines were more famous than Butte's Berkeley Pit. The evolution from underground to open pit is clearly shown, as well as the gigantic scale of the operations (courtesy Anaconda Minerals Company).

and prosperity ignored the environmental atrocities. Sulfur, copper, and arsenic fumes killed grass, flowers, and trees; and cats who licked the grime off their whiskers risked arsenic poisoning. A reporter for the *Anaconda Standard,* on November 21, 1891, wrote, "The atmospheric conditions were just right for complete envelopment of the city in a cloud of smoke and fumes, the air being damp and heavy and almost perfectly calm." From his hilltop view of Butte he could see that "every prominent building and landmark was obscured." A year earlier, the darling of the operatic concert stage, Emma Abbott, had become so frightened by the possibility of losing her voice because of the smoke that she had insisted that heavy blankets be tacked up over all of her hotel windows and transoms. After her concert, she quickly fled town. The smoke grimly dogged the lives of ordinary residents, who had no such escape. From July through October, 1890, 192 deaths occurred, most of them from pneumonia and typhoid. In December, thirty-six deaths were attributed to respiratory diseases.[17] These deaths made hollow mockery of the claims of Clark and others about the healthful qualities of smoke from smelters.

Finally aroused to anger, Butte reacted. The town's health officer went so far as to write to the *Engineering and Mining Journal* in

December, searching for readers who might know a process for the "destruction of gases and smoke." He wrote at the request of the Butte Board of Trade, a step that it would never have taken except in an emergency. The admission that its major industry was threatening the lives of Butte's residents graphically portrayed the desperation of the situation, since no town wanted to have its image so besmirched. Responses to and comments about the inquiry appeared for several months thereafter. Suggestions ranged from building a high smoke-stack (to waft the smoke away) to studying smelting works in Freiburg and Swansea to find out what they had accomplished. The Oakland protestors must have had a good laugh. Nothing had changed very much in two decades. Throughout the rest of 1891, readers of the *Journal* were apprised of what was happening in Butte. The city council adopted a resolution that required smelter people to find some method of "abatement of the smoke nuisance." The maximum $200 fine for not complying gave little evidence of the seriousness of the problem. In August the health officer, Dr. Herbert Robart, went to New York City to investigate an apparatus for consuming smoke and sulfur fumes. His efforts were too little and too late, because in December the local papers reported that the fumes were "unbearable."[18] A suit had been filed against the Boston and Montana Consolidated Copper and Silver Mining Company to stop it from engaging in heap roasting.

Yes, heap roasting, practiced seventy years before in Missouri, was still alive, smoldering and smoking in Montana. To its defense rushed Thomas Couch, superintendent of a prime culprit, who could not see any relationship between smoke and funerals. His firm, the Boston and Montana, had fired up its heaps in December, 1890. Burning sulfur, he argued, supplied a "partial disinfectant" for the filth found "in our valleys." The people in the lowlands, where the smoke hovered at its thickest, were actually healthier, in his estima-tion, than those who suffered the misfortune of living up on the hill, where the "sun shone all the time."[19]

The state of the art of medicine being what it was, doctors in Butte willingly proclaimed that the smoke acted as a disinfectant, destroying "microbes that constitute the germs of disease." They had little idea of what actually caused certain types of illness. Despite several centuries of influenza epidemics, for instance, doctors seemed little closer in the 1890s to determining the cause, prevention, and control of the disease than they had been when it was named in 1743. Thus, what appears to be an idiotic argument, advanced by Couch with support from local physicians, did not seem so illogical. For whatever reason, Butte had suffered few illnesses, so why not credit beneficial properties to the one civic blessing that separated the community from its clean-air neighbors—namely, smelter smoke? People who died in such a healthful climate were shamed. The industry could not let go of the health argument, no matter how much evidence contradicted it.

Undeterred by visible evidence, the defenders of smelters pressed on. Henry Williams, superintendent of the Colorado smelter, defiantly pointed out that his smelter had existed before most of the residents had arrived, and those who came afterward "knew what to expect." The proposed remedies would cause nothing but mischief, and the smelter "might as well close up as use any of them." Charles Palmer, superintendent of the Butte and Boston Mining Company, was less hostile and more practical: "There is no doubt in the world that the greater part of the sulphur can be eliminated from the smoke. But the product is sulphuric acid, and the only places where the sulphur has been eliminated are those places where there is use to be found for the sulphuric acid." Palmer called attention to one of the most telling reasons for not effectively abating the arsenic and sulfur smoke—the cost factor, because there was no market for the resulting product.[20] Pollution abatement had to be achieved within the traditional operations of the marketplace if it were to gain credibility with the mining industry. Butte and Montana offered no market for large amounts of sulfuric acid, and shipment of it continued to be uneconomical. The only alternative was to distribute the smoke over the town and the countryside.

Boston and Montana brazenly chose to ignore a city ordinance against heap roasting when it launched copper roasting. After the abnormal proliferation of deaths and health problems, the mayor ordered that the heap be buried under two feet of sand, and the city sought a permanent injunction prohibiting further roasting. The company's lawyer promptly protested the action on the grounds that the city possessed no authority to pass a smoke ordinance. He vehemently denied that heap roasting or any other smelting operation rendered the "atmosphere of said city unfit for or dangerous to be breathed" or that it endangered the lives or health of the inhabitants in any way.[21] That old war horse, the economic argument, was trotted out once again to bolster the company's plea: to shut down heap roasting (or smelters) would throw men out of work and would damage the economy of the community. The defenses all came to naught; the court supported Butte.

Stymied but far from defeated, the smelters modified as little as possible, while they continued operations. Successfully challenged in one of its bastions, mining could not know that this adverse decision was a precursor of stricter controls. Neither side, though, was fully satisfied with the outcome. An unreconstructed miner, identified only as *B*, wrote to the *Engineering and Mining Journal* in the midst of the fight in December, 1891:

> As regards Butte as a city, its prosperity must depend considerably upon its ability to get along amicably with the great companies operating here. At the present writing the city is suffering from smoke from the smelters, and the real estate men, who think that if there were no smoke in Butte real estate would advance 50% in value, are at the head of a movement to fight the Boston & Montana Company and to interfere with its smelting operations. It is to be deplored that these citizens carry sufficient weight to engender a feeling of hostility against the smelters among a section of the citizens of Butte.[22]

Much more fundamental issues than real-estate values were involved—such as private versus public good, profit versus pollution, and public health—and many more people were concerned than just the salesmen deplored in *B*'s accusation. This blindness to reality afflicted the whole industry.

Conditions in Butte failed to improve a great deal after the struggle during the early 1890s. Union organizer Bill Haywood, no friend of the copper companies, traveled there in 1899 for a union meeting. Approaching the city, he "marveled" at the desolation of the countryside. "The people of this mining camp breathed copper, ate copper, wore copper and were thoroughly saturated with copper. The smoke, fumes and dust penetrated everywhere and settled on everything."[23]

Blatant heap roasting was gone, replaced as much by new techniques as by anything the town had accomplished. The unfinished basic fight—smelting versus the environment—had simply changed locales. Back in 1884 the smelter town of Anaconda had been established twenty-six miles west of Butte. Proudly referred to as a "bustling, prosperous, progressive" city, with the greatest copper-reduction works in the world, Anaconda took some of the smoke problem away from Butte. The mining industry breathed a sigh of relief; the nearby ranchers did not. The second round of the fight would be contested here during the early twentieth century—smelting versus agriculture—duplicating to some degree the California experience with hydraulic mining.

The mining industry's arrogant defense of its "rights" had gained it little sympathy. Its refusal to recognize the total industrial impact and to acknowledge its responsibilities showed a callousness that was all too typical of the era. The industry never came to grips with the basic issues, even when it was successfully challenged and forced to retrench, if ever so slightly. The arguments, both logical and emotional, would carry well into the twentieth century, refined, modified, and polished as the situation required. Nothing had been fully resolved, and the bitterness of the fight had only hardened the existing attitudes. Much that should have been learned went un-heeded. The industry appeared to regard Butte as an isolated incident that would not be repeated. Had they been so inclined, the owners might have looked to Japan, where from 1890 to 1907 an ongoing fight over copper pollution finally forced the government to prohibit the industry from damaging nearby agriculture and streams. The connec-tion touched closer to home than the Butte coppermen compre-hended. During the 1880s, Japanese observers had visited Montana to study copper mining and smelting.[24]

In the conflict in California over debris, the furor in Oakland over smelting, and the controversy in Butte over smoke pollution, the mining industry had for the first time been confronted with major protests. The mixed results did not signal either the beginning of the end, or even the end of the beginning. Mining still dominated—if not unchallenged, then unmastered. Neither the public nor the nation was as yet concerned enough to curb the excesses.

It had been a long, rough climb for the environmental awakening that was occurring, voluntarily or not, within the industry. In two famous mining states, the industry had been challenged and had been forced to back down. No solace could be gained from the fact that these setbacks for mining reflected only local, isolated events. The environmental advances remained local only in their grass-roots elements; they nurtured within them industry-wide implications.

The leadership of the industry did not perceive the challenges to its dominance as being strong enough to force the reconsideration of environmentally damaging practices and policies. Nevertheless, at the height of its nineteenth-century power and prestige, mining had been forced to defend its actions, justify its policies, and modify a few of its cherished beliefs. The next century promised more of the same. A slight breeze of change ruffled the complacency of the mining industry.

CHAPTER SIX

"We Only Want a Square Deal"

To a new century, to a new world, mining had traveled a long way during the past one hundred years, along with the United States. Just as sentimental Victorian melodies fell before the foot-stomping rhythms of ragtime and as rural, agricultural gave way to urban, industrial America, so did the mining industry evolve. For some of the old guard, it was business as usual, with no attention paid to the possibility of change. Our Fairplay, Colorado, dredge superintendent remained unmoved: "Industry is always to be preferred to scenic beauty."[1] But change was coming like a fresh spring breeze, briskly kicking up little whirlwinds and promising a new season.

The first gust hit with suddenness, when the death of William McKinley elevated Theodore Roosevelt to the presidency. The office had not witnessed his animated, hearty style before. Roosevelt, who was deeply interested in natural resources and firmly committed to what became known as conservation, explained:

> We have become rich because of the lavish use of our natural resources and we have just reason to be proud of our growth. But the time has come to inquire seriously what will happen when our forests are gone, when the coal, the iron, the oil, and the gas are exhausted, when the soil has been further impoverished and washed into the streams, polluting the rivers.[2]

He translated those ideas into action and made them popular topics; never before had so much land been set aside for national parks and forests. The president did not fight a lonely crusade. Increasing numbers of Americans, concerned about something that seemed to be vanishing, supported his programs. Perhaps they saw the end of the frontier, which had for so long been a part of the nation's vigor. Perhaps they envisioned the exhaustion of land, oil, and forest reserves. Whatever it might have been, something stirred these people.

Much of the concern came expectedly from individuals like Californian John Muir and his friend and coconservationist Enos A. Mills, in Colorado. Mills was moved to write about the region encompassing Rocky Mountain National Park (which he did so much to help create): "Saving our best scenes is the saving of manhood.

These places encourage everyone to do his best and help all to live comfortably in a beautiful world. Scenery is our noblest resource."[3] His sentiments failed to compel many mining men to man the barricades on behalf of conservation. To them, scenery was still all right in its place, but the place should emphatically not interfere with profits. Consequently, the industry fought the creation of the numerous national forests and objected to some national parks in its attempt to preserve the right to utilize both the forests and minerals for private enterprise. The industry lost more rounds than it won.

Copper king William A. Clark, the old warhorse and multimillionaire from Butte, Montana, and Jerome, Arizona, fought Roosevelt from his position as United States Senator. In an address to the Senate in 1907 he explained his position, clearly delineating the attitude of his generation: "In rearing the great structure of empire on this Western Hemisphere we are obliged to avail ourselves of all the resources at our command. The requirements of this great utilitarian age demand it. Those who succeed us can well take care of themselves."[4]

But parks and forests constituted only one facet of the mining industry's problem. To Roosevelt, conservation meant preservation, protection, and the organized use of the nation's natural resources. He expressed this clearly in a letter to the well-known mining engineer John Hays Hammond:

> Our object is to conserve the foundations of our prosperity. We intend to use these resources; but so use them as to conserve them. No effort should be made to limit the wise and proper development and application of these resources; every effort should be made to prevent destruction, to reduce waste, and to distribute the enjoyment of our natural wealth in such a way as to promote the greatest good of the greatest number for the longest time.[5]

Responses from the mining industry to these words varied. It supported the conservation of what was feared to be the impending exhaustion of some resources. This anxiety, a familiar one today, emerged during the first decade of the century.

An old saying exists in mining lore: "You cannot tell beyond the pick in the end of a mine." When it came to estimating reserves, that adage had been true for much of the history of the industry. Even with advances in methods of exploratory drilling and geology, the science of forecasting reserves remained at almost that same level during the early part of the twentieth century. In the first decade it was feared that the production and consumption of natural resources was increasing at such a rapid rate that mineral supplies "for future use are limited."

Hammond could envision that timber, coal, and oil would rapidly disappear; he conjured up an alarming picture of a starving and shivering population in the not-too-distant future. Andrew Carnegie, who was apprehensive about the same thing, added iron ore and other minerals to the list of resources soon to be depleted. He wrote in 1908 that "no practical man can study our mineral supplies without seeing that they are melting away under our national growth at a geometrically increasing rate." He suggested "ceaseless research," the substitution of some other source of power for coal, and the preservation of the available resources. Roosevelt pleaded for the same things in a special message to the National Conservation Commission, which he helped to create.

> Our mineral resources are limited in quantity and can not be increased or reproduced. With the rapidly increasing rate of consumption the supply will be exhausted while yet the nation is in its infancy unless better methods are devised or substitutes are found.[6]

The commission's report, which was published in three volumes in 1909, makes interesting reading, although it is doubtful that many Americans took the time to study it.

The commission repeated the concerns expressed by Hammond, Carnegie, and Roosevelt; it urged that natural resources be conserved and that waste be stopped. The present generation's use of resources "carries with it a sacred obligation not to waste this precious heritage."[7]

Pulling no punches, the commission warned that while mineral production in 1907 topped $2 billion, the extraction and treatment of waste exceeded $300 million. It did, however, try to allay some of the fears about mineral reserves. Readers tended to be less panicky when they learned that the coal supply should last until about the year 2050 and that four billion tons of iron ore remained (not to worry before 1940). "Entirely inadequate" data prevented estimating the supplies of gold, silver, copper, lead, and zinc. The report cheerfully predicted that further advances in mining and milling techniques and the discovery of new deposits would extend these estimates; in the case of coal, the authors predicted that substitutes (water power, solar energy, alcohol, and other organic fuels) would assume a greater role.[8]

Mining men served on the committee, and their influence can be seen in the practical warning to the advocates of conservation:

1. The present generation have the power and right to use efficiently as much of these resources as it needs.
2. Men of this generation will not mine, extract or use resources in such a manner as to entail continuous financial loss to themselves in order

that something be left for the future. There will be no mineral industry without profits.[9]

The interest of hard-rockers centered on volume 3, which included Waldemer Lindgren's report on gold, silver, zinc, copper, and lead resources, written for the United States Geological Survey. He freely admitted past and present waste, but he also introduced the new theme, which focused on its prevention. The industry clearly had no right "to carelessly waste the metallic treasures of the earth." (Some of J. Ross Browne's ideas, discussed in earlier chapters, were finally finding a home.) Mining would have to police itself, for "no doubt" it would be impractical "under our system" for the government to compel the miners to prevent unnecessary waste by "prescribing certain working methods." Lindgren knew mining people, and he emphatically reiterated what had been said in the first volume: the "standpoint is naturally taken by miners and smelting men that if it can not be done with profit it had better not be done at all."[10]

Pronouncements through reports from the president, and even by Hammond, were one thing, but the reactions of the rank and file (from miner to small operator to mining engineer) were another. The specter of even light-handed regulation by the government proved to be onerous enough to trouble their sleep and bring denouncements of socialism and worse. The president of the American Mining Congress, Bulkeley Wells, made their opinions perfectly clear at the 1910 meeting: "As mining men, we cannot afford to have the Government enact legislation that will make the occupation of mining more hazardous than it is, either respecting the protection of life or the investment of money." Two years before, the *Engineering and Mining Journal* had editorially supported conservation, though with reservations. Waste, particularly the "disgraceful destruction" of forests, should stop, it warned, yet it might be cheaper to leave minerals in the ground than to mine the whole amount, considering the cost. Total conservation looked to be penny-wise and pound-foolish. Then and later, the *Journal* voiced strong opposition to the leasing of mining land and to the government's imposition of a royalty fee to encourage conservation.

With typical progressive enthusiasm, the *Journal* lashed out at speculators and monopolists, who, in its opinion, should be regulated, instead of the miner. Restating a complaint that would rumble down through the decades, it decried the Washington bureaucracy, which grew ever larger but knew so little about the mining industry. In January, 1910, the editor admonished Washington to put its own house in order before involving itself in someone else's domain.[11]

By the second decade of the century, conservation throughout the industry came to be understood as the avoidance of unnecessary waste, "a good thing." "It has been a good work and a good idea, but it has been misunderstood by many well-meaning enthusiasts, and their ill-considered propaganda has done much harm."[12] The "blatant demagogue's wild proposals" would have to yield to a carefully thought-out program of conservation. Conservation would be properly applied to wasteful production; the marketplace would take care of overproduction. By the 1910–20 decade, then, the conservation of natural resources had attained a position that could be eagerly supported by the industry. In fact, the industry discovered that it had already been supporting conservation for decades. Mining pointed with pride, for example, to inventions and improvements in smelting, such as the flotation process and the use of cyanide to recover a higher percentage of valuable ores. These new processes worked so well that old dumps were being reworked in order to recover low-grade ores that had previously been thrown out.

Thus, in just a few years, the industry had subverted the larger national issue to one of its own self-interest. Paradoxically, the conservation of minerals could be implemented even while environmental degradation was persisting.

Several authors who discussed mining and conservation during the years before the United States entered World War I reinforced this self-serving attitude toward conservation. In 1910, Charles Van Hise complimented the mining industry for its saving of minerals, thanks largely to modern methods. He went on to emphasize also the inherent responsibilities: "Mineral resources once dissipated are gone forever." The industry already understood that, but from a perspective of profit, not from one of conservation. A few years later, Richard Ely praised mining men who, "for the most part," had "taken kindly" to the general idea of conservation. Ely sympathized with attempts to apply principles of conservation to specific problems:

> There are far-sighted and public-spirited mining men who favor the general idea of conservation and are ready to take steps in that direction when it becomes clear what is desirable in the interests of general welfare, but who in attempting to apply principles of conservation of their own particular fields have become confused with the multiplicity of factors to be considered.[13]

By 1916/17, articles on conservation were appearing regularly in mining publications; one of the most revealing, entitled "Conservation of Iron Ore," was published in the *Transactions of the American Institute of Mining Engineers* (vol. 53) by Charles Leith. Although he discussed primarily Minnesota's Mesabi Range, his ideas applied to the entire industry. Other than to establish standards, Leith pleaded that no government or other public body should formulate rules. Conservation was not served by requiring the mining industry to spend two dollars in energy and materials in order to save one dollar's worth of minerals for posterity. "Conservation means a sacrifice of the present generation to the future generations whenever it is carried too far. There is a sharp limit to the economic sacrifice that we may reasonably ask the private person to make." Sounding a theme for the industry of the future, Leith argued that conservation

> must promise benefits to general and individual welfare during a period within the range of comprehension of the average man. . . .
> The problem of conservation is so complex that, as the writer sees it, it is practically impossible to lay down the rules of conservation applicable to iron ore as a whole to say nothing of all mineral conditions. What might be intelligent conservation in one case would amount to confiscation or needless sacrifice in another.[14]

Practical conservation was acceptable, provided that it was retained in the hands of private enterprise and was not governmentally regulated or enforced. Leith introduced a new hypothesis when he stated that larger companies had proved to be more conservation-minded than their smaller counterparts. "In this respect [i.e., in not being willing to sacrifice the future to profits], concentration of control has undoubtedly exerted a conserving influence as compared with unrestricted competition working on the principle of *laissez faire.*"[15] Such cold rationale evinced the updated nineteenth-century industrial attitude. Certainly the speculative frenzy of those earlier years needed to be curbed. The government must continue to encourage and even abet mining, and the general public should look only at production and profit—a nice, neat concept, one that mining could wholeheartedly support.

The booming Minnesota Mesabi Range, the heart of America's iron-ore mining, warranted the industry's applause as a classic example of the integration of profits and conservation. Opened to development back in the 1890s, it required steam shovels and open-pit mining to achieve the best possible ore:economics ratio. It also required the railroad, which rode right into the pits. From the point of view of mining, these procedures exhibited clear advantages: they were cost efficient, being much cheaper than underground workings; they worked beautifully on Mesabi ore; they made it possible to attain larger production with fewer miners; and they were simple in execution. These attributes had all been propounded before; now came the application.

The Mesabi pioneered in the use of open-pit mining and machinery. Americans were proud of the technical advances shown in this 1915 photograph of the Fayal open-pit mine near Eveleth, Minnesota (courtesy Minnesota Historical Society, St. Paul).

The industry recognized two advantages of this type of conservation. First was the conservation of ore, since all of it could be removed, without the 10 percent loss incurred in underground operations. Second, the practice of determining well in advance the distribution of grades of ore for the entire deposit made it possible to select and combine those grades so as to leave the lowest possible surplus of undesirable ores.[16] This was conservation that miners could appreciate.

Appreciating it most avidly were the large corporations, which dominated the Mesabi even at this early date. These new and better practices were actually credited to the changed conditions of ownership—the control by a few large steel companies. They could stand the initial cost of the equipment and of the removal of the surface overburden; they could also wait for the profits to materialize, and then congratulate themselves for having so successfully adopted conservation practices.

Conditions on the Mesabi created a model for the final evolution of corporate ownership. Initially, Andrew Carnegie and John D. Rockefeller sought control; then the industrial giant United States Steel came to dominate the district. The open-pit mines constituted only the first step in an integrated operation that helped to make the United States the world leader in the production of iron and steel. Over a longer period of time, the same pattern had evolved in coal mining, where railroads had gained control of the business by the 1890s. In Colorado the pattern was somewhat different, though it ended with the same result when Colorado Fuel and Iron, which was eventually controlled by Rockefeller money, emerged as the major coal producer. Copper mining, evolving in the same way at the same time, served to seal the fate of fuel and base-metal mining for the small operator. The precious metals survived somewhat more independent of dominance by giant corporations, but the drive for efficiency, profit, and modernization had taken its toll on one vestige of nineteenth-century mining.

Those innovations notwithstanding, the majority of miners, companies, and stockholders continued to follow well-worn paths and outmoded ideas. Typical examples were Frank Crampton, who learned mining at Cripple Creek, Colorado, and Goldfield, Nevada, without acquiring any noticeable conscience about the environment, and the stockholders of various companies in Goldfield, who wrote from New York, Iowa, West Virginia, Connecticut, Texas, California, and other states to stockbroker Charles Sprague to inquire about investments or reports on their stock. What reasons had they to be concerned about local environmental conditions? The training of young engineers had not changed noticeably either. Herbert Hoover gave a series of lectures, which were later published, aimed at the interested layman and new mining engineers. His advice ventured no pioneering philosophy. He saw the primary needs as engineering sense, executive ability, financial insight, business experience—no environmental issues crept in. Echoing a familiar refrain, he stressed the short-term nature of most mining operations and emphasized that "mines are operated only to earn immediate profits. No question of public utility enters, so that all mining projects have by necessity to be from the first weighed from a profit point of view alone."[17]

On the other hand, a slowly growing number of other individuals among the rank and file were evincing an environmental consciousness. The seeds planted by the previous generation were bearing fruit, nurtured by committee reports and publications. Environmental supporters were not overzealous in their approach. Leith was right—practical conservation was the most appealing to the miner.

A few examples will suffice to show the transition. John Hays Hammond, who took an active part in the conservation movement, wrote, "I favored the intelligent utilization of natural resources when needed by the present or any other generation." He admitted that there had been gross waste in the exploitation of natural resources. Similarly, a 1907 resolution of the American Mining Congress condemned unnecessary waste and urged the development of resources "for the best interest of the whole people." The Franklin County (Kentucky) Coal Operators Association concurred a few years later, when it called for the proper conservation of coal, which meant "securing a maximum yield of coal per acre," as opposed to existing "low and wasteful" conditions.[18]

Along with these advances came mining's interpretation of conservation, which broadened the definition to encompass benefits to "the whole people," not just to mine owners. It also implied, if ever so subtly, that nonmaterial values such as beauty ought to be considered too.

President Woodrow Wilson ultimately summarized the prevailing mood when he wrote to the secretary of the American Mining Congress in September, 1915. He deeply regretted being unable to address the men who were cooperating "for a wiser conservation of the mineral resources of our country." Conservation, he said, was the "highest use and the least waste" of natural resources, which, once exhausted, never would be replaced.[19]

At that moment the industry had no need to fear Washington's long arms. The federal government was only slowly assuming a role in mining, insofar as it regulated or encouraged conservation and, as Wilson observed, made it serve "the people as a whole." The government's role evolved innocently enough. Some of the impetus came from mining's own requests, which it later regretted. For example, the gold miners wanted the government to build roads in national forests, so they were willing to have their mines taxed up to 1 percent of the gross annual output to finance the plan. Regulations that would accompany the financial aid seemed to be of no concern. This particular scheme came to naught, but it exemplified mining's eagerness for government assistance without fully considering the consequences.[20]

The creation of the Bureau of Mines in 1910 held the potential for bringing government into full involvement with mining. The American Mining Congress had been on record for at least three years in support of the idea of a Bureau of Mines, so the idea came as no surprise. The bureau and the older United States Geological Survey were the two federal agencies that were charged with the development of the nation's mineral resources. One of the original purposes of the bureau—to lessen the waste of resources in mining and metallurgical operations—epitomized the conservation concern of the era. President Wilson, in fact, considered the conservation of human life and resources to be the most important charge of the bureau.

Although the establishment of the bureau and of mine experimental stations received the endorsement of the industry, other activities of the government did not. The withdrawal of Alaska coal lands angered industrial spokesmen. Sounding like his counterparts several generations later, one of them warned that "the greatest of Western problems is how the red tape can be cut to relieve Alaska from restrictions which now hamper its development." J. F. Callbreath, secretary of the American Mining Congress, contended that Congress had failed to act effectively in the withdrawal of the coal lands. "Why? Because they were trying to handle a situation which they did not understand. They were trying to legislate for conditions which were entirely different from what they had known before."[21] Protest had no effect; the deed was done.

With or without a nudge from the government, the mining industry was making an attempt to bend, if ever so slightly, with the breeze of change. It feared that the public did not recognize what mining had accomplished and what it was doing "in the direction of conservation." For the first time, miners showed an inclination to improve their image. As never before, public opinion had attracted the attention of mining; that public was agitating for reform, if for no other reason than a spate of vicious labor strikes between 1900 and 1918. It had been several generations since Americans had taken such an active role in government. They seemed generally to want their state and national governments to become vigorously involved in upholding and protecting the citizens' rights. This charge posed a particularly vexatious problem for the mining industry, which openly exhibited its traditional concern that governmental involvement would threaten private enterprise and profits. Also troubling was the fear that this sudden awakening of popular interest in conservation would be short-lived, leaving behind vague, indiscriminate, and hasty legislation. Mining would then be burdened with the remains of this "new cult." Finally, the suspicion lingered that the furor over conservation was simply part of a larger attack on corporations—all part and parcel of the Progressive Era. Large mining companies were indeed lumped together with their business contemporaries as a potential threat to American democracy.

While discussing developments in southwestern copper, James Douglas summarized a commonly held view: "I am sure that neither our largest mining and metallurgical companies nor ourselves, as their working-agents, are recklessly indifferent to the preservation of those very materials upon which the wealth of the corporations and our own salaries depend."[22] Left to itself, mining would take care of its own, eliminate waste, and make the best use of the natural resources. This concept fortified the industry during the following decades.

Theory and philosophical discussion were one thing; action and reaction were quite another. Miners understood actions much better than words. They still thought of themselves as Henry Clifford described them in his *Rocks in the Road of Fortune* (1908): "These are real men, 'world-workers,' the kind that women really love, those who create our wealth by honest manly toil" (p. 392). They could more easily appreciate something that had an immediate impact. Long-range possibilities were too remote. In this context, two continuing problems kept mining on edge: pollution by smelter smoke and what now had become the dredging issue, an offshoot of the older fight over hydraulic mining.

As one of the newer mining techniques to come into vogue after the turn of the century, dredging allowed the profitable working of what were once considered too-low-grade deposits. That promise of profit ensured the acceptance of dredges, and soon the metallic monsters were clanking in the stream beds of Montana, Oregon, California, and Colorado. Unfortunately, the wake of gravel tailings from them created environmental chaos. Robert Service saw what had happened in Alaska. In his poem "The Prospector" he caught the impact:

> And turning round a bend I heard a roar:
> And there a giant gold-ship of the very newest plan
>   Was tearing chunks of pay-dirt from the shore.
>
> It wallowed in its water-bed; it burrowed, heaved and swung;
> It gnawed its way ahead with grunt and sighs;
>   Its bill of fare was rock and sand; the tailings were its dung; . . .[23]

This horror elicited outrage, particularly in California, where the Anti-Debris Association had already won a fight against hydraulicking.

Familiar criticisms resurfaced; the land was being made unfit for agriculture, water had become unsuitable for any use, and flooding could be the end result. Similar complaints had emerged in Australia and New Zealand somewhat earlier. In 1905 the government of New

Zealand decided against issuing more gold-dredging leases unless the lessees agreed to replace the soil. The reaction of American mining to that kind of governmental interference would have been predictable. Fortunately for dredge men, protests in this country proved to be far less intense, the impact was limited, and governmental reaction was more traditional.[24] Two factors mitigated the impact of dredging—the industry's positive response to questioning and challenges and, more important, the small number of dredges in operation, which made the problem more localized and less compelling. Most Americans, even in the West, faced no peril from a dredging project.

Nevertheless, the mining industry jumped to the defense of dredging in an attempt to deter future complaints. Mining engineer Charles Janin spoke for the industry in support of dredging. After praising the economic benefits to be derived by nearby towns and ranches, Janin pointed out how much of the potential dredge land was useless for other purposes. Conceding that dredging caused some injury to the environment, Janin emphasized the superior advantage of economic benefits. Why, he wondered, did California alone protest the impact of mining when strip mining for coal in Kansas, for phosphate in Tennessee, and for iron in Minnesota had raised no comparable objections? Were the same people who had sold the land now the ones who were leading the fight? Another defender of dredging asked, "So why should anyone cry 'Vandal!' and make faces at the dredge men, if the rock from their 25,000 more-or-less acres goes to help make life possible on the 5,175,000 acres next door?"[25]

The mining engineer–consultant J. P. Hutchins carried the argument further. The land, he reasoned, had already been ruined by previous mining, mostly by Chinese—a historically unjustified racial slur. With more logic, Hutchins pointed out that dredging was efficient in saving gold, and it was cheaper to run than other forms of gold mining. Pulling no punches, he concluded with a blast at those who opposed the dredge: "In California, ill-advised agitation by hysterical devotees of aestheticism, and action by sycophantic blackmailers, have caused some annoyance; but no harm has or can result to any industry doing such inestimable good with such slight accompanying damage."[26]

As much as this combination of sound rationale and dramatic bombast may have satisfied and encouraged those within the industry, reclamation projects proved to be of more long-range significance. Mining finally saw the light, concluding that one way to answer its critics was to develop a use for the mined-out land.

Dredging companies became the American pioneers in this effort, following in the footsteps of New Zealand and Australia. These companies tried several approaches. The first was a cosmetic one— the rock that was left behind in long serpentine piles was removed, crushed, and used in concrete and as railroad ballast and top dressing for roads. This procedure generated profit and eliminated some of the visually offensive mess. It did not, however, restore the land. But that came, too. The removal of the rock made it possible to make better use of the remaining soil, which was claimed to be especially attractive for raising grapevines and fruit trees. As California's mineralogist Lewis Aubury proudly pointed out in 1910, "The utilizing of dredged land for horticultural and agricultural purposes, etc., has been successfully tried in several places in California."[27]

Although tried, the idea generally failed to win acceptance. Several reasons accounted for this: the cost, the location of the dredging operations, and the condition of the soil. In addition, ideas and techniques had not been fully developed to cope with the variety of inherent problems. And although later Americans were shocked by the environmental impact of dredging, their early-twentieth-century ancestors seem to have been less so. With exceptions, they were seldom agitated over this issue for long, and they did not maintain continuing pressure on the companies to devise less devastating methods. Well-intentioned efforts by the industry languished and failed, the victims of waning interest.

Why, then, were the reclamation efforts made? The answer lies clearly in profits, which, it was hoped, would be the end result. Crushed rock or "reclaimed" land, sold even at low cost, brought in money that otherwise would not have fattened the coffers. Unfortunately, the potential market never matched the waiting acres of waste rock, and many dredges worked in such isolated areas as to make it impractical, if not impossible, to transport the crushed product economically. As for reclaimed land, once the early enthusiasm had abated, it was often discovered to be of poor quality. Aubury was eventually forced to conclude that "the soil of most of the dredging lands in California was unproductive and was of little value for any purpose but mining."[28]

Before the excitement had worn off, a 1907 book on dredging published a six-page chapter on reclamation projects in the Sacramento Valley. The author, D'Arcy Weatherbe, saw them as beneficial developments. That pronouncement testified to an industrial break-through; the times were changing, even though at a snail's pace. The reclamation idea caught on elsewhere as well. Startled personnel in the Ohio Division of Forestry received a request early in 1910 for

Smoke, in the nineteenth century, meant progress, industry, and jobs. It also contained deadly compounds of minerals and gases. The odor brought some visitors as near as they cared to come to Hades. Boston and Colorado Smelter, Black Hawk, Colorado (courtesy Colorado Historical Society, Denver).

seedlings to plant on mined land. None of these advances heralded a new environmental era or a sweeping change of heart within the industry. They did prove that mining harbored an empathy that needed to be nurtured, supported, and tenderly loved.

Complaints about smoke pollution rained down on the industry after the turn of the century—and not just from Montana in its long-running fight at Butte. From such widely scattered states as New York, Georgia, New Jersey, Tennessee, Colorado, Nevada, Utah, and California came protests, mostly from nearby communities or farmers. The issue remained as controversial as ever. If the smelters were shut down or were restricted, it was charged, mining as a whole would suffer. Control could be the death knell of mining as it had been known.

Facing law suits, adverse publicity, damage claims, and public criticism, in addition to its involvement in seething political controversy, mining attracted unfavorable attention. Industrial spokesmen rode to its defense with both emotion and logic. Much of what they said reflected their nineteenth-century heritage; some of it was new and occasionally showed statesmanlike consideration of the issues.

Montana warranted its share of attention, though it had shifted from Butte (by 1910, a city of 39,000), where irate citizens had earlier challenged the smelters, to Anaconda, where local farmers and ranchers confronted the industry. Anaconda, as mentioned, had been established as the smelting center to provide at least a partial solution to the problems in Butte. Justification for continuing operations was well thought out by the Anaconda Company and its defenders. They built a show-case plant, using the best and most-modern methods of copper metallurgy. A dust chamber and tall smokestacks were designed to reduce, if not to eliminate, smoke problems; the company claimed to have taken more extensive prevention steps than anyone else. The dust chambers caught and settled harmful particles, and company engineers claimed that the stacks discharged sulfuric-oxide smoke at so great a height that it never reached the ground in sufficient concentration to harm animal or vegetable life. When these improvements failed to perform to the satisfaction of nearby residents, the lawsuit commenced. Remodeling the plant did not quash the complaints. Having done everything possible to reduce pollution, Anaconda could do no more that was economically feasible.[29]

Technologically, Anaconda had built a plant in accordance with the "best known methods and processes" of the era. Its remedial experiments pioneered in the copper-smelting industry. Unable to promise a complete solution, the company worked toward an acceptable one. At this point, opponents of the company jumped in and brought the dispute to a head.

The controversy evolved into a brutal fight. Anaconda took both the high ground and the low in an attempt to defend itself. It paid claims for damage whenever it was "reasonably satisfied" that damage had occurred; these concessions failed to satisfy the protesters. When finally forced into court, the company rehashed the classic arguments. For instance: "We have a perfect right to carry on a legitimate business, and if incidentally we should pollute the atmosphere nobody has the right to complain until specific damage gives him a cause of action."[30]

Business had a right to pollute because it produced revenue in products, wages, and taxes. The economies of Anaconda and Butte depended on mining, as did those of Montana and even the nation. A shutdown would mean a copper deficit in the world market, bringing higher prices. Anaconda based this last statement on the fact that it mined about 11 percent of the world's copper. The company's line of reasoning concluded with the logical assumption that the significance of the smelter overwhelmed that of local farmers and ranchers. The *Engineering and Mining Journal* wholeheartedly concurred. A March 26, 1910, editorial stated frankly: "Even if it does [damage] it is better to suffer some damage than to check a mining industry upon which large cities, we might almost say the state of Montana, are dependent." The nineteenth century still lived.

To the contention that the material escaping up the stacks could be economically converted to sulfuric or some other type of acid, thereby cutting pollution, the company retorted that only a small local market existed and that the amount that would be produced would glut the national market. Having said it could not economically do more to remove pollution and having presented the financial and business justifications for its continued operation, the company rested its case.

Aware of the benefits of improved public relations, Anaconda established its own experimental farms to raise crops and cattle within the shadow of the plant. It promoted agriculture in every way possible in the Deer Lodge Valley, which included sponsoring a fair. As would be expected, the town of Anaconda was praised for its pleasant, healthful atmosphere. Never before had a mining company gone to such lengths to polish its public image or to justify its operations and its very existence.[31]

Not content, however, Anaconda marshaled its tremendous economic and political power. While admitting that there were some ongoing problems, it attempted at the same time to purchase land in the direction that the wind blew the smoke in an unsuccessful effort to stop the complaints. Company-controlled or company-owned newspapers jumped to its defense and sought to discredit the "smoke farmers." Anyone who was found to have a relative involved in the farmers' association lost his job with the company forthwith. Montana's politicians found themselves pressured and bribed.

The company won the bitter fight, but it hardly had time to relish its victory before finding itself embroiled with the federal government over charges of smoke damage to trees in nearby national forests. Anaconda and Uncle Sam reached an agreement that called for continued investigation and experimentation by a "fumes committee," so named by one of its members, John Hays Hammond. This expedient lasted into the 1920s, when a different governmental and business climate reduced pressure on Anaconda.[32] The company manifested the staying power to win, and it did. To its credit, some strides had been made to reduce the smoke pollution.

Ducktown, Tennessee's controversy over pollution was almost as long running as Montana's. The 1850s brought the development of the mines and the first smelter, thereby opening an era that was ended by the Civil War. After the war, the mines functioned sporadically until the completion of a railroad into Ducktown, which

One of the worst cases of smelter pollution occurred in the Ducktown, Tennessee, district, where acid smoke seared the land. Out of this mess grew a landmark court case (from W. Emmons et al., *Ducktown Mining District*, p. 14).

had previously been isolated by mountains. The Ducktown Sulphur, Copper and Iron Company started full-scale mining and, after experimentation, opened a successful reduction works. It was joined by the Tennessee Copper Company, among others, which also built a smelting plant. Both attained full operation by 1900 in a small four-by-six-mile area. Extensive activity produced airborne pollution of comparable proportions. It drifted over neighboring lands and fields that also involved the nearby states of North Carolina and Georgia.

Muted local protests exemplified a fact of economic life: the mines promised a new age in this part of Tennessee, a land of poor soil and long-term isolation that had been only slowly settled. As one person explained, "Thus it is not surprising that no effective protest was offered when the smelters began emitting their sulphurous fumes, which killed the vegetation and made the soil barren for miles around."[33]

Protest did come—from Georgia. Ducktown Sulphur and Tennessee Copper were hauled into federal court in 1905 in an attempt to put a stop to their polluting. The mining interests made an initial concession by halting heap roasting in 1905, but that did not solve the problem. The case dragged on for a decade. The arguments and protests paralleled those that had previously been presented. In 1907, Tennessee Copper agreed "not to produce damaging smoke" during the active cotton-growing season. That was followed in 1913 by an agreement among Ducktown mine owners to pay the state of Georgia $16,500 annually to reimburse farmers for damages. None of these reforms ended the litigation. The United States Supreme Court, in May, 1915, issued an injunction to prevent the "diffusing of sulphurous fumes over the Georgia border."[34]

The mining industry lost a round of the fight over smelter smoke, but it won a compensation—sulfuric-acid plants. Situated near eastern manufacturing centers, Ducktown found its product competitive, something that Butte could not achieve. J. Parke Channing, a mining engineer who worked in Tennessee, praised the companies for saving what had previously been a waste and a nuisance. The industry concurred in that assessment, then let the matter rest. Far-sighted people had hoped that the sulfuric-acid plant, in addition to producing profits, would do more "to prevent further destruction of the vegetation and the soil in the copper smelting districts; to save the water power storage pools downstream from being filled with sediment due to excessive erosion." The problem was eased, though not with the expected results. Earl Case, who studied the locale a decade later, concluded that more success had been achieved in utilizing a valuable constituent that had previously gone to waste than in preventing further damage to the surrounding vegetation and soil.[35]

Obviously, the technology tried in Tennessee did not provide the miracle answer; as yet, no foolproof solution existed. Mining's economic and political hold was strong in this area; the Ducktown case was an exception, mostly because of its location near other states, one of which took the mining industry to court. As long as these firms were the principal employer, taxpayer, and economic force, they would ride high, which boded ill for the environment and for themselves in the long run.

In Utah the smelters found themselves in an equally tense situation. The companies had at first agreed to compensate farmers who brought suit for damaged crops; they also installed a bag system, cooling chambers, and other devices in an attempt to reduce the pollutants. When these remedies fell short of resolving the problems and the lawsuits, the companies threatened the ultimate step—they would relocate. Local merchants promptly rallied to the cause of the mining companies. Interestingly, other towns made a pitch to attract the smelters because of the economic benefits to be derived.

Much emotionalism surfaced on both sides. A visitor to the Salt Lake City smelters said he expected to see the vicinity a "desert waste," but he did not observe anything of the kind. "It is not to be denied that some damage has been done," he wrote to the *Engineer-*

ing and Mining Journal in September, 1907. This the smelters readily admitted, but the writer seemed to be equally certain that the damage had been "greatly exaggerated." Opinions such as these comforted the spokesmen for the industry but carried little or no weight with the protesters. In the end the plants were moved to greater distances from cities and farms, a costly alternative unless the old smelter happened to be near the end of its useful life and was ready for replacement anyway.

The charges that were leveled against owners of smelters in Utah were similar to those already discussed. In 1913 the Park City mining man George Dern defended his interests when smoke became a local political issue. It was not true, he argued, that the company "wilfully, maliciously and with a cold regard to the rights of the people made fumes that were injurious to health." It had made an "honest, earnest effort to control" the problem and had been "reasonably successful." Mining was a legitimate industry, he went on to emphasize, and the company owed the stockholders a return on their money; no dividends would come from a closed smelter. Did the voters really want to close the mining operation, thereby putting local people out of work and hurting the entire community? "We do not ask for charity," Dern stated. "We only want a square deal. . . . Nobody regrets more than I do that our smoke has proved a source of annoyance, and if any additional remedies can be found in the future, we will adopt them as fast as we are able to do so."[36]

That "square deal" seemed to be an elusive entity in the eyes of mining men. They had been willing to experiment with new methods; some had worked, but many had not. Nothing about the problem was new; only the emphasis on it was. Progress had been made, but an ultimate answer remained out of reach. The industry had shown a willingness to invest its money in efforts to find one. A reported $1 million, for instance, had been spent to construct Ducktown's acid plant. When forced to do so, mining and smelter men had gone to court to defend their practices but had found themselves on the losing side unnervingly often. Aware of the times, they expended money and effort to inform the public of its stake in the outcome of litigation, as well as the industrial costs and hardships that were involved with these cases. Montana and California, in particular, provide good examples of this kind of endeavor. In response to the harassment, mining had moved, adjusted, stood pat, or closed its plants, the last a somewhat self-defeating tactic unless the plant had become obsolete.

Thanks to smelter smoke, mining was receiving a bad press in large urban areas, some of which had never been dependent on the

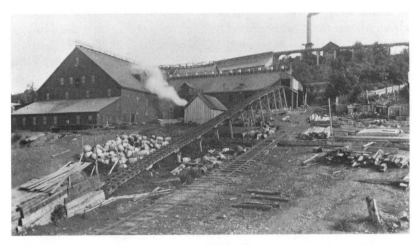

Mills and smelters produced a variety of pollutants, even though this looks to be a quiet day at the Atlantic Copper Mill at Houghton, Michigan. Noise from these mills could be heard several miles away (courtesy Michigan State Archives, Lansing).

industry. Others were less dependent than they once had been. When the wind blew in the right direction, New York City suffered the same type of smoke pollution from neighboring New Jersey smelters that had angered Georgia in the Ducktown case. The nuisance generated considerable complaint, but the threat never seemed to be as widespread as it had been farther south. Although no costly lawsuits resulted, the publicity did mining's reputation no good. In Denver, one resident sued the American Smelting and Refining Company over the sulfur fumes belching from the Globe Smelter. The press virtually ignored the case, and the company kept operating in its usual fashion.

San Francisco, once mining's golden city, found itself in a situation similar to that of Oakland thirty years before. The issues proved to be the same only insofar as they pitted ASARCO against local residents.[37] Ironically, after spending a large amount of money on preliminary work before scrapping the whole project, the company was sued by a disgruntled group of supporters for not carrying through with the building. The plaintiffs had sold land to the company at a reduced price with the understanding that a large plant would be built; obviously they planned to benefit from speculation in nearby land. Mining found itself in a no-win situation. Although this harassment proved to be a mere pin prick in the total picture, it cost the industry both time and money, kept its lawyers busy, and helped to create a tarnished image of the industry in the mind of the urban public. These people knew little about the significance of mining, only what they read, saw, or smelled.

The reader should not assume that mining and smelting alone were criticized in this outbreak of antismoke agitation. Railroads, power plants, steel works, and others also drew unwanted attention, primarily because of their use of coal. New York City had its Anti-Smoke League, and inventors tried a plethora of devices, such as John Parsons's "smoke-eating machine." Inconsistent success, which was generally minimal, met those endeavors.[38] Not alone did the mining industry seek solutions to the "unsolvable."

One ramification of the antismoke agitation directly affected coal mining. Coal smoke polluted the air everywhere in the United States; it settled indiscriminately over clotheslines and fresh snow; coal was not a "clean" source of fuel. As a result, Americans looked to cleaner fuels, which were coming on the market—fuel oil and natural gas. These newcomers posed a severe threat to the future of coal mining, and the always-obvious smoke jeopardized the life of mine offices and tipples (the surface buildings of a coal mine). Americans preferred to shift their allegiance rather than to await some vague promise to clean up their smoky environment.

The obvious first step in meeting the competition—cost-reduction methods—boded ill for both the miner and the environment. Owners, who were desperate to retain their share of the business and trade, would scorn any ideas that might increase costs.

Confrontation did not serve the industry well; more to its liking, if the pollution issue had to be brought up, was the reaction of some residents of Sullivan County in western Indiana. In this coal-mining region, complaints arose about streams being polluted by refuse from various coal mines. The seriousness of the situation alarmed the local residents, who complained to state authorities. Rather than taking their complaints to the courts, however, the citizens (according to the *Engineering and Mining Journal*, May 31, 1902) were "making every effort to solve it [the problem] without working hardship upon the mines." This was the type of complaint and reaction with which the industry could cope.

Prosperous mining times and exhilarating new discoveries, accompanied by the appearance of well-heeled purchasers, including United States Steel, dampened the interest in cleaning streams. These entrepreneurs purchased local mines, intent on putting them on a much sounder financial basis. The thought of reform simply evaporated for the moment. Sullivan County prospered with new jobs and growth, and so did the coal companies. The best defense, in cases such as these, was booming prosperity. West Virginia, for instance, had a banner year in 1903, with 39,452 men working in the mines and coke ovens and with production up to record levels throughout the state. Under circumstances like these it was hard to see mining as much of a local threat.

The coal industry also hoped that it had found a partial answer to the complaints about urban smoke in what was described as "smokeless districts," several of which were found in Indiana. The production of "low volatile bituminous coal" mined there, unfortunately, hardly made a dent in the total market.[39] This glimmer of hope died.

With equal enthusiasm, coal spokesmen pointed to a USGS study being conducted in 1903/4 on the Lackawanna and Susquehanna rivers. Raw sewage from towns such as Scranton and Wilkes-Barre oozed into these streams. The first reports seemed to indicate that acidic mine waste and drainage water, which also percolated into the rivers, killed the "putrescible matter."[40] Perhaps it did, but relying on one pollutant to counter another failed to answer the fundamental question and left the environment of the rivers more to wishful thinking than to workable solutions.

Little consolation came from knowing that other countries were dealing with similar problems without success. New Zealand, which did pioneer work in legislation on dredging, had its troubles with coal mining. Miners sluiced rubbish into streams, the *Mines Record* for December, 1901, reported; and an owner near Reefton burned his "shaly rubbish" until the inspector ordered him to desist. Revelations like these did not temper the criticism of American coal miners who practiced similar methods.

Even after all this talk, expense, and effort to defend its interests and its image, the question remained of whether the industry would permanently change. Ligon Johnson, a counsel for some of the smelters, hoped so, and his 1918 article "The History and Legal Phases of the Smoke Problem" clearly summarized the new context. Johnson argued that whether to blame "smoke farmers" for the litigation was not the issue—that was history. Attempts to buy peace by paying claims for damage, whether attributable to smelters or not, could not be considered a permanent remedy. The smelters needed to be innovated, without making wild claims of success that only borrowed trouble for the future. The ultimate goal had to be to prevent the "excessive loss of toxic solids." Specialists—a smoke engineer, for instance—must be hired, something that Johnson considered to be a necessity, rather than a luxury. The visual problem of smoke should be forthrightly addressed. Smoke by itself, after all, was not the harmful agent; it was the dense smoke that made people uneasy and generated concern. "The best way to take care of trouble is to prevent its starting."[41]

Johnson's words conveyed sound advice from beginning to end; the degree to which it would be heeded depended upon future developments. Name-calling, emotionalism, oversimplified generalizations, and the arbitrary blame of one group or another would no longer suffice for the industry. Nor would reliance on the economic justification of dollar significance to the region. In very few states did mining still maintain the political and economic muscle it had once flexed. Pennsylvania and Montana stood as obvious exceptions. Innovations and modifications were going to have to be made. The future lay with the industry; it had been successfully challenged throughout the United States. It would have to take public attitudes into consideration from now on.

As America was preparing to enter World War I, the mining industry could look back on the early years of the century with considerable pride. Production had matched the demands of industry and of the American people. Mining methods had been modernized; along with dredging, strip and open-pit operations were coming of age, particularly in the Mesabi Range. Innovations of the 1890s had won acceptance. Even the automobile had found its place, as mining engineer Robert Livermore rhapsodized: "Nowadays motors are the common means of locomotion all over the west, and in places where formerly one used to prepare for a long expedition, now he whisked out and back the same day. It is a godsend to the mining engineer and no mistake."[42]

New methods of milling and smelting permitted old dumps and tailings piles to be reworked profitably and to save ore that had once been thrown out. They also allowed lower-grade ores, taken directly from the mine, to be refined successfully, thus neatly coinciding with the current definition of conservation—the prevention of waste. A few tentative steps had been taken beyond these, and as long as they promised profit, interest was maintained. It should not be assumed that mining wholeheartedly accepted its environmental responsibilities and obligations, even under the pressure of promoters of conservation. Too little time had passed since the glory days of the nineteenth century for that transformation to have come; attitudes were too ingrained. The more typical reaction was still to ignore the topic and to continue business as usual, whether in Utah's copper mines or in the limestone quarries of the Portland Cement industry in Wayne County, Michigan.

If mining had wanted a square deal from the American public, it had generally been dealt one. The public overwhelmingly approved of the industry's activities. Having successfully marched into the new century, evolved into a new mining era, and weathered a conservation crisis, the industry looked ahead with enthusiasm and optimism. Environmental concern still seemed to be more of an academic exercise than a practical necessity.

CHAPTER SEVEN

Reprieve!

"Over There," woman suffrage, the Charleston, Model Ts, big bull market, "Brother Can You Spare a Dime," the New Deal, the Good Neighbor, and a peacetime military draft—all crowded into the exhilarating years from 1917 through 1940. Seldom have Americans experienced so many changes, both at home and abroad, in so short a time; never before had they been so aware of them, thanks to two other popular newcomers—the movies and radio.

Changes came to mining also, though not so exciting as these. Nor did the industry's discoveries attract the same headlines they had a generation before. Mining was now accepted as a traditional part of American industry. Emerging as a corporation-controlled, cautiously run big business, it could not expect to hold the public's attention more than any other industry. The memories of rushes, prospectors and burros, opportunity for the little man, mining camps, and rich strikes had receded. To many miners, those days seemed like only yesterday, but mining had decidedly reached the twentieth century.

The imprint of the early years of the century heavily influenced the industry. As America entered World War I in 1917, mining was still caught up in the web of the conservation/environmental controversy, raised during the preceding progressive reform era. In 1917/18 the federal government coordinated and controlled American business as never before by means of a group of quickly established war boards. Mining patriotically pitched in to help beat the "Hun," but some of its leaders took the opportunity to lash out at growing governmental interference. During congressional hearings on a proposed national security and defense bill in 1918, Harry Day, a mine owner from Wallace, Idaho, seized the opportunity he had apparently been awaiting for some time. Governmental policy, he charged, "bewildered, annoyed and mistreated" the producer and the buyer. "Now, the whole policy of the Government, especially in respect to metals, has been not a harmonious one, but a harsh, ugly one, a threat all the time. It is not good."[1] Day and others were exasperated because the past decade had produced too much regulation to suit their nineteenth-century tastes.

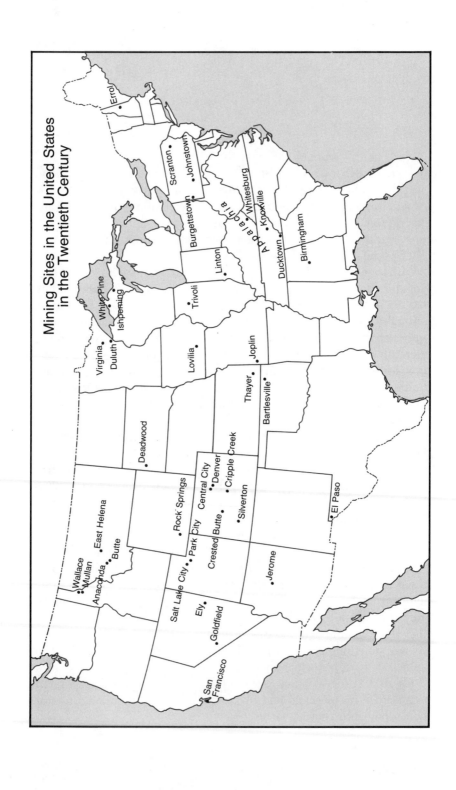

Mining Sites in the United States
in the Twentieth Century

Day had no need to worry—the tide was beginning to turn. One indication was made obvious by these hearings. Although they covered a multitude of topics related to the war and minerals, conservation was not one of them. Conservation had been tolerable a few years earlier; now, expanded production had become a greater necessity. Majority opinion within the industry concurred. Miners wanted little or no governmental regulation, a trend that had grown ominously over the industry since 1900.

The dawn of change in World War I became the morning of a new day in the 1920s. American business began to regain a portion of the influence it had lost. Washington either ignored or did not enforce laws that so recently had been enacted. The American public generally abandoned its reforming spirit and turned to other more lucrative and interesting pursuits. Even though mining no longer dealt from a position of political and economic strength, as it had during past decades, it could not have wished for a more fortunate development.

The mining industry had done little to create or deserve this turnabout. America had raced through a reforming cycle and now wished to enjoy a "national binge." The same thing had happened before in American history, when another reform period had waned (i.e., after the Civil War). At the same time, a mood of nostalgia was gripping Americans, who yearned for the golden age of business and business leadership. Why not "turn back the clock" and seek "normalcy," as President Warren G. Harding had suggested? The country did just that, and for the last time, mining could virtually ignore environmental matters at only slight risk. Signs of the transformation appeared from many directions. Proceedings of the American Mining Congress and the Mining and Metallurgical Society of America, as well as those of local groups like the Lake Superior Mining Institute, no longer included environment-related topics and papers. The *Bibliography on Mined-Land Reclamation* listed only one article in 1928 and did not list another until 1940. The editors of *Engineering and Mining Journal* thought the issue was of so little consequence that from January, 1930, through December, 1940, they wrote only three editorials about the environment. Each dealt with the same general topic, stream pollution. Mining engineers continued the practice of ignoring environmental matters in their reports.[2] Stockholders typically continued to be interested only in profits, and mining tried to accommodate them.

Books about mining relegated few pages to discussions of the environment. In his 1922 book *Coal*, Elwood Moore merely mentioned that it was difficult to dispose of overburden in some regions and that abandoned pits were objectionable. Two volumes of collected articles from the *Engineering and Mining Journal* during the 1930s omitted the subject, as might have been expected from the editorial trend. The only thing that Robert Peele could think to note in his *Mining Engineers' Handbook* was the necessity of providing ample space for a tailings dump, for the reason that it would lengthen the life of a mill.[3] The sudden change of emphasis was startling but understandable.

The unknown author of a booster pamphlet for the once-famous (1880s) Gunnison County of Colorado asked his readers to imagine the world trying to exist without metals. Without the prospector and mining, the writer argued, there would be no railroad, no automobile, and no "flying machine." "Condemn, if you can, the prospector, the miner or the mining business." Neither the public nor the government was in a mood to condemn or to press for reform.[4]

The industry willingly regressed in actions and attitudes to a more comfortable stance. Environmental concerns had never become deeply entrenched, nor had the mining faction that was involved with them gained any real ascendancy. The pattern for the next forty years was established during the first two decades of the twentieth century: pressure on, concern up; pressure off, industrial involvement down. The public's permissive attitude reinforced the mining industry's policy of profit above all. With the end of speculative frenzy and the mad scramble for wealth, mining reverted to its familiar exploitive pattern, minus some of the manifest-destiny trappings of the last quarter of the nineteenth century. The depression of the 1930s did nothing to stem the antienvironmental tide. What it did was to revive placer- and small-mining operations, thereby adding to the problem in some states.

Again the policy of short-term benefits took precedence over environmental and conservation considerations. No more clearly was this evident than in dredging, in open-pit and strip mining, and in the hope of reviving hydraulic mining. Arguments in support of dredging had not changed from those of years before: the profitable working of lower-grade gravel, the direct benefits of wages and purchases, and the indirect benefits of dividends and gold production to the nation's economy. During the depression, dredging was promoted as a way of creating jobs and stimulating the economy. Support for open-pit projects proved similar, whether the mine was near Knoxville, Tennessee, or Jerome, Arizona.[5]

Hydraulicking and strip mining required somewhat more justification. The former never had much of a chance; even during the depths of the depression its track record was too damaging. A few die-hards thought it could be resumed, without "fear of damage," to revive some of the depressed California mining counties. This was recommended in the twenties, before the crash of 1929. Dams would store the debris and also benefit navigation; jobs would, of course, be created, and local business would be stimulated. The state legislature killed a bill to purchase dam sites, and that ended the matter. Mining had lost out.

Coal mining, which was hurting because of inroads that natural gas and oil had made into the fuel market, also took it on the environmental chin. John Hays Hammond chaired a commission, which in 1925 issued a 3,000-page three-volume report. The commissioners concluded, among other things, that "the normal effect of digging coal is to turn the earth's covering inside out, and what comes out in the process is not alone wealth producing, comfort-conserving hard coal but the enormous tonnage of dirt, rock and waste that form the great culm banks and waste heaps." These upheavals threatened nearby coal communities and created an ugly scar on the physical environment.[6]

Scranton, Pennsylvania, amply illustrated the problem with twenty-three dusty, dirty, black monstrous piles of waste that occupied land needed for home building and that visually polluted, threatened health, and posed other problems. Surface concerns were not the only ones, however; the commission further cautioned that underground mining held the potential for surface cave-ins and settling. The industry had been warned, but the era was not ripe for extensive effort, and the problem was of such magnitude that little was accomplished. The threat lay in wait for a future generation to confront.[7]

Strip mining moved ahead full throttle nonetheless. J. B. Warriner, chief engineer for the Pennsylvania Lehigh Coal Company, presented a cogent argument to support stripping. Sounding a familiar refrain, Warriner stated that stripping offered an economical solution to the problem of producing the largest quantity of coal for the least expenditure. Strip mining increased the total output, and it recovered coal that was unobtainable by other methods. In his 1918 opinion, that last point was a solid contribution to conservation. Twenty-two years later, a former mayor of Linton, Indiana, banker J. E. Turner, came to the defense of the strip mining that had so benefited the southern part of his state:

> In the past fifteen or twenty years we have been enjoying our "mess of pottage" represented in the thousands of dollars brought into this community from the sale of lands at good prices, and the many thousands more from payrolls of our employed men in this industry.

And so far we have not suffered from lack of income—not noticeably—from the lands taken from our agricultural belt. Furthermore, as years go by, we do not hear so much about the unsightly appearance of the areas "ravished by the monster shovels."[8]

The Indiana Coal Producers Association, which published the pamphlet featuring Turner's comments, hammered hard on the theme that strip mining made better use of the land. Not only did it produce coal of greater value than that of previous agricultural harvests, but it also left the land more productive than farming did, after the mining had been finished and the trees had been planted. This was the epitome of conservation and reclamation—you could have your cake and eat it too.

Coal operators in neighboring Kentucky and Illinois not only agreed with this rationale but also expanded upon it. Strip mining used fewer workers and experienced fewer accidents than did regular coal mining, an incontrovertible statement because of the absence of gas, explosive dust, and cramped underground working spaces. Strip mines went into production faster and used less complicated mining processes. Illinois miners were overwhelmingly convinced; from 1920 to 1945, strip-mined coal jumped from less than 1 percent to 22 percent, while the rest of the industry stagnated. Neighboring states were no slower in accepting the technology and method.[9]

From mining's point of view, these facts clinched the case for stripping. Having proved its greater productivity (recovery of nearly 100 percent of the coal) and increased economy, it won its case. "Strip mining is a means of preventing waste of a natural resource which cannot be replaced." This was, Warriner argued, "true conservation."[10]

Whether they realized it or not, the strip miners had planted a time bomb, which eventually would threaten the entire industry. Even their spokesmen were not so callous as to ignore the environmental violence inherent in stripping. Warriner worried briefly about drainage and about surface floods in the Pennsylvania fields; then he concluded that the problem inherited from "early day mining" was so great that current operations did not add much threat. Kentucky miners, at least on paper, expressed concern that stripping, "unless carefully engineered and controlled," was destructive to the terrain and led to stream pollution. Within a generation, their opponents would be amused to think that they had conceded even that much.

Unlike underground workings, strip mining was always visible to the public and therefore was open to instant inspection, evaluation, and criticism by its watchdogs. Mining repeatedly countered this liability by arguing that it was no worse a polluter or a threat to the land than any other process. Those palliatives might have soothed a pained conscience, but even the most insensitive strip operator could not help but realize that his powerful steam shovel was permanently scarring the land.

Although its environmental posture had seemed to regress since prewar days, mining could not ignore that first major outburst of public resentment over its treatment of the environment; not could it ignore persistent warnings from within the industry. Because of these, mining continued to move toward a clearer environmental attitude and a cleaner public image. The increased pressure was also evident in Turner's allusion to "monster shovels." He pleaded, and the industry asked for time to solve the problems. A simple plea for time was not good enough, even during the 1920s and 1930s. More evidence of good faith had to come, and it did, in several ways, from planting trees to increased public-relations campaigns.

A reforestation program promised to restore the land and to provide additional income. Abandoned open cuts were converted to lakes, creating a recreational boom and conserving water for general and industrial use. Strip miners in southern Indiana observed that this was particularly significant, because much of the mined land was plainly marginal for agriculture. Bank president Turner waxed eloquent over the change in his neighborhood: "Time has worn down the spoil banks, and the planting of trees and the clearing of the waters in the many lakes have transformed much of the landscape into even a more pleasing picture—if we view it in a purely aesthetic way—than it was before." Mining applauded and waited for general public acclaim but could not understand when it was slow in coming.

That kind of shotgun approach would appeal to a broad spectrum of people, from the recreationist and conservationist to the stockholder in the company—or so mining hoped. Naïve and stumbling, mining was making an effort to improve its public image. In the midst of a "rugged background not unlike miniature mountain ranges," the Indiana Coal Producers Association exhorted men and women to seek these coal-mining-made lakes, these places "of beauty to repair their physical bodies and to think." Continuing, it quoted Edmond C. Foust, editor of the *Hoosier Farmer:* "A boy and his dog, a man and his rod and gun, or mother with her knitting in the pleasant shade of these reforested areas, close to nature, will contribute something more beautiful, more useful, to society and gain pleasure at the same time."[11] The association plainly stated the purpose of its 1940 pamphlet *The Story of Open Cut Mining in Indiana:* to stress "phases" of mining of interest to the general public and to show "our contribution to conservation."

These improvements attested to concern and a willingness to try, even if in a small way. The industry exhibited a certain amount of pride. Strip miners in Indiana, Ohio, and Illinois vied with each other to claim the honor of being the first to plant trees. Individual companies, then mining associations, supported the idea; by the early 1940s, Ohio had progressed to the point of making plans to plant in excess of 100 percent of the land stripped each year in order to reclaim acreage that had previously been worked. This was voluntarism at its best, and one cannot deny the initiative of the industry.

Determining who was first to act would be an exercise in antiquarianism. More pertinent to this study is *why* they acted. Speaking at the 1921 commencement of the Colorado School of Mines, Frederick Laist expressed a very real concern: "At the same time, it is wrong to hedge around the resources of this country with red tape so as to repel the capital which must be forthcoming before any benefits can accrue."[12] Red tape, governmental regulation, governmental involvement—these were threats that had lurked in the background ever since the Progressive Era, if not before.

Pressure was already building for state or federal regulation. In 1939, West Virginia became the first state to enact a statute dealing with surface mining. Ohio, Illinois, Kentucky, and Pennsylvania soon fell into line.[13] The point had been reached that companies would have to do something or action could be forced upon them. Mining would no longer have a free hand to exploit the land in the years ahead. Rape and run were becoming unfashionable or, at the very least, questioned.

Like it or not, government was assuming a steadily increasing role in mining. The smelter-smoke fight of the prewar years gave evidence of this. That confrontation had calmed down since then, although smoke was still contaminating the air. The issue had lost the novelty that was required in order to provoke an emotional response at the moment. Enough progress had been made to satisfy many people, certainly mining.

Mining maintained its prior position, as expressed by mining engineer Edward Mathewson, a specialist in lead and copper smelting: "Each smelter plant has its own particular smoke problem and it will not be solved until there is a market for all the byproducts that can be obtained from smoke." The ideal marriage of technology and economics had not been consummated as yet. For the folks out in East Helena, Montana, in 1929, the controversy had no meaning; they gloried in the American Smelting and Refining Company's plant, with its 400-foot smokestack, the tallest in the country, and the "largest blast furnace and lead smelting plant in the United States."[14] Mining appreciated that kind of civic enthusiasm.

The heated question that the industry now confronted involved stream pollution, which ruined agricultural land and irrigation water, eroded the soil, threatened communities' sources of drinking water, and degraded the scenic, recreational, and aesthetic values of streams and rivers. The government intervened; once more mining had to explain its philosophy and actions. The smoke cases opened the door to regulation, but the stream-pollution cases brought regulation nearer to realization. Protection of the public interest demanded that preventive measures be taken.

Initially, the familiar pattern unfolded regarding mine drainage and stream pollution. Investigations and then reports focused attention on a spectrum broader than the local scene. Then the wrenching economic crash of 1929, followed by the worst depression in the nation's history led to the election of Franklin Roosevelt as president in 1932 and to his formulation of the New Deal. Little did Americans or the mining industry suspect what those programs would mean to them.

The president's personal interest in conservation began long before his nomination and election. Several members of his cabinet held similar views, and the ranks of New Dealers in Washington contained people with the same sentiments. Consequently, environmental ideas and conservation again gained ascendancy on the banks of the Potomac, most obviously in such significant programs as the Civilian Conservation Corps and the Tennessee Valley Authority. Conservation programs would have made even more progress had the nation not been immersed in such hard times. As it was, the New Deal confronted such a great variety of problems that Roosevelt resorted to increasing federal power and to multiplying federal agencies to try to find some solutions. The laissez-faire philosophy of the business-friendly 1920s disappeared almost overnight.

Mining never assumed an important role in the New Deal program, but the momentum from Washington directly or indirectly affected it. By creating the Securities Exchange Commission, establishing the Public Works Administration, suspending annual assessment work that was needed in order to maintain the ownership of unpatented claims, sponsoring schools to learn how to pan, and supporting the unions, the New Deal involved itself in mining's business. The government raised the price of gold and, most significant, revived regulation, which set a precedent for state and local governments to follow. Government would play a momentous role in business and industry from then on. The new philosophy encouraged action on long-standing issues such as stream pollution.

Disputes over stream pollution hit mining in such widely separated states as Colorado, Pennsylvania, Oregon, and South Dakota. The worst predicament involved Pennsylvania's western coal fields, which polluted the Ohio River basin, especially the Pittsburgh region. Acid water drained from active and inactive mines. The magnitude of the problem can be seen in the figures from 1920/21. Some twelve hundred operating coal mines drained an estimated 450 million tons of water per year that contained 1,575,000 tons of sulfuric acid. When the "considerable discharge" of the large number of abandoned mines (estimates of which ran as high as six thousand) is added to those numbers, the extent of the problem comes into sharp focus.[15]

The defense from the mining industry evolved in a predictable manner. It stressed that it was not solely to blame—tanneries, chemical works, oil wells, and blast furnaces also contributed their share of pollution. Some truth lay in that argument, and even more in the one that dealt with cleanup expenses. Charles Dorrence, vice-president of Hudson Coal Company, estimated that the initial expenditure to neutralize acid water from his firm's thirty mines would be $39 million, with an annual operating cost of about half that. To neutralize the sulfuric acid would add about fifty cents per ton to the consumer's bill. The small-mining operation faced an insurmountable barrier in the face of such costs. Furthermore, the coal industry reasoned, it should not be blamed for drainage that simply emerged as an unexpected outgrowth of industrial development. It was being asked to shoulder the entire responsibility for a problem that resulted from actions to benefit the public, the state, and the nation.[16] And last, there was the question of who was responsible for those abandoned mines whose owners were dead or whose companies no longer existed.

The miners had not seriously considered the drainage problem before, nor had they weighed alternative solutions. Caught in a bind not entirely of their own making, they badly needed some direction. The author of one study of the mine-drainage problem, Andrew Crichton of Johnstown, Pennsylvania, gave some insight into their predicament when he explained, "The subject has been given little serious attention, or until recently, it has been little understood."[17] The wishes of the coal industry in water-related matters were paramount in Pennsylvania (the *Sanderson* case showed that); as a result, little had been accomplished in pinpointing the causes of the drainage problem.

Industry spokesmen acknowledged that remedies needed to be found, but they cautioned against "severe and precipitate action." They feared, correctly, that the government would move if the mining industry did not. Bills were already being introduced in Congress to produce some action. Professor of mining engineering C. M. Young, who did research on stream pollution, stressed a theme with which at least some of the coal leaders agreed:

> In my opinion it would be much better for the parties most interested, that is the coal and iron industries, to take steps toward finding a solution which will at least be tolerable. It is surely unwise for these interests, which will be most severely affected by prohibitive actions, to be unprepared for such [federal] action. There can be no plea of ignorance of conditions and if the state of the streams so arouses public opinion as to bring about severe action it is quite possible that hardships will be brought upon these industries.[18]

These words would come back to haunt coal mining; as the issue faded away, so did the best intentions to put them into action.

Coal miners warned that the "public must either suffer the inconvenience or meet the cost of combating it." They accurately predicted that American interest would wane. During the 1920s, reports, discussions, plans (some highly expensive), recommendations, and legislative bills all focused on coal-mine drainage and how to clean it up or at least moderate it. In the end, the potential cost, a lack of leadership in the federal government, and the failure of continued public interest allowed the industry to delay taking action. The problem proved to be too staggering, the ramifications too unclear. The necessary knowledge and skills were as yet undeveloped. Unlike the earlier California fight over hydraulic mining, no unrelenting pressure had been brought to bear on one segment of mining.

If the problem was staggering then, what would it develop into? Forty years later (1967), Pennsylvania's Senator Joseph Clark testified in the United States Senate's hearings on water pollution. Some two thousand miles of waters in his state alone were being blighted by mine-acid drainage; to that figure could be added those of all the states in the Ohio basin and other coal regions.[19]

Coal mining prevailed in this instance. It may be condemned for having been short-sighted and for bending just enough to placate critics, but on this crucial issue it is easy to understand why it dominated. Coal, a powerful economic force in Pennsylvania, wielded political clout. Just how powerful became clear in 1937, when the state finally passed a pure-stream law that specifically excluded drainage of acid from mines. The industry correctly judged that the public, the state, and the federal government did not have the desire or the staying power to get to the heart of the issue to find an answer. The 1925 report of the Federal Coal Commission concluded: "Unless, therefore, the removal of the culm piles and silt beds, the bolstering and artificial settling of the undermined surfaces, and the restoration of the streams to their pristine purity, result in more net profit, or at least in no net loss, to the coal operators, no efforts in that direction can be expected."[20] Critics of mining saw only industrial cynicism in that kind of attitude, because they never did believe that an answer would be found to satisfy both profits and environmental needs.

Industry spokesmen propounded the legitimate argument that no economically feasible or otherwise satisfactory solution had yet been proposed. They were also correct in asserting that more reliable data needed to be obtained on which to base legislation in order to prevent the laws from becoming a burden to coal mining and to the public. The spokesmen admitted the magnitude of the pollution and understood that it caused inconvenience and expense. Beyond that, coal mining would not go. It rested its case firmly on nineteenth-century attitudes; the climate of the 1920s did not precipitate change.

Little would be accomplished during the 1920s and 1930s to alleviate the problem of pollution from acid drainage. The industry bought some time, as public interest waned and the federal government shied away from regulation during the 1920s. In the 1930s, economic conditions worsened enough to preclude adding burdens to an already depressed industry. Mining had postponed the day of reckoning, but it alone could not be blamed for the lack of remedial action.

Meanwhile in Colorado, a battle similar to the one in Pennsylvania was being waged with much less fanfare. It involved the hard-rock mining segment of the industry. The struggle seemed reminiscent of the earlier fight in California, since both of them pitted farmers against miners. As in California, mining's influence had diminished dramatically, both economically and politically. By the 1930s, when the issue came to a head in the Clear Creek Valley drainage (encompassing the once famous Georgetown and Central City districts), Colorado's mining industry had seen better days.

It was more than just an agriculture versus mining conflict, however. As in Pennsylvania, this pollution threatened domestic water supplies and the public use of streams. The confrontation became heated during the 1930s depression, when small mining operations proliferated as people returned to rework old districts in hopes of finding a meager income, encouraged by the raising of the price of gold to $35 per ounce. Many of these mines and some small milling operations made no provision, or only weak ones, for impounding their tailings, which eventually drained into the streams.[21] Since territorial days, Colorado had had statutes that outlawed stream pollution, and mining companies now found themselves in court. The key case was *W. W. Wilmore, et al.* v. *Chain O'Mines, Inc., et al.*

Briefly, this case involved having downstream farmers sue upstream mill owners. The latter stood accused of discharging mill tailings and slime into Clear Creek. Born of a combination of confidence and desperation and firmly rooted in nineteenth-century attitudes, the companies' defense showed ingenuity, heavy-handedness, candor, and shrewdness. Company lawyers stressed these main points, after admitting to having deposited tailings and slime in the creeks:

1. Tailings were not injurious.
2. Usage and custom had permitted depositing slime and tailings in this watershed for many years.
3. The plaintiffs had acquiesced by reason of having failed for an unreasonable time to take steps to prevent this pollution.
4. The cost of developing a suitable depositing place outside of the streams was in excess of the profits of the operation.[22]

The defense pounded on the theme that farmers, when they purchased the land in question, knew about the custom of discharging and had raised no objections when new mills were constructed. Consequently, they had no legal recourse.

Nothing particularly new emerged from this defense. It reinforced hard-line, uncompromising positions and, in fact, reiterated the arguments of the 1909 litigation. The earlier case involved a complaining homesteader on Willow Creek, near Creede, Colorado. Mining lost two arguments in this trial. The defense that the water the mill used was artificially produced as the result of mining and was given to the defendant for its milling purposes had been demolished in court. So had an evasive tactic—the defendant milling company claimed to be an agent of the mine owners, whose ores it was treating under contract; therefore, it was not liable. Obviously, the nineteenth century stood on the docket in both instances. Mining lost again. In March, 1935, the Colorado Supreme Court upheld the lower court's injunction and enjoined the milling companies from polluting the streams' water. Two judges dissented. Chief Justice Charles Butler's dissenting opinion provided only hollow consolation:

> The holding in this case, if adhered to, would seriously and unjustly cripple the mining and milling industry, one of the great industries of

this state; an industry that caused the settlement of this region, and to which the state owes its birth in 1876, its financial salvation during the panic of 1893, and a large measure of its prosperity at all times.[23]

The mining industry prized sentiments such as these, reminiscent as they were of its glorious past. But this was 1935.

The farmers' victory set mining back. The *Engineering and Mining Journal* hoped that perhaps a lesson had been learned: litigation, it admonished, was a poor weapon—conference and compromise offered a better solution, "if the contestants are not too obstinate." That was a very big *if*. Over a year later, in November, 1936, the journal's editor reported increased objections to stream pollution from any form of industrial waste. Two bills that were introduced in the last session of Congress to prohibit stream pollution had failed to pass, the *Journal* pointed out, only because of lack of agreement on a supervising agency.[24]

Confrontation could be avoided by resourceful individuals. Mining proved this with other examples. In 1929, Charles Chase, superintendent of the Shenandoah-Dives Mine and Mayflower Mill near Silverton, Colorado, was planning for pollution control. He explained why: "Because of my personal repugnance for the lack of consideration of the public interest involved in this practice, I undertook to withhold from the Animas [River] the tailings of our new project." That kind of position could have advanced the industry a long way. Instead, the industry persisted in the practice of discharging tailings into the nearest available stream in the San Juan region. Experiencing the financial strains of the 1930s, Chase nevertheless continued his pollution-control efforts, as he said, "at a cost within our reach."[25] Chase devised tailings ponds that worked.

Chase was fortunate to have supportive stockholders, who were not interested in money alone. In 1946 he wrote, "I have always remembered an expression of one of our largest owners in our early days; 'It is a shame to spoil such a beautiful stream.'"[26] This rare combination of caring stockholders and a concerned superintendent pointed to the direction that mining had to go.

In Oregon, mining was befriended by the state. After farmers, as well as recreational and sportsmen's groups, obtained an injunction to keep mining from polluting the Rogue River drainage, Oregon sponsored a study of the situation. Interest in the matter was motivated by the near collapse of placer and lode mining in southwestern Oregon as a result of the injunction. The study concluded that debris was not inimical to fish and fish life, which encouraged the *Engineering and Mining Journal* (1938) to hope that scientific investigation, not popular clamor based on uninformed opinion, would lead to ultimate solutions. The editor could not resist a slap at the opposition, to whom a "crystal clear" stream had become an obsession.[27] Those opponents appeared to be unreasoning in their demands to control mining's effluents.

In the Black Hills of South Dakota, the large Homestake Mining Company found itself in court over debris. The company had formulated varied approaches to resolving disputes. When possible, Homestake negotiated settlements with farmers along Whitewood Creek, who were entitled to compensation according to their principal lawyer, Chambers Kellar. When taken to court, Homestake overpowered the plaintiffs by hiring experts, taking photographs, running tests, and doing everything in its power to strengthen its case. The defendants went so far as to introduce fish as evidence in one case, fish that had been caught in an area of the stream that the plaintiffs claimed had been ruined for fishing by debris. The "catfish were, of course, removed before they could deteriorate to a point where their odoriferous presence would be too much for the court, the jury, or counsel," remembered one of the lawyers, Kenneth Kellar. The company's ace in the hole, however, was an 1881 South Dakota statute that gave mining companies the right to deposit mine and mill tailings in the adjoining stream.[28] The Homestake Company won the 1930s fish case, but its willingness to attempt to solve the disputes without a legal hassle was encouraging.

Stream pollution would not go away; mining could not escape the problems related to it. Only a few exceptional companies and individuals would act on their own; the rest would react to the prevailing public and governmental opinions. Far too few Charles Chases or Richard Hugheses existed. In 1876, Hughes had prospected along Whitewood Creek, one of the finest streams that he had encountered in the Black Hills. He reflected in 1927 on the shameful appearance of this lovely stream after it had collected half a century's worth of town refuse and mine tailings: "It is much to be regretted that a great part of the district's charm thus has been sacrificed."[29] Hughes had been part of it; this pioneer had traveled full circle.

The industry received mixed signals both from its own people and from the public during the 1920s and the 1930s. Attention to the environment surfaced in Indiana and Colorado; almost everywhere else, signs indicated that traditional ways and attitudes remained as strong as ever. A revival of the Tri-State lead-mining district (Missouri, Oklahoma, Kansas) in the mid thirties spawned news stories about dewatering mines, sinking shafts, new equipment, the reworking of tailings, and hopes of renewed activity. A PWA project that involved diking, damming, and ditching around "old mines" war-

During the hard times of the 1930s, placer mining made a comeback, as people tried to earn a living by reworking old mining districts. Auraria, Georgia, had first been mined a century before this man worked the Boggs Branch Gold Mine (courtesy Georgia Department of Archives and History, Atlanta).

ranted only passing mention.[30] The reopening of a Michigan gold mine near Ishpeming in 1937 sparked interest and anticipation, and stories of stripping operations on the Mesabi pointed to improved iron-mining conditions.

A June, 1937, article in the *Engineering and Mining Journal*, "The South Looks Up," exemplified the publication's editorial policy. The article featured the present and future of southern mines, pointing especially to Birmingham, Alabama, as "a steelmaker's dream," with ore, coal, and limestone operations all compacted together. The output of 1937 promised to double that of 1934—welcome news to the miner, the stockholder, and the general public, because it meant revived mining, rising profits, more jobs, improved business, and increased taxes. Mining was making a comeback and was recognizing, as the *Journal* stated, "what the situation today requires."[31]

Meanwhile, two books published during the early 1930s posed fundamental questions that the industry would confront sooner or later. Malcolm Ross examined the impact that coal mining had had on the people of West Virginia and Kentucky, with their concentrations of wealth, coal-district poverty, absentee ownership, and boom-and-bust economic cycles. In poignant and bittersweet chapters he analyzed the miners, the people, the operators, and the human toll that coal mining extracted. With unusual insight he wrote: "It is futile to blame individuals. To our immediate ancestors, investment in coal companies meant the chance for personal fortune, or Creation of a Great Industrial Empire, depending on their habits of thought." Ross understood one of the basic principles that so many reformers ignored: "The desire for privilege is not to be wheedled out of humanity by moral upbraidings."[32]

Ross's study focused on people; Lewis Mumford dissected the industry in *Technics and Civilization*. Although willing to concede that there had been genuine heroism among miners and a personal pride in their achievements, he saw only brutalization: "Mine:blast:dump: crush:extract:exhaust—there was indeed something devilish and sinister about the whole business. Life flourishes finally only in an environment of the living." Mumford denounced the miner's notion of value, which he felt tended to be, like the financier's, purely an abstract and quantitative one. The miner worked, not for love or for nourishment, but to make his pile, the "classic curse of Midas." Not content with present condemnation, Mumford reached back into history and took Agricola to task for his lame defense of mining. Mumford had no more sympathy for those who had followed in Agricola's footsteps. The indictment of mining, he claimed, was "an unanswerable one." From the Rand to the Klondike to the modern iron mines of Minnesota, "the routine of the mine involves an unflinching assault upon the physical environment: every stage in it is a magnification of power."[33]

Unfortunately, mining entrepreneurs neither completely understood nor heeded these admonitions; they had most likely not even read Mumford and perhaps held only a nodding acquaintance with Ross. The industry should have paid closer attention—the issues these two men addressed spoke of something more profound than profits and progress. The depression days of the 1930s were not the best time to bring up philosophical questions such as these, but the time was coming when the mining industry must face them.

Mining virtually went its own way in the years from World War I to the early 1930s, despite occasional setbacks. Perhaps to some unreconstructed individuals it seemed that the tide had been reversed, that conventional ways and philosophies would prevail. The reform climate of the decade 1910–19 had withered before the blare of the twenties and the depression-locked thirties. Governmental strategy shifted from regulation to partnership. Then came the New Deal, with reliance on both but with emphasis on regulation. By 1934, for instance, the Bureau of Mines worked with the industry to ''reduce or prevent'' waste, to conserve the country's resources, to disseminate and analyze data, to assist large- and small-mine operators, and to safeguard the miners' health and lives. Only the most stubborn of individualists could fail to see that the times were changing again and that mining had better start to prepare for those changes.

Even during these years, the environmentally intent group within the industry grew, assuming more leadership, both within and outside of mining. Mining lawyer William Colby, an early associate of John Muir's, served on the board of directors of the Sierra Club for forty-nine years. The first director of the United States Park Service, Stephen T. Mather, made part of his fortune in borax mining; and a later director, Horace Albright, was also involved in mining and mining law. These men served as two-way streets, carrying mining's attitudes out and outsiders' attitudes into the industry. Each faction gained by the efforts of these individuals and others like them.

That old man of the mountain T. A. Rickard, who had been closely associated with mining for more than forty years, published his history of world mining, *Man and Metals,* in 1932. Although his environmental consciousness might not have matured, he had several things to say that the industry needed to hear. History, he believed, was a philosophy that teaches by example: ''We have more examples than our predecessors; shall we heed them no better. The history of mining, like all other history thunders a warning.''[34] Environmentally, history had knocked, not thundered, a warning. Time was running short for mining to respond.

CHAPTER EIGHT

"A Tradition That Endured Far Too Long"

The 1940s and the 1950s—years of change, decades of quiescence—were a puzzling mixture of past and future, as Americans and the United States groped their way toward a dim destiny. The mining industry mirrored these conflicting trends and by 1960 was far more removed from 1940 than a mere twenty years.

American mining found itself tied much more closely to the international market, exactly as the United States found itself mired more deeply in the quicksand of a smaller political world. Some of the newly independent nations harbored large reserves of natural resources, enough to affect the price of copper and other minerals. Governmental subsidies to foreign companies also undermined the United States' position at home and abroad. Independent producers increasingly discovered that they were being undersold in the market, which hurt, especially when imports flooded into the country. The industry continued the trends toward technological intensity and corporate domination, both at the expense of the smaller operator, who encountered nearly unmanageable costs and competition. Unions played a more dominant role in mine operations, thanks to the New Deal and to changing public opinion. The owner no longer ruled in his own domain, a fact of life that had been totally unforeseen a generation before.

Coal mining, confronted by the decades-old competition from oil and natural gas, receded to a mere shadow of its former national significance. Mining's political influence went the way of the coal industry, fading in both statehouse and congressional chambers. Even its local role waned, as Americans looked to new economic worlds to conquer. Impoverished, "old" mining took another blow in the West, when tourism came to many of the remaining communities and generated more profit than the industry that had first created the attractions.

Mining passed two milestones during these years—the one-hundred-year anniversaries of the 1849 California gold rush and the 1859 Pike's Peak rush. The *Engineering and Mining Journal* for January, 1948, saluted the centennial of Marshall's discovery of gold at Sutter's

Mill and the industry that this made famous: "One cannot but be proud of an industry like mining that has come so far and done so much in the last hundred years. Great as the demands upon it have been, the mining industry of the United States has not failed to meet them." These two rushes, the largest and most glamorous of them all, had focused the country's attention on mining and had set the pace for the rest of the nineteenth century. Many technical advances had been made during those one hundred years, and mining's position had also evolved significantly since those invigorating days.

But in some crucial, fundamental respects, little had changed, and the men of 1849 and 1859 would have felt right at home. The profit motive still held sway, and the exploitation of natural resources by private enterprise for private profit was being carried on with as much zeal as ever. The myth of the superabundant, inexhaustible mineral resources lived on. The theory of "mine and run" continued to prevail, though it had been curtailed somewhat from its rampant youth. As Robert Browning once remarked, "The story always old and always new."

These benefits, which predated 1849 and were accentuated by it, proved to be the very ones that seriously threatened the environment, molded mining's policies, and shaped its reaction to criticism. Signs of change could be seen, but they were coming at a pace that could generously be described as leisurely. In the end, the old won out over the new, tradition over innovation, and indifference over concern and awareness.

There would never be another 1849 or 1859. Similarities notwithstanding, history would not repeat itself—World War II saw to that. Neither Americans nor the mining industry of 1945 fully comprehended the impact of the war. Whatever else may be said about the long-range significance of the war, it can be stated unequivocally that the mining industry acquired a partner in the federal government. Neither a marriage of love nor a willing adoption, the alliance was forged from circumstances beyond the control of mining. When Washington, in the name of the war effort, could shut down nonessential mineral mines by refusing operators the access to replacements or materials (as it did in the Gold Limitation Order, L-280, in October, 1942), then the new order of things was clear. Wartime exigencies justified the closing of gold and silver mines in order to transfer men, materials, and experience to more strategic molybdenum, coal, and copper facilities. A host of new federal agencies and acts made their impact on mining, ranging from favoring larger and more efficient operations to building roads, purchasing war-needed minerals, and sponsoring scientific research.

The national interest outweighed private interests; earlier-day miners would have arisen in horrified indignation and wrath.

Then came the uranium boom—stimulated by World War II and accelerated by the cold war—which centered in Arizona, Utah, New Mexico, and Colorado during the late 1940s and the early 1950s and provided the last hurrah for mining in the old tradition. The same hustle and bustle of the nineteenth-century rush to riches reemerged, with predictable results. Once it was over, the land had been rutted with roads, prospected, littered, and mined, all in the name of profit, but with one striking difference—the banner of national security lay over the wasteland. More uranium mined meant more atomic bombs would be made. The United States would thus be militarily stronger in the battle against communism in the cold war. The miner's new partner, Uncle Sam, kept his finger in every pot, from exploration to milling. Washington encouraged and condoned. When the rush subsided and a semblance of quiet returned to those isolated deserts and plateaus, the now familiar impact on the land remained, with one addition—piles of radioactive tailings and their attendant problems. Possible environmental repercussions, compounded by the strange properties of uranium, had generated little anxiety. But the wind had been sowed once more; this time the whirlwind would be reaped much sooner.

In addition to the Bureau of Mines and the United States Geological Survey, the miners and the mining companies now had to reckon with Uncle Sam and his ever-growing number of agencies, rules, and regulations. The small operator could only temporarily avoid the proliferating restrictions. It was just a matter of time before the federal government would become involved with the environment; only the lack of public outcry stood between mining and that day. Miners were forced to keep an eye on Washington, the international price of ore, the world situation, and the rising costs of mining, as well as on their own work.[1] Mining no longer was a relatively insulated business, free of outside pressures.

Public agitation on behalf of environment/conservation and mining issues did not increase noticeably during the 1940s and the early 1950s. The awakening came gradually in the mid and late fifties. Converts joined the cause; organization strengthened; public relations improved; and environmentalists took their case more aggressively to the uncommitted. Until then they had not attracted the publicity or the emotional issues necessary to incite the hitherto complacent public. The social/political situation was not conducive to mounting a campaign, nor had Americans shown a willingness to accept the sacrifices that would surely be required of them. They had sacrificed and suffered enough during the depression and the war; now they wanted a taste of the "good life." The postwar years gave to many the opportunity for better jobs and higher salaries. Demands for raw materials and energy accelerated as Americans reaffirmed their love of material things. Mining helped to support these desires, and for at least some portions of the industry the ore market expanded as it never had before. Understandably, interest in backing conservation and environmental issues waned; and mining was not castigated as a "threat" to the quality of life. As a producer of America's "good life," it seemed foolish to deter mining, one of the gaggle of geese that were laying the golden eggs.

Affluence, indifference, and technological change led Americans to waste their resource heritage prodigiously, in a manner that was reminiscent of the post–Civil War years, but on a larger scale. Mining was asked only to keep those metals, fuels, and dividends coming. Miners and mining companies responded predictably to the wishes of their stockholders and the public.

The environment/conservation consciousness never completely disappeared; coal mining came under the most frequent scrutiny. The blatant stripping of coal created widespread public apprehension, particularly in the eastern states, where strippers had been digging away for decades. The wartime demands gave new impetus to strip mining. The urgency of that situation diminished the determination to restore or reclaim the mined-out land immediately. Reclamation, still in its infancy, had no proven methods, nor did it have any time to spare for experimentation. The "mine and run" line of reasoning appeared to have regained its popularity. A later study concluded: "As a result, land abuse was fairly common, and unfortunately, a tradition was established that endured far too long."[2] Strip mining, which was labor intensive and economical—a winning combination from the industry's view—retained its adherents after the war.

But the ripped, unsightly land and polluted streams stayed there for all to see. Damned for this damage, the strip miners were also denounced for having caused floods and for having forced people off their land, as well as for menacing public health, disrupting trade, and "allegedly" harboring reptiles and vermin in their mines. Even uranium mining took a slap at its rival, proclaiming that nuclear power could end the rape of the land by coal miners. Not since the hydraulic and smoke controversies had mining found itself so severely condemned. Agitated voters pressured state legislatures and managed to win some victories, even during the war; Illinois (1943) and Pennsylvania (1945) passed laws for the reclamation of strip-mined land. The mining industry objected, but with little effect.

Transportation and mining collaborated to produce the minerals and fuel that America needs. They also have jointly scarred the land, as this 1970 coal-mining operation in Northumberland County, Pennsylvania, illustrates (courtesy Pennsylvania Historical and Museum Commission, Harrisburg).

Conceding nothing, Illinois strip miners promptly went to court to challenge the constitutionality of the law. They sounded like true descendants of the nineteenth century in denouncing the law as impractical, costly, and a threat to "wipe out the margin of profit." The state legislature, they claimed, had exceeded its authority and had passed an act that was "indefinite, uncertain and incapable of enforcement." Not satisfied with merely rehashing the old, they attacked the intent of the law as being impractical. Leveling the ridges so that the contour of the land was returned approximately to what it once had been would not produce productive farm land, they argued; it would actually make it less desirable for grazing, forestry, and recreational purposes. The damage done by strip mining was similar to, but no greater than, that of open-pit and shaft coal mining and sand and gravel operations, complained the plaintiffs; yet the statute discriminated because it applied only to coal strip mines. Furthermore, "ninety-six percent of strip mining companies" were engaged in long-term reclamation projects that were more "valuable" than the one concocted by the legislature.[3] Let mining take care of its own.

Regardless of the transparency of some of the arguments, the Illinois Supreme Court held that the law was unconstitutional because it was an invasion of the private property rights of owners of mineral estates. Mining had won again, which only served to strengthen the determination of some owners to ride roughshod over the opposition. These were the ones who would rather see "smoke and full dinner pails" than restoration and idleness; who opposed all "wild-eyed" conservationists and their theories; who believed that relatively little land would be strip mined compared to all the acres of any state; who saw the land as worthless anyway and believed the profits from coal mining would far surpass the previous contributions of marginal farming. Truly, they constituted the unreconstructed host.

In spite of this militant segment, some coal companies were involved in reclamation, perpetuating the trend of the preceding decades. Unquestionably, a purported 96 percent stretched the truth, but it was happening. Men like James Hillman, president of the Harmon Creek Coal Corporation, serve as outstanding examples. Mining near Burgettstown, Pennsylvania, Hillman firmly believed that a company that made a living from the land had a responsibility to restore it to as good a condition as it was before the mining started. "Restoration is an obligation," asserted this devout conservationist.[4] Hillman's dedication to reclamation was unusual, as was that of his company.

Hillman, however, did not stand alone; others took the same stand. The recreational theme that was promoted by operators in southern Indiana provided a popular justification for planting trees and for creating lakes out of stripped areas. This remedy, of course, allowed companies to spend less than what was required to return the land to a semblance of its original condition. A growing number of miners appreciated the public-relations benefits to be derived from undertaking a minimum of "practical" measures. The W. P. Stahlman Coal Company of Corsica, Pennsylvania, found profit in reclamation. In the 1950s it bulldozed the "spoil peaks" that had been left after strip mining; it then planted pine trees and soon sustained a flourishing Christmas-tree business. In Kentucky, some of the strip-mining companies formed the Kentucky Reclamation Association, their purpose being to give technical advice to its members. They organized to promote the "best use of all land," to cooperate with federal and state agencies that had similar purposes, and to encourage the production of timber.[5]

The reasons that spurred this kind of interest and involvement varied considerably, ranging from a feeling of obligation to the need for improved public relations. Those reclamation schemes that somehow returned a profit—recreation, timber, stock raising, and the like—held the most appeal for coal operators. When they made money, it meant that local and state governments collected revenue through taxes, a point that they never let their critics forget. Both the initial operation and the aftermath, if handled judiciously, improved the tax base, according to the spokesmen for the mining industry.

Strip mining received by far the most attention during these years. It grew and prospered, as other elements of the industry suffered setbacks. The mining of precious metal, which had long been out of the general public's eye, faced a multitude of problems. Criticism of its disdain for the environment prompted little discussion throughout the industry; other issues demanded more attention.

An example of the types of pressures and of one man's reaction to them is found in Charles Chase, who was still mining near Silverton, Colorado. The problem of having mill tailings pollute the Animas River hounded Chase's operations and heaped both praise and blame on him. He thanked a writer in 1946 for complimenting his efforts to keep tailings out of the river: "We will do our best to be fair." A year later, Chase was moved to write, "I have taken pride in doing this work well, and we expect to do work in the future [in] which we may have pride." The results did not please everyone. Although he had worked to eliminate trouble, his neighbors had ignored it, and downstream residents had difficulty in separating the guilty from the innocent, as the dirty gray-green tailings flowed by and fouled their water. Finally, in 1949, the angered Chase replied to a Colorado Fish and Game accusation: "This company alone, of mine operators in the valley, in conference with downstream farmers, *undertook in 1935 to retain its tailings.* To date expenditure on the project has aggregated $200,083, $18,053 within this calendar year."

Tailings ponds evolved into a great source of erosion and pollution and were aesthetically unsightly. This one sits near Ophir Pass in the Colorado San Juans (courtesy Richard L. Gilbert).

The next year, however, the sportsmen's club of Durango complained about pollution. Chase again took the offensive in a letter to its members in which he stressed the long-time, volunteer nature of his efforts to stop pollution. He concluded thus: "I wish not to continue this profitless controversy. . . . We believe that our record is good and we have every plan of co-operating fully with you."

With what must have been secret satisfaction, in February, 1951, Chase asked the Colorado Fish and Game Commission to trap beavers, whose activities threatened to "imperil" the storage ponds. Over a year later, he was still waiting; the agency's lack of action exhibited a sharp contrast to what it had demanded of him. By then Chase was nearing the end of a San Juan mining career that extended back over fifty years. He wrote to a friend in Durango, "I share with you your satisfaction [in a clear river], having always believed it wrong that the stream should be fouled."[6]

Chase's enlightened attitude put to shame many of his contemporaries. (A rumor that refuses to die accuses some of the other Silverton mining companies of having dumped their tailings into the river at night, so that the discoloration would slip past the community and be safely downstream by morning, when the inspectors would be making their examination.) Having grown up in the nineteenth century, he matured in the twentieth to appreciate mining's responsibility toward the environment. He discovered growing sentiment against mining's activities, and he found his company in the role of the scapegoat, simply because Shenandoah-Dives represented the largest and most obvious local operation. The impatience and anger on both sides can be readily understood; tragically, in most cases, little attempt was made to understand the other side's point of view. Chase's problems portended what would come on a larger scale. Elsewhere in the hard-rock industry, attitudes ranged from Chase's one of accommodation and cooperation to those of stubborn individualism. Unified opposition lay in the future; local protests of the kind that Chase endured were typical. The miners could afford to bide their time and trust that the wind would blow their way once more. Even dredging, which was again giving rise to complaints in California, failed to motivate the industry's determination to solve the problem internally before public pressure would force regulation and action. Mining continued to defend itself with hoary arguments—for example, that the land was of little value otherwise and that the extent of the dredged area was not very large. Analysis of the protest went only as deep as insinuating that this was an emotional, political issue: "The uproar is entirely out of proportion to the importance of the problem."[7] Miners had not learned much from the lessons of history.

The threat of governmental regulation did unify the industry and did bring its spokesmen quickly to the pen and the podium. Never popular, the idea of regulation generated heated opposition as the federal government's role expanded. Testifying before a 1947 Senate hearing on water pollution, Donald Callahan, representing the Idaho Mining Association, the Northwest Mining Association, and the American Mining Congress, bluntly said:

> Historically, in the development of our civilization, streams and bodies of water have been used for the purpose of waste disposal and the public interest has been and now is served by such use. We realize, however, that the public is interested also in maintaining the purity of our streams and bodies of water . . . the question of water pollution is a local problem and we believe that the industry can do much in solving that problem without any compulsory legislation.[8]

Before finishing, Callahan warned about delegating "almost despotic power to political officers," which, if done, would seriously harm the industry, which was "so essential to the security and prosperity of our people."

Other speakers concurred with Callahan's fears of potential federal intervention, a boogeyman of no mean proportions. They painted glowing pictures of what mining was accomplishing and of how local people could handle any problems. Incipient revolters had arisen to be counted—the westerners of the late 1970s had nothing on them. They continued the generations-old love/hate relationship with Washington, which was founded on the firm conviction that the fewer the regulations, the better for mining. Uncle Sam was to give only aid and support, not to dictate what to do or what not to do. The skirmish had ended with a victory, but the battle would be a different story. By 1960, Washington had emerged as a partner of mining, if not yet as an environmental policeman.

Would local control have provided the answer, or did it give just another means of dodging the question and of postponing a solution? Except in a few isolated cases, local control had not worked, and mining had not indicated how it proposed to do better. Growing uneasy once more about federal intrusion, mining grabbed for the most available substitute, local or state control, but not without malice aforethought. When it came to ease of access for domination and manipulation, the home front brooked no comparison. And it was convenient to have a villain to blame one's troubles on; Washington played that role nicely. Miners, like other Americans, would increasingly lash out at bureaucracy, red tape, and federal meddling. Hiss the villain; cheer the hero—a real-life melodrama was unfolding.

The status-quo arsenal of the mining industry was fortified by the emerging emphasis on the industry's strategic importance to national security. This ingenious idea evolved into an emotional issue as the cold war became a part of American life. For the moment, this potentially two-sided theory assisted mining. An industry that was so important to national security, however, would logically be most subject to governmental control. Whether the spokesmen for the industry were thinking that far ahead is unclear.

A frustrating fact of reclamation—namely, that programs and methods were still being formulated and tested—nagged at everybody. It sometimes took decades for reclamation to achieve noticeable results. Impatient Americans found this delay hard to accept, and miners were no more inclined to wait stoically—they wanted a return for their investment. The failure of reclamation to produce overnight success created frustration and some bitter "We told you so's." Sam Dickinson, who for twenty years was supervisor of lands and forestry for the Erie Mining Company north of Duluth, Minnesota, asserted that research, planning, flexibility, and patience were the answers. Programs based on them "show what can be accomplished by the determined cooperation of owners and management to keep mining compatible with the environment."[9] Stewardship of land and natural resources was the logical solution, a fact that too few mining people comprehended.

If more men like Dickinson, Chase, and Hillman had taken positions of leadership, mining would have moved toward steward-ship. That would take time, which was running out for the industry. Relatively few companies and individuals to date had expressed a desire to give more than token recognition and service to environ-mental issues. What would rouse them to action had not yet been discovered. The time for action was near at hand, however. An incident in upper Michigan exemplified the onrushing dilemma. Copper miners there were seeking permission to mine in part of the Porcupine Mountains State Park (near White Pine). Comprising some seventy-five square miles of virgin hardwood forests, this wilderness park maintained an area along Lake Superior in virtually the same condition as when the first French *coureurs de bois* had seen it centuries before.

A section of the park harbored low-grade copper, which is not unusual for this region. In the mid fifties, copper-mining interests requested permission to mine in the park and under the adjoining lake. What had seemed until now a routine request stirred up a storm of protests among conservation groups and other alarmed citizens throughout the state and the nation. By late 1958, over 90 percent of the letters to the State Conservation Department protested this action. Suddenly Porcupine versus mining had become a national cause célèbre in certain circles.

Copper miners fought back. They talked of only 900 acres out of 58,000 being affected, of a $6 million annual payroll, of increased local tax revenue and a royalty to the state of three-quarters of a million dollars. All of these would bestow a windfall to unemployment-beleaguered Upper Michigan. Not overlooked was the fact that tax revenues and royalties could be used to improve other state parks.

The mining faction rallied supporters—business folk, chambers of commerce, city councils, Rotary Clubs—all from the Upper Penin-sula. The support that the industry attracted came to little. The damage to public relations had already been done, and the opposition had been marshaled. Mining seemed to be unable to shake its nineteenth-century indifference. An editorial in *Nature Magazine* summarized the position of the opposition: "We have always ques-tioned any attempt to place a price tag on the values inherent in a park or comparable area . . . wilderness and wilderness values are irreplaceable." Another writer called mining's rationale for development "the siren song." Where were the discussions of the impact on workers, access roads, power lines, and waste? This last item the company planned to dump in Lake Superior, thereby creating another environmental horror. The same writer went on to say: "I thought it would be a sacrilege indeed to build a mine on the doorstep of such a cathedral."[10]

Here, unnoticed by mining, was a last warning and the opening shot of the barrage that was yet to come. Now well-organized environmental groups, encouraged by growing public support for the protection of natural resources, could challenge mining with a greater chance of success. Economic considerations would not suffice much longer. Old ways and old ideas die hard, and their influence extends well beyond their vitality. The fight over the Porcupines pointed to the imminent hostilities that mining would confront.

That the industry was caught by surprise is understandable. President Dwight Eisenhower, late in his second term, established a commission to report on goals for America during the upcoming decade of the sixties. That group delivered its report in November, 1960. The commission listed fifteen major goals for national concern and action; the environment was not one of them. Only five short paragraphs, out of 372 pages, dealt with air and water pollution.[11] This minimal attention to the environment epitomized the lack of general public consciousness of the subject and its ramifications as the 1950s ended. The Truman and Eisenhower administrations had responded to this apathy by ignoring the environment as one of their primary considerations.

As the 1960s began, mining crossed a watershed in its history, an event that went unnoticed at the time. No triumphal procession heralded the passage, no headlines announced the crossing. The year 1960 could claim no singular credit for the occasion. The quiet, unnoticed, unfelt, long-coming milestone would be recognized later. Mining's years of tranquillity would be wistfully remembered by old-timers as a cherished age. Previous disagreements, bickering, and troubles would be forgotten as the new realities emerged.

The attitudes and industrial philosophy of the nineteenth century had fit well into the twentieth for six decades. Now, like old shoes, they seemed threadbare and unseemly to wear in public. Plentiful warnings failed to alarm mining, which had chosen to ignore them or wish them away. The time of judgment had come; the day of postponement had passed. The dawn of national environmental concern had broken; environmentalism was "in."

Americans were beginning to respond belatedly to problems that had become a national embarrassment. The social costs of environmental damage had been largely ignored and unaccounted for. No longer would they be overlooked; a new era was at hand.

CHAPTER NINE

Environmental Whirlwind

The 1960s brought the inevitable collision of three groups, two of which came from within the mining industry. The environmentalists, who were gaining support with each passing month, converted the conflict into political power and challenged mining everywhere in the United States. Mining's "hard liners" moved predictably to repel the audacious attacks, damning the "radicals" at every turn; but the hard liners foundered. Environmentalists within the industry, the third group, came into their own at last, alarmed, nevertheless, by the intensity of this onslaught on their livelihood. Their day had come— the heritage of Rossiter Raymond and J. Ross Browne would have its hour—but no one had envisioned the catastrophic events it would bring. Caught off guard, even mining's environmentalists found themselves on the defensive.

The storm that had been coming for years, the great environmental awakening, was now at hand, not only in the United States but throughout the world. A popular cause had been born; a multitude of factors could take credit for its birth. Books such as Rachel L. Carson's *Silent Spring* and Harry M. Caudill's *Night Comes to the Cumberlands* popularized the subject and frightened their readers. Increased knowledge about the environment and about industrial impact on it intensified the public's consciousness of the threat that pollution posed to all Americans. During the Kennedy and Johnson years, the federal government became more actively involved than it had been since the two Roosevelts.

Even a brief survey of the enacted legislation gives a clear indication of its sweep and its impact on mining. The 1963 Clean Air Act awarded the federal government the enforcement power over air pollution. The Water Quality Act of 1965 strengthened the enforcement process and provided for federal approval of ambient standards on interstate waters. The 1967 Air Quality Act was the first federal legislation designed to control lead emission. And the capstone legislation, the National Environmental Policy Act of 1969 (during the Nixon administration), which represented the most pervasive environmental law ever enacted by a United States Congress, was signed into law on January 1, 1970. This act created the Environmental Protection Agency, which, along with its environmental-impact statements, came to be distrusted and roundly despised by a great many miners and mine companies.

This 1969 legislation firmly established environmental quality as a leading national priority by stating a policy to protect it. The contrast with the report that had been given to President Eisenhower in 1960 should not go unnoticed. More than anything else previous to it, the new legislation graphically portrayed what had evolved during the 1960s when the state of the environment had become virtually a popular fad. Furthermore, this legislation made environmental protection part of the mandate for all federal agencies, bringing Washington in on all mining operations, big and small.

Growing activism among the nation's youth had focused on the environmental movement as one of its "causes," and adherents took the issue to the campus and to the streets. Suddenly, television brought into every home the sight of crowds protesting environmentally callous practices. For dedicated environmentalists, the long years of playing the role of Paul Revere were reaping dividends. Americans were coming to realize that an environment that was conducive solely to survival and to maintaining the good life at all costs was not enough. The land must do more than simply support life and the affluence of modern society—it had to offer beauty, renewal, and a sustaining thread to the future. "Conservation," "ecology," and "environment" enjoyed a dramatic rise in popularity. The surge of public anxiety and press coverage was unprecedented.

Mining, and industry as a whole, found themselves under a general attack by "Spaceship Earthers." Technology, the delight of previous generations, was challenged as a major threat to Earth. Uncontrolled technology had devoured raw materials and had created waste products in vast quantities. Economic institutions had engendered ecologically destructive practices and had exploited nature, as well as man. In the words of Ian G. Barbour, "We have allowed technology to be an instrument of private profit and assumed that it would lead to human welfare."[1] He and others hammered on the theme that "man is inseparable from nature." Mining had a moral obligation to protect the environment and to conserve the heritage for future generations.

The miner under the ground and the geologist above it had never heard themselves denounced in these philosophical terms. Values clashed against values, and mining suffered. The industry could deal more comfortably with specific complaints, even some old ones that now had a comforting ring to them.

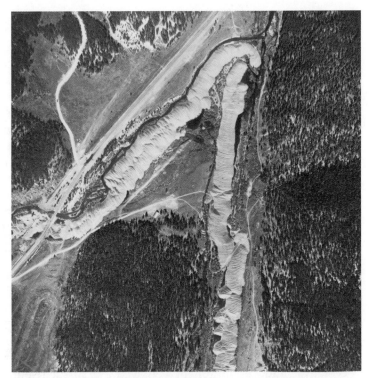

The remains from mining activity range from the picturesque to the grotesque, a source of the tourist dollar and a contributor of pollution. A bird's-eye view of the junction of Colorado's Blue and Swan rivers presents a graphic illustration of dung from dredges (courtesy Kucera & Associates, Denver).

This mine near South Pass, Wyoming, is one of many that dot the western landscape, most of which are not so well preserved (courtesy Richard L. Gilbert).

Clear Creek lived up to its name before miners arrived in 1859; in 1951 it showed the heritage of placer mining. Black Hawk, beyond, lies free of smelter smoke and waits a new bonanza—the tourist (courtesy United States Forest Service).

A coal mine once operated here in Northumberland County, Pennsylvania; only scattered relics and stream pollution served as an epitaph in 1971 (courtesy Pennsylvania Historical and Museum Commission, Harrisburg).

During the decade, renewed public interest in air pollution that was related to coal burning angered Americans, who increasingly channeled their complaints through organized conservation groups and public-health officials. Even that time-worn issue of smelter smoke came back for more criticism in areas where smelters had retained a toe hold. Because attempts at regulation at the state level had done little to abate the problems, federal controls now seemed to be the answer.[2] By the end of the sixties the environmental movement was "fashionable," and Washington was serving as the guardian to save America from Americans.

Criticism of mining came from expected quarters about expected things. It seemed now, however, as if almost everyone wanted to get into the act. One westerner complained, "It is not right that a prospector can drive a bulldozer onto the public land, dig a bunch of damn holes, and then just leave them." Another critic admonished the mining industry and its apologists to quit conjuring up and clinging to the image of the grizzled prospector rustling a grubstake; "Instead, join us in facing the problems of our time." Not even the prospector was immune! Earlier efforts at environmental reclamation were called "bits of expediency." Or as Bernard T. Carter, director of fisheries for Kentucky, explained, "The big catch is that the coal companies are not in the reclamation business, and their efforts to date have not been ones which can be pointed to with pride." Arnold Miller, president of the United Mine Workers, leveled this blast: "The moral is simple; beware of industrialists bearing gifts. Fifty years ago they promised to develop Appalachia, and they left it in wreckage. Now they promise to develop the Northern Plains. They will leave it in ruins." Elementary-school textbooks painted mining in less than glowing colors. For example, one discussed the deep, ugly holes and pits, the scraped surface: "When the supply of minerals was exhausted, the miners moved on. They left the land scarred, covered with waste rock, and unfit to live on. The same unhappy story can be told about early oil and gas drilling."[3]

Mining reeled under the barrage of condemnation. The environmental options that had formerly been open to it had been slammed shut; its future was no longer within its grasp. Miners could usually count on the public eventually to lose interest; that expectation no longer seemed viable. Now the miners were reaping the consequences of their indifference, insensitivity, expediency, and gross exploitation. Environmental involvement, demanded today, should have come yesterday—tomorrow might be too late. Postponement would not be tolerated. Traditional attitudes had their foundations ripped out from under them, and mining came to be seen as one of America's environmental villains.

Americans, seemingly as one, suddenly discovered the strip miner. More specifically, they hit upon Appalachia, a time bomb that had been lying in wait for a generation to explode in the industry's face. It blew up on TV screens and in politicians' lexicons during the presidential campaign of 1960 and stayed there through the Kennedy years and during President Lyndon Johnson's War on Poverty. Horrified citizens would not soon forget those words and pictures. Reclamation and public-relations efforts of previous decades carried little weight. The country had found a rascal of no mean proportions in the strip miner; *raper, polluter,* and *exploiter* were some of the more polite terms used to describe this fiend.

Appalachia actually stretched through the mountainous counties from Pennsylvania into Alabama, but in the public's eye it centered exclusively in the eastern-Kentucky counties and those of neighboring West Virginia. An area that had long been devoted to coal mining, characterized by good times and bad, it remained isolated, poverty riddled, and politically powerless under the domination of coal companies. During the 1880s, uncomprehending mountaineers had sold the mineral rights under their land for fifty cents an acre or less. The new owners were given the right to do whatever was "convenient or necessary" to extract the coal; the deeds contained what seemed to be a harmless clause that absolved the company of all liability for any damages that might result from mining operations.

The traditional underground coal mines, when they came in the twentieth century, provided more jobs and better wages than the local citizens had ever earned before. Then, during the 1950s and the 1960s, the strip miners arrived, and those old mineral deeds took on new meaning. What had once been rolling, wooded mountain land looked like this to one horrified viewer who observed strip-mined devastation near Hazard, Kentucky:

> Huge gashes have been ripped out of the mountainsides and lie raw and exposed with no green cover. To judge by the vast unrelieved stretches of yellow clay, baked iron-hard by the sun and speckled with greasy dark splotches where poisonous acid has seeped through, nothing will ever grow there again. . . .
>
> It is as though the entire landscape, as far as the eye can see, had gone through a hideous convulsion or been ravaged by some crazed monster.[4]

Though a far cry from the nineteenth-century observations of destruction by placer mining, the description somehow seemed hauntingly familiar.

This time, mining did not escape—criticism bombarded it from all corners of the United States, and the coal industry was rocked back onto its heels. The whole industry soon found itself under a siege of public condemnation, as other despicable examples, past, present, and future, were dug up and flaunted by critics. In Florida it was found that a company was planning to dredge Lake Okeechobee, despite pleas to desist by public and governmental groups. In Georgia, another company's plans to mine the offshore sea bottom for phosphate aroused intense controversy once the intentions and scope of the plans had become clear.

Magazines as diverse as *American Heritage,* the *Saturday Review, American Forests,* and *Field and Stream* published antimining editorials and articles. Literate Americans could hardly avoid reading about mining, and they soon became abundantly aware of its environmental transgressions. Questions were hurled at mining: Why had it been so destructive? Why had not more reclamation been done? Why had mining acted in such a cavalier fashion? Why? Why? Why? Mining was scarcely given time to respond before it was inundated with more questions.

Jolted by the adverse attention, the industry responded. In Kentucky it prevailed in the state's supreme court in the case of *Martin* v. *Kentucky Oak Mining Co.* In an opinion handed down on June 21, 1968, the majority opinion held that the owner of underlying minerals may totally ruin the surface without the consent of the man who owns and tills the land. Undaunted by that legal setback, the opponents, led by folk-hero–lawyer Harry Caudill from Whitesburg, continued to press their case. The strip miners did not advance their cause appreciably when they resorted to slander, typified by one operator's slur: "I went to college with Harry Caudill. He was a sonofabitch then and he's a sonofabitch now."[5] It was darkly hinted that anyone who spoke out against coal mining was somehow in league with the Communists.

Strip mining resorted to its tried-and-true defense as being the best, cheapest, and safest method of mining. Also emphasized were its impact on the local economy and the detriment to the county and the state should strip mining be driven out of business. Several grains of truth lay within those arguments, but they did not sit well in the 1960s. The underlying theme—the justification of profligacy based upon the superabundance of resources—also won no converts; neither did the kindred supposition that, given enough time, all wrongs could be righted and that time existed. Mining failed to understand the obsessive nature of its opponents' concern, which also encompassed the waste of human resources that resulted from mining practices and from environmental impact.

It did no good to point to the accomplishments of reclamation. Most efforts were patchwork at best; at too many Kentucky mines, nothing at all had been done. Colorful brochures and costly advertising did nothing to enhance mining's image—"conscience ads," one opponent called them. Even the 1966 Kentucky strip-mining laws, hailed as the best in the country, provided no succor. One antagonist described them as a little like legalizing rape, as long as the rapist agrees to restore the victim to her original condition.[6]

A study of those years makes it obvious that Kentucky strip miners, blinded by inbred jargon and attitudes, failed to grasp the idea that many Americans found something fundamentally wrong with that occupation. Tragically, neither side sympathized with or understood the other. Aphorisms would no longer suffice; old methods provided meager bandages. Something more was needed. Appalachia became the symbol of what had gone wrong with nineteenth-century practices that lingered into the mid twentieth century. Mining had become entrapped by its own rhetoric and experience. In the second half of the twentieth century, that excuse no longer served to justify the actions of the industry.

Local turmoil did not convince the national coal industry to change its ways quickly enough to prevent a country-wide attack on it. In 1963, Joseph Lee, general counsel for the Central Pennsylvania Open Pit Mining Association, showed the frustration of the times: "Unfortunately, outspoken critics of the industry in general have adopted the policy of blandly accusing the industry of contaminating Pennsylvania's streams and destroying Pennsylvania's abundant forest reserves and game population. More sober minds recognize that such accusations are false and misleading." Sober minds were in short supply just then. Another spokesman for mining called attention to the fact that natural resources were the "backbone of the nation's economy."[7] He might as well have asked the incoming tide to roll back.

Strip mining's defense, already mobilized, was quickly challenged and defeated. The public would not buy the argument that environmental problems could be attributed to a few careless, thoughtless strippers or to the sins of the past. The evidence of damage precluded the belief that "conscientious" strip miners with community spirit actually existed. Mining continued to insist that they did and that their successes pointed to salvation for the future. The tried-and-true arguments—economic benefits, the poor quality of the mined land, and that the criticism was unfair and uninformed—

fell at the start of the battle, and the showcase reclamation projects were routed almost as fast.

The ramparts had fallen in what had literally become a war. Strip miners vainly took the offensive to blunt the fury of criticism. Benson Lingle, president of his namesake Pennsylvania coal company, pointed with pride to his family's history, emphasizing that strip mining on marginal farm land had finally allowed a small profit from the property. Lingle argued that he should not be deprived of his rights to the "use and benefit of our privately owned property. We are not destroying this land. It is far more valuable after stripping and reclamation than it was before." History, another miner asserted, showed that malpractices could be found in society in general, and mining should not be singled out. Hugh Montgomery, in his 1962 article "Conscientious Coal Stripping," admitted that the accusations of critics were justified; mining had earned its unsavory reputation. On the other hand, he urged those critics to recognize the growing sense of responsibility on the part of strip miners.[8]

More to the liking of the die-hards within mining were the comments made by the vice-president of the Consolidation Coal Company at the American Mining Congress in 1968. Attacking conservationists who demanded that strip miners do a better job of restoring what they tore up, he unloaded: "Stupid idiots, socialists, and Commies who don't know what they're talking about. I think it is our bounden duty to knock them down and subject them to the ridicule they deserve."[9] That kind of vituperation built only walls, not bridges of understanding.

Only slightly less provocative was a full-page advertisement defending the coal industry, which appeared in 1966:

> If you want an instant end to air pollution stop driving your car, then turn off your oil burner, brick up your fireplace, bundle your leaves, box your trash, refuse delivery of anything by truck, boycott trains, buses and cabs. Don't use anything which requires oil, gas, coal or atomic energy in its manufacture.[10]

If the reader had by then failed to realize that coal was not solely responsible for the country's pollution and environmental problems, the last line spelled out the industry's pitch: "Coal is a minor cause of this contamination, but the coal industry is working hard to clean the air."

All of this rhetoric proved to be far too blatant for Norman Cousins, editor of the *Saturday Review*. He wrote a blistering editorial in the October 8, 1966, issue, demanding that the industry apologize to the American people for insulting their intelligence. It was difficult to imagine "a more maladroit, frivolous, or misleading statement on a major national problem." He summed up a lot of people's reaction when he concluded, "Once a man talks like a fool, everything he may have said becomes suspect."[11]

The mining industry's defense collapsed under the barrage of criticism. The national industry's arguments and remedies, like those of Kentucky, attracted little public attention and served to little effect. This was a generation in search of instant results; it was disinclined to learn from history, and it did not have the patience to wait any longer for changes that the industry had been promising since the turn of the century. The public wanted action, action that it knew how to initiate through federal regulation. Mining had traveled this road before. The president of the R. S. Carlin Company expressed that firm's opinion: business "should be helped and not burdened with restrictions, whether it be coal operations or any other industry. I say let us all strive to make America grow and prosper." That striving came in a way that mining did not approve. No longer could it insulate itself in patriotism and profit. Once again, miners sat in on congressional hearings, and spokesmen for them defended their interests before an increasingly hostile public, press, and Congress.

These congressional hearings produced a mixed bag of results for the industry as well as the public. In June, July, and August, 1967, for example, the Senate Subcommittee on Air and Water Pollution heard testimony. Spokesmen for the industry came forth to present their case and to defend their actions. They had the opportunity to discuss the work of the Bituminous Coal Research Laboratory, a research affiliate of the National Coal Association, which had devoted a quarter-century of study to acid drainage. This group had also cooperated with the Bureau of Mines on a number of projects and had sponsored symposiums, along with its independent research. Witnesses pointed with pride to Illinois for its significant work on acid drainage and the reclamation of mine spoil.[12] They praised the "conscientious reclamation" of surface-mined land and lauded the role of coal mining in the growth of American industry. That these improvements came, in some cases, at the expense of stream pollution they admitted, but until recently, little thought had been given to environmental conditions that paralleled growth.

All of these accomplishments were well and good, but they failed to erase from the public's mind such comments as those from Jim Quigley, commissioner of the Federal Water Pollution Control Administration. In recalling his Pennsylvania boyhood, he said that he was at least twelve years old before he learned that creeks flowed in colors other than black and orange.[13] That recollection proved to be newsworthy; twenty-five years of research, without a practical solution, did not. Mining's justification for its actions, even though Americans in general had benefited from them, created few headlines. The public wanted more than platitudes, homilies, and history.

Action translated into laws. States were the first line of defense, but testimony in 1968 disclosed that only fourteen had laws about surface mining. Secretary of the Interior Stewart L. Udall, meanwhile, called attention to the fact that every state had some surface-mining activities. A representative of the Sierra Club pointed out that none of the "pending bills comes near to meeting the challenge."[14] This left only one possible regulatory body with enough clout to force action—the federal government.

Although some individuals still thought, like Joseph Abdnor, that federal controls were "unnecessary, undesirable and impractical," that attitude could never again prevail. Federal controls were a fact of life; the only question was how strong they would become. More enlightened was the 1967 testimony of James Boyer, the project director for research on bituminous coal. He correctly accused the industry, the government, and the public of jointly seeking rapid industrialization, while giving little thought to the concurrent environmental repercussions. Admitting that the problem was serious, Boyer argued, "It has only been during the past ten years that combined efforts of industry and Government have been accelerated sufficiently to produce significant—although not yet adequate—technological advances." Operating mining companies were not always the prime villains—he estimated that up to 90 percent of the acid discharge, a major factor in stream pollution, drained from abandoned mines. The industry was making headway on a problem that was not its alone, and Boyer wanted the federal government to share the cost of installing and maintaining pollution-control devices.[15] Boyer offered strip mining's most reasoned, logical answer to criticism. Evidence from states in which companies actively promoted reclamation programs strengthened his argument. These mining men were willing to accept some federal control, if money came with it.

Conferences and voluntary agreements by coal companies had been the earlier solution to reclamation. Now government, federal and state, would be an environmental partner with the industry. The mining industry continued to argue that proliferating agencies and strong legislation unreasonably curtailed and obstructed it. Environmentalists violently disagreed. But the choice had been made—no one would escape the day of reckoning.

For a while, hard-rock mining seemed to be leading a charmed life in comparison to its strip-mining cousins. Eventually, however, hard-rock mining came in for its share of public criticism, though never to the extent that was directed toward the strippers. The defense that it mustered duplicated what has already been described; for example, a vice-president of Kennecott Copper underscored the fact that mining furnishes America with the materials that are required for future expansion and growth. This was only a variation on a theme that had been heard for the last generation, and it was repeated in R. S. Carlin's cry that all should "strive to make America grow and prosper."[16]

As late as the 1960s, such mining giants as AMAX and Homestake were ignoring the turmoil and were publishing annual reports that would have delighted the nineteenth-century investor. At the same time, the number of environmental articles published in the *Mining Congress Journal* jumped from one in 1963 to fourteen in 1970; *environment* became a new category in the index. Mining's conservation/environmental movement, which had lagged behind its traditional profit-at-all-cost brethren, now received its greatest impetus; this indicated the change in national priorities. If mining hoped to regain some of its lost status and to clean up a besmirched image, this element would have to surge to the forefront.

As the 1960s wound to a bitter end, mining hardly had time to catch its collective breath. It reeled from coast-to-coast exposure on TV, at hearings, and in books, articles, debates, letters, and protests. Never before had it experienced such a tumultuous era. The stark contrast to the previous century defied understanding, and those who had once been hailed as makers of modern America now retreated before an angered public, who looked upon them as environmental Genghis Khans.

Neither side listened unemotionally to the other, nor did the tried-and-true nineteenth-century responses muster much support or sympathy anywhere. Mining and its critics failed to understand each other's positions, and in that failure came the conflict of the sixties. The country seemed to have changed its national priorities within a decade, from development toward conservation. Mining, once a favored, if not pampered, institution, slipped into public disfavor; the momentum had swung to its opponents.

As if that were not bad enough, members of the industry were working at cross-purposes with one another; some were ready and willing to adjust to changing times and needs, while others dug in to fight a bitter rear-guard action. Out of the ashes of the sixties had to come a new effort. The industry could no longer rely on its significance to the American economy or on the superabundance of minerals to explain its actions. Nor could industry spokesmen bow to capitalism and laissez-faire idealism. Time alone would not solve the problem. The seventies were going to be soul-searching and thought-provoking for the industry.

CHAPTER TEN

A Vision, a Hope for the Future

The shouting, the name calling, and the public condemnation left their scars on mining and shaped the industry's responses in the 1970s. Mining has not forgotten that upheaval. Defenders hoped that the corner had been turned and that an environmental consciousness had been awakened. Critics, on the other hand, did not believe that the decade of the sixties could erase positions that had been hardened by centuries of exploitation of minerals and the land. Industry champions sensed a new surge of support that would carry mining back to its position as a mainstay of American progress and development. Who was right?

For environmental concern to surge anywhere meant that its advocates had to overcome opposition from mine and company offices; old ways and old ideas would not die without a struggle. Unreconstructed individuals continued to vilify the detractors of mining with as much emotion, wrath, and rancor as ever. They could not let go of their favorite epithets—"idiots, socialists and Commies"—and they threw in a few new ones for good measure. One defender claimed that the "new breed of conservationists who have been waxing so eloquent about the Kodiak bear and the Nevada pupfish had better get concerned about the survival of the American public which is the ultimate endangered species." Two other miners also castigated the "enemy":

> It may be interesting to list some of the attackers of the mining industry. . . . These include a real mishmash of welfare, anti-establishment, loudmouths and hippies, muckrakers (politicians), so-called intellectuals, share-the-wealthers, antipollutionists and ecologists, and plain rabble rousers. These groups have some things in common; leftist leanings, a contempt for hard work, and extreme pessimism and disrespect for the ability of the aggressive individual. . . . The mining industry has nothing to apologize for, and least of all to the longhairs. . . . An open pit mine is a beautiful thing to look at. I say to the Sierra Club, if they want to do something about a scene that hurts their eyeballs, then they ought to restore an ugly thing like a washed out creek.

Denver's *Mining Record* took up the cause through its cracker-barrel philosopher, Prunes the burro. Prunes brayed loudly:

In some parts of the country, strip mining operations should be welcome. It would be the only scenery available.

50 years ago smoke was a sign of progress; now it's a dirty word!

If the old time miners had been forced to replant the trees and restock the trout streams like today, they'd never have made it!

I want a front row seat when the Environmentalists start digging for coal to satisfy their energy needs![1]

Nonwriters who felt the need to express their opinion in no uncertain terms displayed one of those ever-popular bumper stickers: "Ban Mining. Let the Bastards Freeze to Death in the Dark."

The critics of mining voiced their opinions also, equally as emotionally and often just as illogically. West Virginia's Congressman Ken Hechler hit a sensitive nerve when he said: "I have seen what havoc and obliteration are left in the wake of strip mining. It has ripped the guts out of our mountains, polluted our streams with acid and silt, uprooted our trees and forests, devastated the land, seriously disturbed or destroyed wildlife habitat, left miles of ugly high walls . . . and left a trail of utter despair for many honest and hardworking people." Appalachia would not go away. Harry Caudill wrote in *Watches of the Night* (1976), "If lessons are to be learned anywhere in America about this crucial clash and its deadly consequences it is here, and from the Cumberland experience the rest of the country should derive guidance in what to avoid if men and mines are to coexist."[2]

No letup came in governmental regulation, which proliferated during the seventies. Laws evolved in a variety of packages: the Mineral Policy Act of 1970, the Threatened and Endangered Species Act of 1973, the Federal Land Policy and Management Act and the National Park System Mining Regulation Act of 1976. All of them affected and regulated mining's activity. Reclamation became a catch word. With the abandoned-mine reclamation fund, Washington even reached out to help mining through the states. The new policies led to some confusion, many headaches, and yards of red tape. One miner sputtered that when it came to the environment, he was forced to deal with the Forest Service and with the Bureau of Land Management on the federal level. After that the state Commission on Water-Quality Control, the Public-Health Department, and the Division of Mines clamored to have their say; and finally the local county's zoning board demanded its toll. The complicated procedures sometimes created a frustrating, time-consuming, and costly adventure through the bureaucratic maze.

So pervasive became the environmental issue that even in the pages of "friendly" publications, miners could find articles stating both the pros and cons of their activities. *Business Week*, for example, published articles entitled "The EPA Is in a Bind in West Virginia" and "A Clash along the Yellowstone: Coal vs. Moose."[3] Mining could not escape the issue, which hung like a cloud over the industry's present and future.

The impact of the controversy went far beyond vocal or printed criticism. Franklin Yoffe, who attempted to mine diatomite from Lake Umbagog near Errol, New Hampshire, ran afoul of "environmental extremists," who took to the newspaper and public meetings to create enough protest to force the state to refuse his request. In Minnesota, mining companies that were prospecting for copper and nickel around the Minnesota Boundary Waters Canoe Area found themselves in court when the Isaak Walton League filed suit to stop their activities. In handing down his decision, the United States district judge said, "There can be no question that full mineral development and mining will destroy and negate the wilderness or most of it."[4] Mining had lost again. Decisions like that drove the industry's extremists into a fervor of useless verbosity and posturing.

Fortunately for mining, the influence of this belligerent group waned. Moderates presented the case for mining more effectively and moved the industry toward accommodation. Even the *Mining Record* came around, once it had recovered from its early 1970s shock and anger. That pattern was typical for many others within the industry.

The swiftness of change created some incredulity. The director of the Bureau of Mines, Elburt Osborn, came west in 1971 to give the keynote address at the Western Resources Conference in Golden, Colorado. Ten years earlier, a meeting such as that would have "been inconceivable to most of us," he observed. There they sat, listening to three days of papers on environmental problems, "as if it were the most natural thing in the world."[5]

The case for mining was built on the tradition of mining's national significance: "The public needs to be reminded that agriculture and mining together are the two basic industries upon which all others depend." The American Mining Congress admitted that mistakes had been made. Workable, reasonable solutions and policies must now be found to ameliorate environmental impact; no longer would dangerous, temporary ones be tolerated. The folly of over-regulation, accompanied by warnings of dire calamities if current trends should persist, continued to be emphasized. The spokesmen for mining repeatedly asked if consumers would be willing to pay the increased costs of restrictions and regulations and whether they would assume a role in improving the environment. Their pleas for more time fell on ears that were no more receptive than they had been during the sixties.[6]

For the first time in its history, mining generally admitted blame for creating environmental damage and for shirking its responsibilities for restoration once the operations were concluded. Elburt Osborn stated well the new perspective of mining: "It is vitally important that we care—not just about damage caused directly by the mineral industries, but about the indirect consequences too." Failure to do this, Osborn warned, would force the industry to "suffer infinitely more restrictions on freedom of operation than exist today."[7] Putting its own house in order and improving its public image, especially among the youth, meant that mining must combine tradition and innovative ideas.

Osborn and others correctly reasoned that the mining industry's freedom to make policy decisions for the public "was never a right—only a luxury." The old days were gone; regulations curbed all aspects of the industry, and lawsuits proliferated alarmingly when mining appeared to flout them. Some of the restrictions helped; some hindered; some only confused. One must sympathize with the mining engineer who complained in the mid 1970s that he had to obtain a permit to have a tailings pond and another one *not* to have a tailings pond and was required to deal with several agencies in the process.

The small operator rebelled at these restrictions, as did his larger compatriot—all to little avail. State and federal regulations forced mining to defer to the environment. A "rising concern over increasingly excessive governmental regulation of the mining industry" prevailed. Realistically, governmental action was necessary to catch the industry's attention, to convince the industry that it had to be a steward of the land and its resources. For too long, mining had danced to its own tune. The governmental kick in the pants, though painful, had the desired result. In Bartlesville, Oklahoma, the National Zinc Company applied for a permit to construct a zinc plant. Included in its plan was a detailed report on how environmental, safety, and health standards would be met. ASARCO launched a four-year program to bring its El Paso, Texas, smelter into conformity with state and federal air-quality standards. A strip-mining company near Thayer, Kansas, was required to reclaim the land as it went along; and the Midland Coal Company organized a task force that was responsible for the reclamation of mined areas before the company even began to work near Trivoli, Illinois. Before turning a shovelful of Wyoming coal, the Spring Creek Coal Company was required to draft an environmental statement to cover the entire projected twenty-five-year period of operation.[8] State and federal governments forced mining to fulfill its responsibilities. To some companies, regulation brought only discouragement. To others, who saw public scrutiny as a challenge, it brought the opportunity to continue mining through satisfactory compliance.

Mining's leaders began to realize that the industry could not stand as an "anachronism of anarchy," as Mike Frome had labeled it only a few years before. Mining's spokesmen could no longer merely sabotage bills on the state and national levels; now they would have to propose constructive measures and exhibit more understanding and a willingness to compromise. Mining could not persist in "the exercise of primeval political power and pressure to subvert the will of the people."[9] The industry appeared to be learning this lesson as the 1970s progressed, except for a few die-hards who managed to inflict a great deal of damage to public relations.

The distress of miners arose largely from the fact that the public seemed to be imposing excessive demands on the industry, to the point of virtually shutting it down. They were justifiably afraid that the average American did not fully understand what he was asking of mining. To counteract these demands, the industry worked to improve its public relations and to educate the general public throughout the seventies. Typical of its efforts was this statement in 1976: "Mining operations, including smelting and refining, can be pursued without environmental damage on this awesome scale. They can meet necessary standards for protection of human health. Still, some environmental disturbance is inevitable, if there is to be minerals production. The public must recognize this inescapable fact."[10]

Some of the public never did accept that fact, nor would they admit that mining was essential to the economic health of the United States. A compromise, or a trade-off, had to be found. James Wilson, president of the Rocky Mountain Energy Company, perceived that somewhere between the prospectors, who wanted to prospect everywhere, and the extreme environmentalists, who seemed totally indifferent to the nation's needs, lay the future of mining. That angle of repose had not yet been reached.

Recovering from the initial assaults on it, the industry had regained some of its confidence by the end of the decade. The *Mining Record* for February 14, 1979, could proclaim that mining too often was painted as the "villain destroyer" of the environment, when actually the "opposite is true." The time had arrived, the editor insisted, to evaluate laws and policies and to weigh the role of bureaucracy. Through education, conservation, enlightenment, and the sound management of resources, the environment and the ecological balance of nature could be preserved. These enlightened ideas indicated that a lesson was being learned.

Having been mauled by the media for nearly two decades, mining became keenly aware of the potentialities and problems of public relations. Its leaders redoubled their efforts to present the case for mining, using traditional and contemporary arguments and techniques. It was to be hoped that their efforts indicated a legitimate change of attitude this time, not a cynical, window-dressing approach that had characterized so many of their past actions.

The Falcon Coal Company of Lexington, Kentucky, epitomizing the traditional approach, featured a vineyard and abundant grapes as part of its reclamation project in the eastern part of the state. In a joint effort with a winery, the company believed its project to be a first of its kind, certainly in Kentucky. The industry also continued to play upon the theme that mining was not the single, nor even a major, source of pollution. Pollution was everybody's problem, so it was proclaimed from speakers' podiums and by magazine advertisements.[11]

Presenting mining's case to America's youth required special measures, and some success was achieved. Efforts expended in that direction could be expected to be particularly fruitful; today's youth would be tomorrow's more enlightened middle-aged consumer. An upbeat tempo invigorated an old idea: "Everyone must recognize that the *cost* as well as the *benefit* will be his." And along the same line, "the public must also understand that it, too, must play a role in improving that quality."[12]

The entire spectrum of the industry—base, coal, and precious metals—pleaded strongly for public understanding of the intrinsic conflict between mining and the environment. Typical of this promotion was the aforementioned statement that appeared in a pamphlet at mid decade, *What Mining Means to Americans:* "Some environmental disturbance is inevitable, if there is to be minerals production." Americans needed to realize that the ultimate test should be whether what was gained from regulation would prove to be more valuable than what was lost, warned another spokesman, because damage would result either way.[13]

Mining tried to answer the "Spaceship Earthers" too, although the industry always seemed uncomfortable when it ventured into their philosophical realms. Grappling with ethereal issues had never been a strong point of the industry. George Monroe, president of the Phelps Dodge Corporation, attempted to reassure the critics when he reminded his audience at a speech in Colorado Springs that mineral development would be as important to the welfare of Americans in the future as it had been in the past. Mining could and should be conducted in such a manner as to minimize the damage to the environment, which, he confessed, had not always been the procedure in earlier years. A year later, in September, 1974, the *Mining Record* spoke in a similar vein about the essential significance of those two basic industries—agriculture and mining. In terms of benefit to the nation, mining was essential, another defender asserted.

By the end of the decade, mining had come closer to coping with some of the issues of moral responsibility. Ideas such as the sound management of resources, conservation, and environmental education came together in mining's vocabulary, and even that once-hard-to-swallow phrase—the ecological balance of nature—seemed less threatening. Mining would be in the vanguard of environmental progress, a writer felt, if it was not dictated into ecological overkill by enthusiastic environmentalists or strangled by laws.[14]

No one succeeded in squarely confronting the issues that such writers as Ian Barbour and Helen Hunt Jackson raised; perhaps no one was temperamentally able to do so yet. Allan Bird, a down-to-earth mine manager in Silverton, Colorado, touched upon one of the reasons. When asked about the destruction of trees by the expansion of a tailings pond, he responded: "The EPA people looked at it. The water quality people looked at it. They all approved the plans. It was a situation where it was the choice of preserving 30 acres of willows or putting a town out of work."[15] That conflict, as old as mining itself, had surfaced long before Jackson had traveled to O-Be-Joyful Creek so many years ago. The company had, at least, met governmental standards, which were much too lenient in the opinion of vocal opponents.

Mining hoped for both an immediate and long-range impact with its public-relations strategy. The industry needed to launch its campaign on a national scale and, insofar as possible, to coordinate it industry-wide. Deeds, however, were required to back up promises.

Realizing that the best defense could be a good offense, mining launched an attack of its own. The amount of land that had been disturbed by mining, the industry claimed, represented only a small percentage of the total of the United States, an amount far smaller, for example, than the national or the state park systems. It was, one author argued, an area only about one-sixth of that devoted to highways and approximately equal to the acreage being used in the country's airports.[16] Discussing air pollution, industry spokesmen pointed out that the largest percentage of it was natural, not man-made. Of the remainder, mining contributed only a small percentage.

More subtly, Richard Schmidt analyzed coal versus the environment in a series of lectures, which were later published. One of his major themes centered on distinguishing between environmental change and environmental damage. Change, an alteration of relatively short duration, could be reversed under proper attention and "legitimate control." The root of the environmental controversy, he believed, rested directly upon distinguishing between change and damage. Damage he defined as an impact on the physical environment that was beyond the reach of controls and was perhaps irreversible.[17] Whether his kind of philosophical debate altered much thinking cannot be measured. The fact that mining would take that type of approach indicated its desire for future discussions along similar lines. Words, it seemed, were at last being translated into action.

Mining now needed to take some positive action, whether motivated by a change of heart or by a forced accommodation to public opinion or the law. The small-scale, financially weaker miners and companies found themselves at a disadvantage when thrust against corporations. Those larger companies took most of the blame for the problems, but they also had most of the resources for making the changes that the times required. The financial impotence of the small miner threatened him with extinction.

A sampling of new approaches illustrates how environmental ideas were catching on within mining. An Exxon advertisement in *Sports Illustrated* in 1978 emphasized "Continuous Reclamation Mining"—Exxon's way of surface-mining coal without permanently scarring the land. Anaconda Copper finally converted to the idea that environmental conservation had become an integral part of business responsibility. The company won an award for water-quality treatment; the amount of money that Anaconda spent on land reclamation and air-quality improvement showed that Anaconda was paying more than lip service to its responsibilities. The Homestake Company followed the same path. In its various mining operations throughout the country, Homestake devised environmental programs, at the same time shrewdly informing its stockholders that these required a great deal of effort and expense, money out of their dividends.[18]

Kennecott published the pamphlet "Our Environment," which described what the company was accomplishing in Utah with environmental programs. Beautifully illustrated, it explained the company's plans for improvements in smelters and mine environments and its revegetation program for restoring dumps and company land. Publications by other companies did likewise in an aggressive attempt to tell mining's side of the story.[19] The investing public needed to know where "the buck stopped." Some companies willingly followed the example of the aforementioned environmental vanguard; others did so begrudgingly.

One of the most progressive environmental plans, clearly a guide for the future, was proposed by AMAX at several of its Colorado mines. The chairman of the company's board, Ian MacGregor, had set the theme for the seventies when he had written in 1971, "[We] are also responsive members of the community, alert to public demand for environment control." Mining, he concluded, must not be forced into a take-it-or-leave-it choice: "Private companies and the public can work together to help retain or achieve quality environments in the midst of industry activity." MacGregor pledged that AMAX's philosophy would be "to evaluate development plans with full consideration of their impact on the environment that created and must sustain them."

AMAX moved quickly to make good on those fine words. At its Urad molybdenum mine, which closed in 1974, the company began land reclamation that would ensure future public use. Land that had been disturbed by mining dating back to the nineteenth century was restored at the same time as that which AMAX had despoiled during its less than ten years of operation. By 1981, $7 million had been spent on this project, which won a National Environmental Industry Award. It was hailed as "the first full scale program in the United States to stabilize and reclaim surface areas disturbed by hard-rock mining."

Reclaiming the past was not enough. From the very first planning stages of its new Henderson molybdenum mine (70 miles west of Denver), AMAX worked under the concept "that the mineral wealth of this earth can be utilized for human progress in complete harmony with conservation and recreation." Calling it "The Experiment in Ecology," the company began in 1966 to create what has become a prototype environmental program, one designed to continue beyond the life of the Henderson Mine. By 1979, AMAX had an environmental-services department working throughout the world; the company spent $47 million in 1978 and $38 million in 1979 on various projects.[20] AMAX epitomized the fundamental changes that were coming to the industry. Without doubt, this company had originally taken up the cause in response to public pressure and governmental regulation, but it had subsequently manifested a genuine respect for the environment and for its responsibility toward it. Stewardship was becoming an essential policy.

Momentum had shifted to the environmental faction within the industry and had begun a steady ascendancy, a long-overdue change.

Mining engineers were offered a selection of academic courses on the subject: environmental law, air pollution, ecology for engineers, mine environment planning, reclamation practices—even a major in environmental geology. The subject catalog for the library at the Colorado School of Mines contained nearly two drawers full of cards on environmental topics. The *Mining Congress Journal* and other publications steadily increased the number of articles on the subject during the 1970s, and the Mining Congress convention at Los Angeles in 1979 held four sessions on environmental or reclamation topics, the papers from which were later published.[21] The new generation of mining professionals was being steeped in environmental topics.

As the 1970s drew to a close, a growing realization permeated the industry—from miner to superintendent to engineer to owner—that environmental attentiveness had come to stay. In twenty years the mining industry had been asked to change the attitudes of two thousand years and, all things considered, had done remarkably well. A transformation of that magnitude did not come without considerable upheaval. By 1980 the environmental group within mining had not totally prevailed, but a determined start had been made. Many miles still had to be traveled to attain a complete reformation.

Mining received a mixed set of signals regarding its significance to national security and the future, a circumstance that, for a while, changed the context of discussions about the environment. After the oil embargo (1973) and the resulting apprehension about energy dependence, questions arose about the increased production of coal, oil shale, and oil. A crisis atmosphere prompted Washington to respond with plans, agencies, and money. In states that had large projected reserves of coal and oil shale (e.g., New Mexico, Wyoming, Colorado, and Montana), mining appeared to have at least a tentative green light to proceed with new projects, unfettered by the environmental safeguards that had come to weigh over more normal operations.

Had national priorities trumped environmental ones? Would the government now provide more financial help and less regulation? And what would be the industry's position vis-à-vis the environment and energy independence? These questions haunted mining men and the states in which they were operating or planned to operate. No answers came immediately. For a short time, the energy crisis created agitation by Americans who soon lost interest when it seemed to go away. Congress and the president became bogged down in discussions and failed to provide long-range planning, or even a general direction. Mining, meanwhile, tried to provide answers and to fend off the advancing environmentalists.

In its defense, it should be said that mining stood at the bar, a victim of the times. It became a convenient scapegoat when public awareness was finally awakened. Americans suddenly discovered the threat to the environment, and they moved with a vengeance to remove it. At times, it appeared that any means justified the ends, that the country felt a collective guilt and sought repentance for its past sins. Certainly the public had to assume much of the responsibility for the attitudes and actions of the mining industry. The enemy had indeed been met, and "he is us."

Had mining paid more heed in the 1950s and the early 1960s, some of the subsequent pressure would not have been so heavy. But mining had ignored the signals, and now the public provided an unreliable barometer to indicate the trends of the new era. Most Americans had no comprehension of the technology, nor had they any idea of the cost and the length of time necessary for making changes. Patience was not one of their virtues either. With insight and a hint of cynicism, one defender of mining stated that the most important aspect of reclamation lay in physical appearance. Almost by itself it determined whether public approval would be forthcoming. An unattractive project would never be acceptable. On the other hand, the layman accepted anything that appealed to the eye, even though it might not accomplish adequate conservation.[22]

Uneven accomplishments characterized these two decades. In Pennsylvania, Illinois, Idaho, and elsewhere, abandoned mines continued to pollute; exorbitantly expensive remedies precluded action. The relatively new environmental laws and regulations (few came before the 1950s) did not totally meet the expectations of either side. Some mining companies worked actively with the public, environmental groups, and the government to conserve the environment; others did as little as possible or simply abandoned the fight. Distrust, foundering hopes, and disappointments gave rise to a kind of guerrilla warfare that harassed, delayed, or halted mining.[23] Mutual disillusionment thwarted efforts to reach détente.

A classic confrontation unfolded in Colorado's Elk Mountains at Crested Butte, once a coal-mining town. After the closing of the "Big Mine" in 1952, Crested Butte evolved into a ski resort, most of whose residents had no ties to mining. As a result, they greeted with something less than enthusiasm AMAX's announcement that it intended to develop a large molybdenum mine on nearby Mount Emmons. Even though the company had amply demonstrated environmental leadership and corporate sensitivity, "as rare in these climes as Spanish moss," the battle lines were quickly drawn.

Meetings to present plans, express views, and hear out arguments deteriorated into stormy scrimmages. Newspaper and magazine articles brought national attention and notoriety to Crested Butte. The debate pivoted on the crucial matter of the quality of life. What impact would two thousand construction workers, fourteen hundred miners, roads, mills, tailings piles, and sudden growth have on the town, its three hundred or so residents, and its beautiful site? Rock Springs, Wyoming, was cited as an example of a town where uncontrolled and unplanned development had produced its worst, thanks to mining activity.

AMAX counterattacked with its best artillery. It met with various county, state, and federal agencies and spent hundreds of thousands of dollars on surveys of cultural resources; reviews of historic districts; studies of water resources, wildlife, fish, vegetation, and soils; and statements on environmental impact. Never before had the area, the people, the flora, and the fauna been so carefully studied and so thoroughly discussed.[24] But the vocal and alarmed residents continued to fight, in an effort to preserve their way of life. At the end of the decade, the two factions were locked in a stalemate, with AMAX promising to make this a precedent-setting environmental-versus-mining project, and the opponents in Crested Butte doubting the benevolent intent and purpose of any and all plans.

No winner emerged. Patricia Petty, the editor of *Mines Magazine,* summarized the frustration that the industry felt in this kind of situation. She compared Ely, Nevada, to Crested Butte. In 1981, Ely, true to its copper-mining heritage, accepted an open-pit gold-mining operation, which would employ about 140 people. Depressed and struggling to stay alive, Ely was determined to become a part of America's mainstream. Crested Butte, on the other hand, Petty charged, scorned mining and miners and regarded the industry as its enemy. "Ely isn't the prettiest town in the world, but somehow I prefer it to the beautiful Crested Butte—it's a contributing part of our Western World."[25]

The industry was perhaps learning its last lesson: its uncontested domain had been taken away. The Crested Buttes of the world saw mining, even under the best of conditions, as an ogre, despite all of its promises of good behavior. The heritage of mining's past and the promises for its future meant little to this new generation. The industry had no choice but to press on environmentally without losing its temper, despite the provocations.

The questions and the concerns that were raised by the tumult of the 1960s and by the books by Ross and Mumford in the 1930s and the ones by Browne and Jackson in the nineteenth century were not resolved in the 1970s. A start had been made, and a consciousness had been acquired; and in those lay hope for the future. Mining could not be expected to change overnight, but on a broad front, from classroom to mine shaft, a reformation was coming. The industry would have to crawl before it could walk and would have to walk before it could run. And it would have to run before it could turn the vision of the future into reality.

The people of no vision are the people with no future. When today becomes yesterday, tomorrow is today. Suddenly yesterday's plans become today's reality. Mining, if it expects to survive in the 1980s and beyond, cannot ignore the heritage of yesterday, the here-and-now of today, or the hopes for tomorrow. One decade, of course, does not a generation make, nor does it give a clear indication of mining's commitment to a new path. It is too early yet to expect a complete transformation in attitude and action toward environmental matters. Nor is less than a decade enough to evaluate the success of the mining industry's public-relations campaign to educate the public.

There can be no doubt that the environmental consciousness of mining was raised by the 1960s and 1970s and that attention was focused on practical and realistic solutions to problems. The majority of the industry seems to have accepted the new rules under which it must work and has set out to comply with them. There seem to be fewer who argue that mining's freedom to make policy decisions for Americans is a right. From Death Valley to the Great Plains to the Atlantic Coast, the battle has been fought.[26] Issues have been polarized, contestants have been embittered, and communities have been frightened where environmentalists and miners contended. As yet not enough time has passed to bring the two sides into a relationship of confidence, trust, and respect. Still, when the 1980s arrived, mining had come a long way in ten years.

EPILOGUE: THE 1980s

More than halfway through the decade, mining has had the time to evaluate the progression of environmental events over the past twenty years. This self-examination stems from a much-weakened position. Never before in the twentieth century has the industry been in such a depressed condition. Foreign competition, lower prices, and a diminished demand for minerals have spelled trouble for the entire industry. Increased costs, arising from environmental solicitude and governmental regulation, also have played a role, although they do not loom so large as some mining spokesmen would have their listeners believe.

The oil crisis has passed into history, along with plans to develop coal and oil shale in the western states. Environmental topics that were raised by this crisis were never dealt with satisfactorily. Mining did not receive a clear answer to the question of whether environmental considerations would stand in the way of national needs. A growing dependency on imported minerals over domestic production has not been resolved. The mining of lower-grade, higher-sulfur coal can stimulate local economies and revive dormant coal mines, but the process has the potential for polluting the atmosphere. Is the cost to the environment worth it? Is reliance on foreign copper and smelters in countries where environmental problems do not create political liabilities strategically wise? Can that reliance put the United States in jeopardy in times of crisis? Neither mining nor the government can unilaterally answer these questions. The American people somehow have to be galvanized by the issues and spurred to action.

Like the oil crisis, Crested Butte—Colorado's most publicized environmental dispute—moved off the front pages, as AMAX retired from the fight. With depressed molybdenum prices and world competition, more wrangling seemed futile. The mine was not needed. Many of the young leaders of Crested Butte, newcomers who opposed mining and AMAX, moved on to other jobs and interests. They left behind a community with an uncertain future and an embittered segment of old-timers from its mining heritage. "I'm not surprised, not in the least," said one. "They treated the town like a toy."

163

The environment stayed on the front page, at least early in the decade. The election of Ronald Reagan as president in 1980 placed in Washington an administration that was much more sympathetic to private rights. Reagan's secretary of the interior, James Watt, embroiled himself in myriad disputes with environmentalists, before he eventually resigned. Those unreconstructed miners cheered some of Watt's ideas about opening up mineral lands, easing mineral-leasing practices, and reducing regulations. Watt's opponents warned about the danger of returning to the earlier stance of disregard for the environment. Without question, Washington's climate had turned lukewarm toward regulation of the environment and conservation, and the general public seems to have become much less interested in environmental issues than it had appeared to be in the recent past.

That Watt's legacy lives on is abundantly clear in the fight over forests, parks, and wildlife refuges, which involve some 209 million acres from Alaska to Florida. The controversy, though not new, gained momentum during Watt's turbulent administration. Former Assistant Secretary of Agriculture John Crowell calculated that the cost of maintaining enough trees to support a pair of spotted owls was $600,000 a year—a price that was too high, he bluntly told the National Audubon Society. Both men called for opening more federal land to industry. This exacerbated the animosity between ranching, mining, timbering, and energy companies, on the one hand, and environmentalists and conservationists on the other. The former groups seized the opportunity to be more aggressive. Stanley Dempsey, a member of the Public Lands Committee of the American Mining Congress, spoke at a recent hearing of the President's Commission on Americans Outdoors. Dempsey urged that the public recognize and appreciate the need to provide for the exploration, identification, and development of mineral deposits on public lands, "within the framework of responsible multiple-use management."[1] This clash of values will only intensify as resources on private lands are depleted.

At almost the same time (June, 1986), the Environmental Protection Agency (EPA) announced that it was relaxing rules that would have placed mining wastes under the "hazardous wastes" designation and under strict EPA controls. The agency proposed instead to place mining wastes under the less stringent "solid waste" category. Idaho's Senator Steve Symms was pleased: "This will release mining companies from rule changes which many people in the mining industry called the 'finishing blow' to an industry faced with tough foreign competition and low metal prices."[2]

Once again the industry is receiving ambiguous signals from the public and from the government, sometimes loud and clear, other times quiet and murky. The climate is reminiscent of the Progressive Era prior to World War I, when it was feared that popular interest in conservation would prove short-lived, leaving behind vague and hastily drawn legislation. The "new cult" of environmentalism is threatening to slip into the same pattern during the 1980s.

The attack on mining has continued. Carolyn Merchant wrote passionately in *Death of Nature* (1980) about the historic concept of the mining industry's rape of Mother Earth and about the avarice, vice, and violence associated with the industry. Few miners read her book; many conservationists did and concurred with her assessment. Miners preferred the messages emanating from James Watt.

One of the few constants over the past three decades has been change. Yesterday's guideposts may or may not serve for today and tomorrow; mining and its leaders are in a quandary. Mining will never be able to return to its free-wheeling days. Environmental stewardship is here to stay; only the form that it should take is a subject of debate. The corner was turned in the 1960s, and the environmental studies, reclamation plans, hydrological data, and related investigations are now an inseparable part of industrial operations. They will continue to create protests and hardships. In May, 1986, Harry F. Magnuson, president of the Clayton Silver Mines at Clayton, Idaho, charged that the serious problems faced by mining can be traced largely to the result "of actions and policies initiated by the federal government."[3] Right or wrong, his charge found a receptive audience in many camps.

When Anaconda Copper closed its smelter at Anaconda, Montana, and began to ship its copper ore to Japan to be refined, a shock wave rolled through the industry. An article in the *Mining Record* for January 27, 1982, blamed "unrealistic laws and regulations" for pressuring companies into difficult situations. Yet the same issue carried this comment: "With mutual understanding and cooperation the mining industry can better serve its purposes, to the greater benefit of the community, the environment, and our country."

This theme was reiterated by the Homestake Mining Company in its annual report for 1985, entitled "A Tradition of Leadership":

> Virtually every human activity disturbs our environment to some extent. Mining is among the more visible ones. Recognizing this and its obligations to protect public interests while continuing to serve its shareholders, Homestake has become a leader in developing and applying environmental quality controls to the mining industry that are both effective and economically practical.[4]

In recent years the mining industry has worked hard at reclamation. It is costly, time consuming, and not always successful in the public's eye. These before and after photos show what can be done in the Colorado Rockies. The Urad project won AMAX an environmental award (courtesy AMAX).

The Star Coal Mine dragline operation, near Lovilia, Iowa (top),
displays the impact of modern technology on the land (courtesy Bill
Gillette). With awareness, sensitivity, and planning, that same land can
be reclaimed. The Star Coal Company reclaimed this strip-mined land
in the 1970s (center; courtesy Bill Gillette). Another reclaimed strip-
mining site in the Midwest presents a pastoral view, with cattle grazing
and a fishing lake beyond (courtesy AMAX). The amount of land to be
reclaimed and the stream pollution to be cleaned up are staggering, and
the American public, as well as the industry, must be willing to make
the sacrifices to achieve these goals.

The endless conflict goes on; the basic questions are still unresolved. Where, then, are mining, the United States, and the environment headed?

L. E. Weible, president of the St. Joe Lead Company, who was the keynote speaker at the Eighty-seventh National Western Mining Conference (1984), gave this assessment:

> The mining industry has always been faced with many diverse challenges. Recently additional challenges have been placed on the industry through decreased demand, oversupply from foreign subsidized competitors, materials substitution and government land and environmental regulation. Indeed, the challenges are significant. However, the mining industry and its products remain vital to our industrial society and the standard of living to which we have become accustomed.[5]

An analysis of the past two hundred years of mining in the United States helps to explain the actions of the mining industry and why it has held its stubborn opinions to the present day. Such analysis illustrates that neither sinners nor saints have dominated one side or the other. Sincere, hard-working people, trying to do the best they could under circumstances that were not all of their own making, were not intent on being villainous. To paint miners as destroying "Huns" and to accuse them of "raping and pillaging" is unfair historically. The past should serve as a fund of collective wisdom and experiences from which to draw and as a standard by which to measure current realities. From the past we can learn ways to plan for the future.

Mining must surely carry its share of the responsibility for past policies. But so must the American people and their government. We all became too enamored of technology and its ability to produce the better life at less cost. As the nineteenth century stressed technology, so has the twentieth; only in the present generation has technological impact on people and their earth become more universally understood.

In the last twenty years the mining industry has tried to accommodate to shifting environmental times. Perhaps the volatile 1960s and the emotional early 1970s were necessary in order to shake the industry out of its complacency and its rut of tradition into a new path that emphasized careful stewardship, without ignoring profits. In the end, the two must form a partnership, as Homestake is trying to achieve.

It is still unclear whether Americans are willing to pay the bills for preservation. The final decision rests with all of us who must stand the increased costs and perhaps adjust to a less affluent life style. Pogo correctly pointed the finger at us as the enemy. If we are not to be the enemy, we must prove that we have in our hands and hearts the ability and the desire to reconcile mining with the environment.

It is not yet evident, either, whether the government, most likely the federal one, is willing to underwrite the enormous expense of cleaning up previous environmental pollution and damage. The industry can reasonably be expected to pay for current and future programs; it should not be expected to finance reclamation for the past two hundred years. Although environmental impact may have increased over the last century, it did not suddenly begin with the California gold rush or with Montana copper.

The nineteenth-century heritage lingers with mining today, muted perhaps, but still very much present. The industry must continuously strive to educate itself environmentally and to educate the public to mining's programs and purposes. Both groups need to exercise patience; the past has taught that lesson, if nothing else. Environmental miracles do not come overnight, nor do fundamental changes in industrial thinking.

Even in the depths of mining's current depression, amid predictions that the industry will never recover, a strong dose of that nineteenth-century elixir—optimism—has cropped up to encourage the faithful. That mining will rebound appears highly probable, as nearly a certainty as were the cycles of mining booms a hundred years ago. Those who assume that the problems will evaporate with the demise of the industry need to reconsider their position. The industry will survive EPA, the Sierra Club, and adverse environmental publicity, as well as its present doldrums.

As a friend of mining so aptly expressed it recently, "You can build a tooth paste factory anywhere you want; mining has to be carried on in certain defined areas." Unfortunately, some of those defined areas happen to be environmentally sensitive or subject to visual pollution. The mountain cannot be moved; the miner must go to the mountain. "You can only screw up Colorado once"—or Pennsylvania or Illinois or Alaska. The problem is clear; the solution remains hazy. It will not be found in the shrill, emotional comments of the "zanies" on either the environmental or the mining side. The answer will come from a compromise, a trade-off, between the extreme views of both sides. A hundred years ago, Clarence King wrote: "There is always a point beyond which saving costs more than it is worth." He could not have had the present situation in mind when he made that statement, but the basic observation stands as true now as it did then.

Mining and the American people have to plan for the long term, so that generations one hundred or more years from now will find ''a future not by default, but by design.'' That truth is both as old as yesterday and as young as tomorrow; amid the apocalyptic visions of the Book of Revelation comes this warning: ''Do not harm the earth or the sea or the trees.'' We carry the future on our shoulders—an awesome responsibility. Fortunately, man's spirit does not perish; it rolls on like a river to the sea. Like a river, this spirit is refreshed by the enthusiasm and outlook of each new generation.

The mining industry and the American people must willingly assume the burden of stewardship for the land and its natural resources. Then, and only then, will the fundamental lesson of the past two hundred years be learned. In the words of Colorado's Senator Gary Hart, ''The easy path is the beaten path, but the beaten path seldom leads to the future.''

NOTES

PROLOGUE

1. George MacDonald, *Poetical Works of George MacDonald*, 2 vols. (London: Chatto & Windus, 1893), 2:160.

CHAPTER ONE. BOOMING, DIGGING, AND DUMPING

1. Henry R. Schoolcraft, *Journal of a tour into the Interior of Missouri and Arkansaw* . . . (London: W. Lewis, 1821), pp. 3–4, and *A View of the Lead Mines of Missouri* . . . (New York: Charles Wiley, 1819), pp. 64–65 and 89; and George W. Featherstonhaugh, *Excursion through the Slave States* (New York: Harper, 1844), p. 74.

2. Josiah Gregg, *Commerce of the Prairies* (reprint, Norman: University of Oklahoma Press, 1954), p. 119.

3. George W. Featherstonhaugh, *A Canoe Voyage up the Minnay Soto*, 2 vols. (London: Richard Bentley, 1847), 2:251 and 331; J. B. Warriner, "Anthracite Stripping," *Transactions of the American Institute of Mining Engineers*, 1918, p. 159.

4. Clark to his brother, Dec. 30, 1864, Henry Harmon Clark Papers, Montana Historical Society; and L. P. Brockett, *Our Western Empire* (Philadelphia: Bradley, 1881), pp. 106–7.

5. Rossiter Raymond, *Statistics of Mines and Mining* (Washington, D.C.: Government Printing Office, 1873), p. 283.

6. Mary H. Foote, "New Almaden: or A California Mining Camp," *Scribner's Monthly Magazine*, Feb., 1878, p. 480; and James Rusling, *Across America: or The Great West and the Pacific Coast* (New York: Sheldon, 1874), pp. 66 and 72.

7. John Muir, *Steep Trails* (Boston: Houghton Mifflin, 1918), pp. 198–203.

8. Harvey to his parents, Sept. 26, 1850, and Harvey Diary, Aug. 17, 1850, Charles H. Harvey Papers, Library of Congress.

9. Samuel Bowles, *The Switzerland of America* (Springfield, Mass.: Bowles, 1869), p. 103; Sidney Glazer, ed., "A Michigan Correspondent in Colorado, 1878," *Colorado Magazine*, July, 1960, p. 211; and Alexander K. McClure, *Three Thousand Miles through the Rocky Mountains* (Philadelphia: Lippincott, 1869), p. 312.

10. Mark Twain, *Roughing It* (Hartford, Conn.: American Publishing, 1872), p. 253; "Galena and Its Lead Mines," *Harper's New Monthly Magazine*, May, 1866, pp. 689 and 690; Robert D. Billinger, *Pennsylvania's Coal Industry* (Gettysburg: Pennsylvania Historical Association, 1954), pp. 16 and 25; Eli Bowen, *The Pictorial Sketch-Book of Pennsylvania* (Philadelphia: W. Bromwell, 1853), p. 173; and "Gold Mining in Georgia," *Harper's New Monthly Magazine*, Sept., 1879, p. 513.

11. J. Ross Browne, *A Peep at Washoe* (reprint, Balboa Island, Calif.: Paisano, 1959), p. 77.

12. Bronson Keeler, *Leadville and Its Silver Mines* (Chicago: Perry Bros., 1879), p. 29.

13. Carl Henrich, "The Ducktown Ore-Deposits and Treatment of Duck-town Copper-Ores," *Transactions of the American Institute of Mining Engineers* (photocopy in my possession), p. 228; T. A. Rickard, *Interviews with Mining Engineers* (San Francisco, Calif.: Mining & Scientific Press, 1922), p. 315; Francis Farquhar, ed., *Up and down California in 1860–1864: The Journal of William H. Brewer* (Berkeley: University of California Press, 1966), pp. 142–43; and J. Ross Browne, *Mining Adventures: California and Nevada, 1863–65* (reprint, Balboa Island, Calif.: Paisano, 1961), pp. 192–94.

14. Schoolcraft, *View of the Lead Mines*, pp. 93–94 and 97; and T. Eggleston, "Boston and Colorado Smelting Works," *American Institute of Mining . . . Engineers Transactions*, 1876, pp. 280–81.

15. *Summering in Colorado* (Denver, Colo.: Richards, 1874), p. 24; Glazer, "Michigan Correspondent," p. 215; and *Engineering and Mining Journal*, Sept. 23, 1877, p. 236.

16. Harvey to his family, May 22, 1879, Harvey Papers.

17. Dan De Quille, *History of the Big Bonanza* (Hartford, Conn.: American Publishing, 1877), pp. 215–16, 238, and 245; see also Eliot Lord, *Comstock Mining and Miners* (reprint, Berkeley, Calif.: Howell-North, 1959), p. 351; and Henry Clifford, *Rocks in the Road to Fortune: or The Unsound Side of Mining* (New York: Gotham, 1908), p. 86.

18. De Quille, *History of the Big Bonanza*, pp. 215–16 and 245.

19. Rossiter W. Raymond, *Statistics of Mines and Mining* (Washington, D.C.: Government Printing Office, 1870), pp. 342–43; see also G. Thomas Ingham, *Digging Gold among the Rockies* (Philadelphia: Cottage Library, 1881), pp. 329–30.

20. *Engineering and Mining Journal*, Apr. 12, 1879, p. 258; and Schoolcraft, *View of the Lead Mines*, p. 42.

21. Raymond, *Statistics* (1870), pp. 476–77.

22. Sara Titus, ed., *This Is a Fine Day* (Long Beach, Calif.: Seaside Printing, 1959), p. 49; Irving Howbert, *Memories of a Lifetime in the Pike's Peak Region* (New York: Putnam, 1925), p. 34; and T. A. Rickard, *Across the San Juan Mountains* (New York: Engineering and Mining Journal, 1903), p. 80.

23. "Gold Mining in Georgia," p. 517; and Carl Wheat, ed., *The Shirley Letters from the California Mines, 1851–1852* (New York: Alfred A. Knopf, 1970), p. 212.

24. George Kulp, *Coal: Its Antiquity . . . in the Wyoming Valley* (Wilkes-Barre, Pa.: Wyoming Historical & Geological Society, 1890), p. 14; Demas Barnes, *From the Atlantic to the Pacific* (New York: Van Nostrand, 1866), p. 80; De Quille, *History of the Big Bonanza*, p. 347; and Hill to his wife, June 7, 1865, Nathaniel P. Hill Papers, Colorado Historical Society.

25. Browne, *Mining Adventures*, pp. 26 and 111; George F. Becker, *Geology of the Comstock Lode and the Washoe District* (Washington, D.C.: Government Printing Office, 1883), pp. 5–6; John Tice, *Over the Plains . . .* (St. Louis, Mo.: Industrial Age Printing, 1872), p. 228; and *The Fruits of the Bonanza* (San Francisco, Calif.: n.p., 1878), pp. 37–38.

26. Joseph Grinnell, *Gold Hunting in Alaska* (Chicago: Cook, 1901), p. 88; and Lanier McKee, *The Land of Nome* (New York: Grafton, 1902), pp. 43–50, 79, and 93–94.

27. Wheat, *Shirley Letters*, p. 50; and Twain, *Roughing It*, p. 304.

28. Henry Blake, "Historical Sketch of Madison County, Montana Territory," *Contributions to the Historical Society of Montana*, 1896, p. 87; De Quille, *History of the Big Bonanza*, p. 343; John J. Powell, *Nevada: The Land of Silver* (San Francisco, Calif.: Bacon, 1876), pp. 238–39; and Liston E. Leyendecker, "Young Man Gone West: George M. Pullman's Letters from the Colorado Goldfields," *Chicago History*, Winter, 1978/79, p. 214.

29. Three recent books discuss the relationship between work, job, and owner in the mining industry: see Ronald C. Brown, *Hard-Rock Miners: The Intermountain West, 1860–1920* (College Station: Texas A & M University Press, 1979), chap. 5; Mark Wyman, *Hard-Rock Epic* (Berkeley: University of California Press, 1979), chap. 4; and Richard E. Lingenfelter, *The Hardrock Miners* (Berkeley: University of California Press, 1974), chap. 1.

30. Featherstonhaugh, *Canoe Voyage*, 2:72.

31. *Colorado Miner* (Georgetown), July 28, 1869.

32. William Brewer, *Rocky Mountain Letters, 1869* (Denver: Colorado Mountain Club, 1930), p. 43.

33. Muir, *Steep Trails*, p. 195.

34. Percy Fritz, "The Mining Districts of Boulder County, Colorado" (Ph.D. diss., University of Colorado, 1933), p. 50. I examined mining laws from various districts in Arizona, Montana, Utah, Idaho, Colorado, Nevada, and California. For state laws see Andrew Roy, *The Coal Mines . . . Ventilating Mines* (Cleveland, Ohio: Robison, Savage, 1876), pp. 360–64; James H. Hawley, ed., *History of Idaho* (Chicago: S. J. Clarke, 1920), vol. 1, p. 493; Charles Shamel, *Mining, Mineral and Geological Law* (New York: Hill, 1907); *Proceedings of the Constitutional Convention . . . for the State of Colorado* (Denver, Colo.: Smith-Brooks, 1907); *Proceedings and Debates of the Constitutional Convention* (Helena, Mont.: State Publishing, 1921); and Curtis H. Lindley, *A Treatise on the American Law Relating to Mines and Mineral Lands*, 2 vols. (San Francisco, Calif.: Bancroft-Whitney, 1903), 1:30–53 and 2:1779–1906.

CHAPTER TWO. "WE WERE GIANTS"

1. Pliny the Elder, *The History of the World*, trans. Philemon Holland (Carbondale: Southern Illinois University Press, 1962), pp. 361–62, and *Natural History*, trans. Loyd Haberly (New York: Frederick Ungar, 1957), pp. 177 and 179.

2. Paul R. Lieder et al., eds., *British Poetry and Prose* (Boston: Houghton Mifflin, 1950), vol. 1, offers an overview of this era and these poets. Carolyn Merchant, in *The Death of Nature* (San Francisco, Calif.: Harper & Row, 1980), pp. 29–41, presents a stimulating discussion on the evolution of the concept of mining and Mother Earth.

3. *The Memorial of Fray Alonso de Benavides*, trans. Mrs. Edward Ayer (Chicago: privately printed, 1916), p. 217; F.C., *The Compleat Collier: . . .* (London: G. Conyers, 1708); and Samuel G. Hermelin, *Report about the Mines in the United States of America, 1783*, trans. Amandus Johnson (Philadelphia: John Morton Memorial Museum, 1931), pp. 11–13, 22, 24–25, and 46.

4. Georgius Agricola, *De re metallica*, trans. Herbert Hoover and Lou Hoover (London: Mining Magazine, 1912), p. 14.

5. T. A. Rickard, *Man and Metals*, 2 vols. (reprint, New York: Arno, 1974), 2:1049.

6. Fletcher M. Green, "Gold Mining: A Forgotten Industry of Ante-Bellum North Carolina," *North Carolina Historical Review,* Jan., 1937, p. 10.

7. Clark to his brother, Nov. 11, 1864, Clark Papers; Twain, *Roughing It,* pp. 193–94; Richard Hughes, *Pioneer Years in the Black Hills* (Glendale, Calif.: Arthur H. Clark, 1957), pp. 19–23; and Hill to his wife, Aug. 15, 1865, Hill Papers.

8. John Muir, *The Mountains of California,* 2 vols. (New York: Houghton Mifflin, 1916), 2:62–63; and "Coal, and the Coal-Mines of Pennsylvania," *Harper's Monthly,* Aug., 1857, p. 451.

9. J. Ross Browne, *Report on the Mineral Resources of the States and Territories West of the Rocky Mountains* (Washington, D.C.: Government Printing Office, 1868), p. 498.

10. William A. Clark, "Centennial Address on the Origin, Growth and Resources of Montana," *Contributions to the Historical Society of Montana* (Helena, Mont.: State Publishing, 1896), vol. 2, pp. 50–51; and Richard H. Stretch, *Placer Mines and Their Origin* (Seattle, Wash.: Lowman & Hanford, 1897), pp. 22–23.

11. *Mining Magazine,* Apr., 1854, p. 417; *Leadville Democrat,* Jan. 1, 1880; Edwin A. Charlton, *New Hampshire as It Is* (Claremont, N.H.: Tracy & Sanford, 1855), p. 459; and *Programme for the First Annual Exhibition of the National Mining and Industrial Exposition* (Denver, Colo.: Tribune Publishing, 1882), p. 14.

12. Horace Tabor's autobiography, Bancroft Library, University of California, Berkeley, p. 14; and Frederick G. Corning, *Papers from the Notes of an Engineer* (New York: Scientific Publishing Co., 1889), p. 103.

13. George W. Parsons, *The Private Journal of George Whitwell Parsons* (Phoenix: Arizona Statewide Archival and Records Project, 1939), p. 109; see also general entries, Feb. 17–Mar. 19, 1880.

14. McClure, *Three Thousand Miles,* p. 93; Henry Villard, *The Past and Present of the Pike's Peak Gold Regions* (reprint, Princeton, N.J.: Princeton University Press, 1932), pp. 77–78; H. A. Gaston, "The Present and Future of the Mines and Mining in Nevada," Huntington Library; Blake, "Historical Sketch," p. 84; Rusling, *Across America,* p. 65; and Wheat, *Shirley Letters,* p. 213.

15. William H. Keating, *Considerations upon the Art of Mining* (Philadelphia: Carey & Sons, 1821), p. 4; John D. Imboden, *The Coal and Iron Resources of Virginia* (Richmond, Va.: Clemmitt & Jones, 1872), pp. 7 and 27–28; Bowen, *Pictorial Sketch-Book,* pp. 174 and 185; and *Lane Register,* quoted in *True Republican and Sentinel* (Sycamore, Ill.), July 29, 1863.

16. J. Wyman Jones to Yeatman, Oct. 25, 1889, and J. Wetherill to Yeatman, July 27, 1891, Pope Yeatman Collection, American Heritage Center, University of Wyoming; John Arnold Rockwell Collection, John Daniell Collection, and Savage Mining Company Collection, Huntington Library; and Daly to S. Dorsey, Mar. 23, 1880, George Daly Collection, Colorado Historical Society.

17. Josiah D. Whitney, *The Metallic Wealth of the United States . . .* (Philadelphia: Lippincott, 1854), p. 98; *Prospectus of the Geological Survey and Report of the Gregory Gold Mining Company* (New York: n.p., 1863), pp. 7, 16, and 22; Articles of Incorporation, Smuggler Consolidated Mining Company Papers, Colorado Historical Society; *Crown King Mines Company* (New York: Patterson Press, 1903); and Thomas Yenkes to William Coleman, Apr. 1, 1865, Henry Bacon Papers, Huntington Library.

18. Lord, *Comstock Mining*, p. 127; and A. D. Hodges, "Amalgamation at the Comstock Lode, Nevada . . . ," *Transactions of the American Institute of Mining Engineers*, 1890, 1891, vol. 19, p. 207.

19. Clarence King wrote the Introduction to Samuel Emmons and George F. Becker's *Statistics and Technology of the Precious Metals* (Washington, D.C.: Government Printing Office, 1885), pp. vii and viii.

20. Warriner, "Anthracite Stripping," p. 161; *Cleveland Iron Trade Review*, July 21, 1892, quoted by Horace V. Winchell in "The Mesabi Iron-Range," *Transactions of the American Institute of Mining Engineers*, 1893, p. 685; and *The Story of Open Cut Mining in Indiana* (n.p.: Indian Coal Producers Association, 1940), p. 2.

21. King's Introduction to *Statistics and Technology*, pp. vii–x.

22. Ibid., pp. viii–x.

23. Rossiter W. Raymond, *Mineral Resources of the States and Territories* (Washington, D.C.: Government Printing Office, 1869), pp. 230–45.

24. James D. Hague, "Mining Engineering and Mining Law," *Engineering and Mining Journal*, Oct. 20, 1904, p. 3 of reprint.

25. James Fergus, "A Leaf from the Diary of James Fergus," *Contributions to the Historical Society of Montana* (Helena, Mont.: State Publishing, 1896), vol. 2, p. 254; Andrew F. Rolle, ed., *The Road to Virginia City: The Diary of James Knox Polk Miller* (Norman: University of Oklahoma Press, 1960), p. 107; Wheat, *Shirley Letters*, p. 131; and Hague to his parents, Oct. 16, 1861, James D. Hague Collection, Huntington Library.

26. Howard Eavenson, *The First Century and a Quarter of American Coal Industry* (Pittsburgh, Pa.: Waverly, 1942), pp. 179, 292, 294, 302, and 334.

27. *Abstract of the Eleventh Census: 1890* (Washington, D.C.: Government Printing Office, 1894), p. 184.

CHAPTER THREE. "GOING TO COVER MARYSVILLE UP"

1. Jones to his wife, Aug. 3 and 6, 1879, John P. Jones Collection, Huntington Library.

2. Hill to his wife, June 23, 1864, Hill Papers; *Hydraulic Press*, Nov. 6, 1858; and *Mining Age*, July 2, 1892.

3. Twain, *Roughing It*, p. 176.

4. Amasa McCoy, *Conversational Lecture on Mines and Mining in Colorado* (Chicago: International Mining & Exchange Co., 1871), p. 22.

5. The sources for the preceding section are numerous: see, for example, Harvey's diary for 1857/58, Harvey Papers; Joseph Horskey's reminiscences, Montana Historical Society; Daniel E. Conner, *Joseph Reddeford Walker and the Arizona Adventure*, ed. Donald Berthrong (Norman: University of Oklahoma Press, 1956); Keating, *Considerations upon the Art of Mining*; Eli Bowen, *The Coal Regions of Pennsylvania* (Pottsville, Pa.: Carvalho, 1848); Eric Hedburg, "The Missouri and Arkansas Zinc-Mines at the Close of 1900," *Transactions of the American Institute of Mining Engineers*, 1902, pp. 379–404; *Pittsburgh and Boston Mining Company* (Pittsburgh, Pa.: W. Haven, 1866); and Carl Lokke, *Klondike Saga* (Minneapolis: University of Minnesota Press, 1965). Many reports and much correspondence by mining engineers can be found in the Hague Collection, the Daniell Papers, and the Bacon Papers, Huntington Library, and in various papers of mining engineers at the American Heritage Center, University of Wyoming.

6. Walter Van Tilburg Clark, ed., *The Journals of Alfred Doten, 1849–1903*, 3 vols. (Reno: University of Nevada Press, 1973); Lola Homsher, ed., *South Pass, 1868: James Chisholm's Journal of the Wyoming Gold Rush* (Lincoln: University of Nebraska Press, 1960); Anne Ellis, *The Life of an Ordinary Woman* (New York: Houghton Mifflin, 1929); Estelline Bennett, *Old Deadwood Days* (New York: Scribner's Sons, 1935); and Richard Lillard, ed., "A Literate Woman in the Mines: The Diary of Rachel Haskell," *Mississippi Valley Historical Review*, June, 1944, pp. 81–98.

7. Raymond, *Statistics* (1870), p. 343; Sargeant to Hague, Jan. 22, 1889, Hague Collection; and Clark's comments, in *Proceedings*, p. 754.

8. John T. Waldorf, *A Kid on the Comstock* (Palo Alto, Calif.: American West, 1970), pp. 106 and 108.

9. Raymond, *Statistics* (1873), pp. 87–88; and *Crown King*, p. 17.

10. Whitney, *Metallic Wealth*, p. 325.

11. Lord, *Comstock Mining*, p. 116.

12. David Sheridan, *Hard Rock Mining on the Public Land* (Washington, D.C.: Government Printing Office, 1977), pp. iii and 3–4; and *Mining Act of May 10, 1872* (San Francisco, Calif.: Frank Eastman, 1872).

13. Williamson to register and receivers, Aug. 15, 1878, Carl Schurz Papers, Library of Congress.

14. James A. Lake, *Law and Mineral Wealth: The Legal Profile of the Wisconsin Mining Industry* (Madison: University of Wisconsin Press, 1962), p. 185.

15. Morton Horwitz, *The Transformation of American Law, 1780–1860* (Cambridge: Harvard University Press, 1977), p. 102; see also pp. 1, 5, 107, 108, and 139. On p. xv, Horwitz discusses the changing definition of laissez faire. The *American Digest* (St. Paul, Minn.: West, 1902), vol. 34, traces cases to 1896, particularly see pp. 3241 and 3248–50 for decisions in regard to mining.

16. *The Pennsylvania Coal Company* v. *Sanderson and Wife*, 113 Pa 126, 6A, 453 (1886).

17. "*Pittsburgh Coal Company* v. *Sanitary Water Board*," *Environmental Law Reporter*, 1972, p. 20342; Shamel, *Mining*, p. 288; *The American Law of Mining* (New York: Matthew Bender, 1979), vol. 4, pp. 110–11; and *The Pennsylvania Coal Company* v. *Sanderson and Wife*.

18. Daniel Barringer and John S. Adams, *The Law of Mines and Mining in the United States* (St. Paul, Minn.: Keefe-Davidson, 1900), p. 613.

19. Robert S. Morrison and Jacob Fillius, *Mining Rights in Colorado* (Denver, Colo.: Chain & Hardy, 1881), pp. 121–22, 213, and 237; Andrew B. Crichton, "What Shall Be Done about the Growing Evil of the Pollution of Streams by Mine Drainage?" *Coal Age*, Mar. 15, 1923, p. 448; T. F. Van Wagenen, *Manual of Hydraulic Mining* (Denver, Colo.: n.p., 1878), p. 57; *American Law of Mining*, vol. 1, pp. 37–38, and vol. 4, pp. 104 and 113–14; and Emmons and Becker, *Statistics*, p. 187.

20. *Mining Record* (Denver), Jan. 31, 1979.

21. G. W. Baker, *Treatment of Gold Ores in Gilpin County, Colorado* (Central City, Colo.: Herald, 1870), pp. 3 and 9.

22. Van Wagenen, *Manual*, p. 11; and *Sutter Banner*, no date, quoted in the *Mining and Scientific Press*, Apr. 4, 1877.

23. *Golden Manual: or The Royal Road to Success* (Philadelphia: Bell, 1891).

24. Matthew Josephson, *The Robber Barons* (New York: Harcourt, 1962), p. 49; Joseph Wall, *Andrew Carnegie* (New York: Oxford University Press,

1970), pp. 197 and 584. Wells is quoted by John A. Garraty in *The New Commonwealth* (New York: Harper, 1968), p. 78.

CHAPTER FOUR. "MINING DESTROYS AND DEVASTATES"

1. Browne, *Report on the Mineral Resources,* p. 9.

2. *Journal of Mining,* Dec. 22, 1866, p. 200; *Engineering and Mining Journal,* Apr. 15, 1876, p. 365; and Tice, *Over the Plains,* p. 123.

3. Whitney, *Metallic Wealth,* p. 77; Barnes, *From the Atlantic,* pp. 73–74. For an overview of forestry policy see Joseph M. Petulla's *American Environmental History* (San Francisco, Calif.: Boyd & Fraser, 1977) and Roderick Nash's *Wilderness and the American Mind* (London: Yale University Press, 1967).

4. Gifford Pinchot, "Mining and the Forest Reserves," *Transactions of the American Institute of Mining Engineers,* 1898, pp. 339–43 and 344–46.

5. G. Michael McCarthy, *Hour of Trial* (Norman: University of Oklahoma Press, 1977), pp. 23–25.

6. Waldorf, *A Kid on the Comstock,* p. 114; and John D. Galloway, *Early Engineering Works Contributory to the Comstock* (Reno: University of Nevada Press, 1947), p. 118.

7. The bylaws of the California Mining District, pp. 6 and 8; and Barringer et al., *Law of Mines,* pp. 613–15.

8. Schoolcraft, *View of the Lead Mines,* p. 29; Persifor Frazer, "Bibliography of Injuries to Vegetation by Furnace-Gases," *Transactions of the American Institute of Mining Engineers,* 1908, pp. 520–21; and George P. Marsh, who in his last edition of *The Earth as Modified by Human Action* (New York: C. Scribner's, 1885) stated that while mining might occasionally disturb the earth's surface, the damage was too slight to deserve the notice of geographers (pp. 604–5).

9. Tice, *Over the Plains,* p. 228; T. A. Rickard, *The Stamp Milling of Gold Ores* (New York: Scientific Publishing, 1897), p. 86; *A Brief Description of the Washoe Smelter* (Anaconda, Mont.: Anaconda Copper, 1907), pp. 5, 9, 25, and 29; Baker, *Treatment of Gold Ores,* pp. 1, 3, and 9; *American Journal of Mining,* June 20, 1868, p. 393, see also May 2 and 30, Aug. 8, 1868; and Emmons, *Geology,* pp. 287 and 294.

10. Roy, *Coal Mines,* p. 80.

11. W. S. Keyes, *Last Chance Bed-Rock Flume* (Helena, Mont.: Wilkinson & Ronan, 1868), p. 5.

12. Henry Hanks, *Second Report of the State Mineralogist* (Sacramento, Calif.: State Printing, 1882), pp. 35–36.

13. Corning, *Papers,* pp. 101–2.

14. De Quille, *History of the Big Bonanza,* p. 222; Samuel H. Daddow, *Coal, Iron, and Oil: or, The Practical American Miner* (Philadelphia: Lippincott, 1866), pp. 425 and 483–84; and "Coal . . . ," *Harper's Monthly,* p. 463.

15. Helen Hunt Jackson, "O-Be-Joyful Creek and Poverty Gulch," *Atlantic Monthly,* Dec., 1883, pp. 755–57.

16. Anne Ridler, ed., *Poems and Some Letters of James Thomson* (London: Centaur, 1963), pp. 245–46; and Isabella Bird, *A Lady's Life in the Rocky Mountains* (reprint, Norman: University of Oklahoma Press, 1960), p. 193.

17. Rossiter W. Raymond, "Historical Sketch of Mining Law," *Mineral Resources of the United States, 1883–84* (Washington, D.C.: Government Printing Office, 1885), pp. 988–89.

18. *Dolores News,* Aug. 28, 1879; Clarence King, *Mountaineering in the Sierra Nevada* (reprint, New York: Lippincott, 1963), p. 292; and Emmons and Becker, *Statistics,* p. xiii.

19. John Birkinbine, "The American Institute of Mining Engineers and the Conservation of Natural Resources," *Transactions of the American Institute of Mining Engineers,* 1909, pp. 417–18.

20. Rusling, *Across America,* p. 440.

21. Raymond, "Historical Sketch," pp. 989 and 1004; see pp. 990–1003 for his development of mining law and its evolution, which provides the basis for his arguments.

22. Hewitt, quoted in Raymond, "Historical Sketch," pp. 989–90.

23. Browne, *Report,* p. 9.

24. Ibid.

25. *The Gold Valley Placer Mining Co.* (Aspen, Colo.: Aspen Leader, 1893), p. 1; Stretch, *Placer Mines,* p. 21; see also Richard H. Stretch, *The Laporte Gold Gravel Mines, Limited* (Glasgow: M'Corquodale, 1882), pp. 19 and 31.

26. K. Ross Toole, *The Rape of the Great Plains: Northwest America, Cattle and Coal* (New York: Atlantic Monthly, 1976), pp. 243–44.

CHAPTER FIVE. THE RUSTLING BREEZE OF CHANGE

1. See Farquhar, *Up and down California,* p. 328; Ingham, *Digging Gold,* pp. 64, 69, and 70; and Raymond, *Statistics* (1873), p. 390.

2. W. Veall to G. Pride, July 30, 1868, Bacon Papers. The argument in defense of hydraulicking was constructed from N. Keith to Barlow, Mar. 23, 1868, Samuel Barlow Collection, Huntington Library; Ingham, *Digging Gold,* p. 64; Raymond, *Statistics* (1870), pp. 475 and 478; Charles Waldeyer, "Hydraulic Mining in California," *Mines and Mining* (Washington, D.C.: Government Printing Office, 1873), p. 391; *Mining and Scientific Press,* Jan. 7, 1871, p. 1; Browne, *Report,* p. 120; Keyes, *Last Chance,* pp. 4 and 6; Gaston, "Present and Future," pp. 6–7; and *Report upon the Property Belonging to the Cedar Creek Hydraulic Mining Company* (n.p.: n.p., 1880), pp. 1 and 11.

3. "Bill of Complaint," *Woodruff* v. *North Bloomfield,* copy in Huntington Library, pp. 4–20.

4. *Mining Debris* (Marysville, Calif.: Anti-Debris Association, 1889), pp. 4–5; *Hydraulic Press,* Nov. 6, 1858; *Mining and Scientific Press,* Feb. 20, 1869, pp. 118–19; Robert L. Kelley, *Gold vs. Grain: The Hydraulic Mining Controversy in California's Sacramento Valley* (Glendale, Calif.: Arthur H. Clark, 1959), pp. 57–58; and *The Yuba Levee . . . Hydraulic Tailings* (San Francisco, Calif.: n.p., 1877), pp. 1–3, 11, 12, and 16.

5. Kelley, *Gold vs. Grain,* pp. 59 and 64; *Mining Debris,* pp. 4–5; H. B. Congdon, comp., *Mining Laws and Forms* (San Francisco, Calif.: Bancroft, 1864), p. 37; and *The American Law of Mining* (New York: Matthew Bender, 1979), vol. 1, pp. 28–30.

6. Kelley, in his *Gold vs. Grain,* presents the farmers' argument in chaps. 2, 3, and 6 and the *Woodruff* case on pp. 229–30 and 237–39. One of the most interesting summaries can be found in John Durst, "Hydraulic Mining: A Need of State Action upon Rivers," *Californian,* Jan., 1881, pp. 10–12.

7. James K. Byrne, *Argument on Motion for a Temporary Injunction* (n.p.: n.p., n.d.), copy in Huntington Library, pp. 2–26, 41, and 53–55.

8. Ibid., pp. 2–26.

9. Ibid., pp. 2–26, 41, and 53–55; *Mining Debris*, p. 9; *Mining and Scientific Press*, Jan. 6, 1877, p. 12; Charles Waldeyer, "Hydraulic Mining in California," pp. 392–94; and *Report . . . Cedar Creek*, pp. 1–2.

10. Byrne, *Argument*, pp. 97–98, see also pp. 24, 35–36, 85, and 87; and *Grass Valley Daily Union*, Dec. 29, 1875, and Jan. 9, 1876, quoted in Kelley, *Gold vs. Grain*, p. 76.

11. *Mining and Scientific Press*, Apr. 4, 1874, p. 214, Jan. 6, 1877, pp. 9 and 12, Mar. 30, 1877, p. 200, and Aug. 17, 1878, pp. 97 and 104; *Engineering and Mining Journal*, Jan. 15, 1876, p. 56, Mar. 25, 1876, p. 300, Apr. 15, 1876, p. 370, and Aug. 4, 1877, p. 89; and Richard H. Stretch, *Report on the Cherokee Flat Blue Gravel and Spring Valley Mining and Irrigating Company's Property* (New York: Mining Record, 1879), pp. 12–13.

12. *Mining Debris*, p. 8; Kelley, *Gold vs. Grain*, pp. 240–42; and Rickard, *Interviews*, pp. 414–15 and 427. In a similar case, *The People* v. *Gold Run*, 66 Cal. 138, the California Supreme Court granted a perpetual injunction against the defendant, who claimed that many millions of dollars' worth of property was being destroyed by such an action (*Mining Debris*, pp. 2–4).

13. Eugene Wilson, *Hydraulic and Placer Mining* (New York: John Wiley & Sons, 1898), pp. iii and 81.

14. *Smelting Works: Objections to Certain Smelting Works in Populous Localities* (Oakland, Calif.: n.p., 1872), pp. 3–4 and 14–17.

15. Ibid., pp. 27 and 31–32.

16. Ibid., p. 4.

17. Donald MacMillan, "A History of the Struggle to Abate Air Pollution from Copper Smelters of the Far West, 1885–1933" (Ph.D. diss., University of Montana, 1973), pp. 16, 18, 20, and 22; and *Butte Miner*, Apr. 21, 1886, quoted in the *Mining and Scientific Press*, May 1, 1886, p. 297.

18. *Engineering and Mining Journal*, Dec. 20, 1890, pp. 711, 727, and 737, Jan. 24, 1891, p. 112, Feb. 7, 1891, p. 176, Aug. 29, 1891, p. 247, and Dec. 26, 1891, p. 733.

19. *Weekly Missoulian*, Nov. 11, 1891, quoted in MacMillan, "History of the Struggle," pp. 79–80.

20. MacMillan, "History of the Struggle," pp. 2, 38, 79–80, and 95; and William S. Greever, *The Bonanza West* (Norman: University of Oklahoma Press, 1963), p. 239. For the medical history of the era see Geoffrey Marks and William K. Beatty, *The Story of Medicine in America* (New York: Charles Scribner's, 1973).

21. MacMillan, "History of the Struggle," p. 95.

22. *Engineering and Mining Journal*, Jan. 2, 1892, p. 58.

23. William D. Haywood, *Bill Haywood's Book: The Autobiography of William D. Haywood* (London: Martin Lawrence, n.d.), p. 83.

24. Alan Stone, "The Vanishing Village: The Ashio Copper Mine Pollution Case, 1890–1907" (Ph.D. diss., University of Washington, 1974), pp. 1–5. For comments on Anaconda see Greever, *Bonanza West*, p. 240; and *Butte City Illustrated, 1890–91* (Butte, Mont.: Inter Mountain, 1891), pp. 81 and 83.

CHAPTER SIX. "WE ONLY WANT A SQUARE DEAL"

1. Erl Ellis, *The Gold Dredging Boats around Breckenridge, Colorado* (Boulder, Colo.: Johnson Publishing, 1967), p. xi.

2. Farida A. Wiley, ed., *Theodore Roosevelt's America* (New York: Doubleday, 1962), p. 293.

3. Enos Mills, *The Rocky Mountain Wonderland* (Boston: Houghton Mifflin, 1915), p. 331; Muir to Mills, Feb. 21, 1910, and Aug. 14, 1912, John Muir Collection, Huntington Library; MacMillan, "History of the Struggle," p. 6; Robert Wiebe, *Businessmen and Reform: A Study of the Progressive Movement* (Chicago: Quadrangle Books, 1968), pp. 11–14 and 212; and McCarthy, *Hour of Trial*, pp. 79–82, and numerous references to mining as part of the anticonservation movement.

4. Quoted in Michael P. Malone, "Midas of the West: The Incredible Career of William Andrews Clark," *Montana*, Autumn, 1983, p. 14.

5. Roosevelt to Hammond (June 1908?), quoted in John Hays Hammond, *The Autobiography of John Hays Hammond* (reprint, New York: Arno, 1974), p. 557.

6. *Report of the National Conservation Commission*, 3 vols. (Washington, D.C.: Government Printing Office, 1909), 1:8; Hammond, *Autobiography*, p. 557; and *Engineering and Mining Journal*, May 23, 1908, p. 1051.

7. *Report of the National Conservation Commission*, 1:26 and 109.

8. Ibid., 1:15–16.

9. Ibid., 1:109.

10. Ibid., 3:523–24 and 557, 1:95–104 and 524.

11. *Engineering and Mining Journal*, May 23, 1908, pp. 1054 and 1061, and Jan. 22, 1910, p. 201.

12. Ibid., Oct. 8, 1910, pp. 710–11, Oct. 15, 1910, p. 756, and June 17, 1911, p. 1189; and *Mining and Scientific Press*, Jan. 12, 1901, p. 35.

13. Charles R. Van Hise, *The Conservation of Natural Resources in the United States* (New York: Macmillan, 1910), pp. 16, 26–27, and 88–89; and Richard Ely et al., *The Foundations of National Prosperity* (New York: Macmillan, 1917), p. 190; see also pp. 7 and 268.

14. Charles K. Leith, "Conservation of Iron Ore," *Transactions of the American Institute of Mining Engineers*, 1914, pp. 79–82.

15. Leith, "Conservation," pp. 280–82.

16. Charles Leith, *The Mesabi Iron-Bearing District of Minnesota* (Washington, D.C.: Government Printing Office, 1903), pp. 25–31 and 283–85; and *Engineering and Mining Journal*, Sept. 6, 1902, p. 302.

17. Frank Crampton, *Deep Enough: A Working Stiff in the Western Mine Camps* (Denver, Colo.: Sage, 1956); Charles S. Sprague Company Letters, Huntington Library; Charles H. Janin Mining Papers, Huntington Library; Horace Patton, *Geology and Ore Deposits of the Bonanza District* (Denver, Colo.: Eames, 1916); Minutes of the Annual Meetings of the Waldorf Mining and Milling Co. (Denver, Colo.: n.p., 1904); and Herbert Hoover, *Principles of Mining* (New York: Hill, 1909), pp. 186–89.

18. Hammond, *Autobiography*, pp. 557–59; Resolution, American Mining Congress, Nov., 1907, Bureau of Mines Records, National Archives; and Franklin County Coal Operators Association Declaration of Purposes, 1915(?), Bureau of Mines Records.

19. Wilson to J. F. Callbreath, Sept., 1915, Bureau of Mines Records, National Archives.

20. J. F. Callbreath's testimony, House of Representatives Committee Hearings, 1916; Callbreath to Franklin Lane, Oct. 17, 1913; and Resolution of the Twenty-second Annual Convention of the American Mining Congress—all in the Bureau of Mines Records.

21. J. F. Callbreath's testimony, House of Representatives Committee Hearings, 1916; "History of the Bureau of Mines" (typed copy); and Experimental Stations Records—all in the Bureau of Mines Records.

22. Birkinbine, "The American Institute of Mining Engineers," pp. 412 and 417; Ely, *Foundations*, p. 187, and Leith's section therein, pp. 187–272; and James Douglas, "Conservation of Natural Resources," *Transactions of the American Institute of Mining Engineers*, 1909, p. 430; see also pp. 419 and 429–31.

23. Robert Service, *Ballads of a Cheechako* (Toronto: William Briggs, 1909), p. 95.

24. *Engineering and Mining Journal*, Apr. 12, 1902, p. 521, Feb. 3, 1906, pp. 221–22, and May 8, 1909, pp. 946–47; Lewis Aubury, *Gold Dredging in California* (Sacramento, Calif.: State Printing, 1910), pp. 242–49; and Clark Spence, "Golden Age of Dredging: The Development of an Industry and Its Environmental Impact," *Western Historical Quarterly*, Oct., 1980, p. 409.

25. Charles Janin, "Proposed Regulating of Gold Dredging," *Mining and Scientific Press*, Mar. 8, 1913, pp. 381–84; and Charles S. Aiken, "Farming for Gold," *Sunset*, Dec. 1, 1909, p. 655.

26. J. P. Hutchins, "Gold Dredging in 1905," *Engineering and Mining Journal*, Jan. 20, 1906, p. 124, and "Tailing Disposal By Gold Dredges," *Engineering and Mining Journal*, Feb. 3, 1906, pp. 124 and 219–23.

27. Aubury, *Gold Dredging*, p. 237.

28. Ibid., p. 241, and see also pp. 224–25 and 236–40; Arthur Dahl, "Turning Boulders into Gold," *World's Work*, Dec., 1912, pp. 214–15 and 218; *Engineering and Mining Journal*, 1907/8; and Spence, "Golden Age," pp. 410 and 414.

29. *Mining and Scientific Press*, 1902; *Engineering and Mining Journal*, 1902–8; and MacMillan, "History of the Struggle," pp. 5, 7, 8, and 133–37.

30. *Inter Mountain*, May 19, 1909, quoted in MacMillan, "History of the Struggle," p. 133; see also *Engineering and Mining Journal*, 1909/10.

31. *Montana: The Most Productive Ore Center of the Inter-Mountain Region* (Butte, Mont.: North American Industrial Review, 1904), pp. 8 and 148; and MacMillan, "History of the Struggle," pp. 163–80.

32. Hammond, *Autobiography*, pp. 562–63; for more on the Anaconda fight see Isaac F. Marcosson, *Anaconda* (New York: Dodd, Mead, 1957), pp. 104–6; and J. K. Haywood, *Injury to Vegetation by Smelter Fumes* (Washington, D.C.: Government Printing Office, 1905), pp. 6–8 and 34.

33. Earl C. Case, *The Valley of East Tennessee: The Adjustment of Industry to Natural Environment* (Nashville, Tenn.: Department of Education, 1925), p. 68, and see also pp. 69–70; and *Engineering and Mining Journal*, 1907.

34. *Engineering and Mining Journal*, May 22, 1915, p. 926, and June 12, 1915, p. 1047.

35. Rickard, *Interviews*, pp. 161–62; Charles H. Fulton, *Metallurgical Smoke* (Washington, D.C.: Government Printing Office, 1915), pp. 83–84; and W. H. Emmons and F. B. Laney, *Geology and Ore Deposits of the Ducktown Mining District, Tennessee* (Washington, D.C.: Government Printing Office, 1926); and Case, *Valley of East Tennessee*, pp. 83 and 110–11.

36. Dern letter, quoted by Newell G. Bringhurst in "The Mining Career of George H. Dern" (Master's thesis, University of Utah, 1967), pp. 170–72. For additional information on Utah see *Engineering and Mining Journal*, 1906–8 and Aug. 8, 1914, p. 241.

37. The *Engineering and Mining Journal* from 1905 to 1915 contains various articles on the smoke problem. This was the peak period of public concern during the early decades of the century. California smelters were inundated by complaints; at least four closed. It reached the point that a suit was instigated against an operating smelting plant on the grounds that damage "would result" (see the issues for July 26, 1913, p. 153, and Jan. 23, 1915, p. 217).

38. See the *New York Times* index, 1905–15, for the scope of the problem and interest in it. In 1915/16, interest waned. Harold C. Livesay and Glenn Porter, in "William Savery and the Wonderful Parsons Smoke-Eating Machine," *Delaware History*, Apr., 1971, pp. 161–76, recount the story of this wonder.

39. *Engineering and Mining Journal*, Oct. 31, 1903, p. 674; and "West Virginia," Jan. 7, 1904, p. 53.

40. *Engineering and Mining Journal*, Feb. 4, 1904, p. 217.

41. Ligon Johnson, "The History and Legal Phases of the Smoke Problem," *Transactions of the American Institute of Mining Engineers*, 1918, p. 211; see also pp. 200–202, 206, 209–10, and 212. For the fight in California see *Engineering and Mining Journal*, 1908–13; Fulton, *Metallurgical Smoke*, pp. 85–87; and Haywood, *Injury*, pp. 22–23.

42. Robert Livermore's log book, Nov. 7, 1916, Robert Livermore Collection, American Heritage Center, University of Wyoming.

CHAPTER SEVEN. REPRIEVE!

1. United States, Senate, *Hearings before the Committee on Mines and Mining* (Washington, D.C.: Government Printing Office, 1918), p. 531.

2. See, e.g., *Transactions of the American Institute of Mining Engineers*, 1921–27; *Proceedings of the Lake Superior Mining Institute* (Ishpeming, Mich.: Lake Superior Mining Institute, 1923); *Proceedings of the Mining and Metallurgical Society of America*, 1931–40; *Bibliography on Mined-Land Reclamation* (Washington, D.C.: Department of the Interior, 1979), p. 1; *Reports of the Proceedings of the American Mining Congress*, 1919, 1920, and 1924; mining reports, 1920s and 1930s, Leverett S. Ropes Papers, Montana Historical Society; various reports by mining engineers, 1922–39, Harley Sill Collection, Huntington Library; mining reports, 1920s, 1930s, Ira B. Joralemon Collection, American Heritage Center, University of Wyoming; Consolidated Virginia Mining Co. Collection, Huntington Library; Northern Belle Extension Mining Co. Papers, Huntington Library; and mining reports, 1918–30, Dyer-Benjovsky Papers, Western Historical Collections, University of Colorado.

3. Elwood Moore, *Coal: Its Properties . . . Distribution* (New York: John Wiley, 1922), p. 266; *Successful Operating Ideas for Mine-Mill and Smelter* (New York: Engineering and Mining Journal, 1936); *Modern Mining and Milling Practice* (New York: Engineering and Mining Journal, ca. 1940); and Robert Peele, *Mining Engineers' Handbook* (New York: Wiley, 1918), p. 1709.

4. *Gunnison County, Colorado* (Pitkin, Colo.: Nelson, ca. 1917), p. 46.

5. H. A. Coy and H. B. Henegar, "Mining Methods of the American Zinc Co. of Tennessee," *Transactions of the American Institute of Mining Engineers*, 1918, p. 36; and E. M. Alenius, *A Brief History of the United Verde Open Pit, Jerome, Arizona* (Tucson: University of Arizona Press, 1968), pp. 1 and 3. For hydraulic mining see Lloyd Root, *Report XXII of the State Mineralogist* (Sacramento, Calif.: State Printing Office, 1927), pp. 44–49 and 108; and *Morning Union* (Grass Valley, Calif.), May 10, 1936.

6. *Report of the United States Coal Commission*, 5 pts. (Washington, D.C.: Government Printing Office, 1925), pt. 1, p. 190, and pt. 2, p. 536.

7. Ibid., pt. 2, p. 536.

8. Warriner, "Anthracite Stripping," pp. 162–63, 180–81, 184–86, and 191–93; *Strip Mining in Kentucky* (Lexington: Kentucky Department of Natural Resources, 1965), pp. 21–23 and 35; Harman D. Graham, "The Economics of Strip Coal Mining . . . Illinois" (Ph.D. diss., University of Illinois, 1947), pp. 1–2; and *Story of Open Cut Mining*, pp. 19 and 20–21.

9. *Strip Mining in Kentucky*, pp. 9 and 23; and Graham, "Economics," p. 1.

10. Warriner, "Anthracite Stripping," p. 181; see also pp. 188–90.

11. Quoted in *Story of Open Cut Mining*, p. 18.

12. Frederick Laist, "An Address to Mining Students," *Mining and Scientific Press*, July 2, 1921, p. 22.

13. *Strip Mining in Kentucky*, p. 24; see also Sullivan, "Voluntary Industry Program," pp. 86–87; "Spoil Reclamation: Assures Good Income without Leveling," *Coal Age*, July, 1946, p. 94; "Strip Reclamation in Eastern Ohio," *Coal Age*, 1941, pp. 114–16; and *Story of Open Cut Mining*, p. 9.

14. Mathewson is quoted by Rickard in *Interviews*, p. 349; and *Helena Mining Review* (Helena, Mont.: n.p., 1929), pp. 25 and 27.

15. C. M. Young, "Pollution of River Water in the Pittsburgh District," *American Water Works Association Journal*, May 8, 1921, p. 206.

16. Andrew Crichton, "Mine-drainage Stream Pollution," *Transactions of the American Institute of Mining Engineers*, 1924, pp. 435–36 and 442–46.

17. Ibid., p. 434.

18. Crichton, "What Shall Be Done," pp. 447–48 and 451; Young, "Pollution of River Water," pp. 201–3; and Young was quoted by Crichton in "Mine-drainage," p. 445.

19. United States, Senate, *Hearings before the Subcommittee on Air and Water Pollution*, 2 vols. (Washington, D.C.: Government Printing Office, 1967), 1:320.

20. *New Ideas in Coal Mining* (New York: Coal Age, 1917), p. 100; *Pittsburgh Coal Company* v. *Sanitary Board*, quoted in *Environmental Law Reporter*, 1972, p. 20339; and *Report of the United States Coal Commission*, pt. 2, p. 537.

21. J. P. Wood, *Report on Mine Tailing Pollution of Clear Creek, Clear Creek–Gilpin Counties, Colorado* (Denver, Colo.: n.p., 1935), pp. 5, 9, 20, 23, 26, 29, and 34.

22. *Wilmore et al.* v. *Chain O'Mines, Inc., et al.*, 96 Colo. 319, 44 P 2d 1024, pp. 321 and 324.

23. Ibid., pp. 330–31, and see also p. 319; *The Humphreys Tunnel and Mining Company* v. *Frank*, 46 Colo. 524, 105 P, 1093, pp. 530–32; see also *Slide Mines, Inc.* v. *Left Hand Ditch Company et al.*, 102 Colo. 69, 77 P 2d 125.

24. *Engineering and Mining Journal*, Apr., 1935, p. 162, and Nov., 1936, p. 546; and *Elk Mountain Pilot* (Crested Butte, Colo.), Mar. 21, 1935.

25. Chase to Lyons, Jan. 25, 1950, in my possession; and *Silverton Standard*, Mar. 6, 1980.

26. Chase to Lyons, Jan. 30, 1946.

27. *Engineering and Mining Journal*, Oct., 1938, p. 38.

28. Kenneth C. Kellar, *Chambers Kellar: Distinguished Gentleman—Great Lawyer—Fiery Rebel* (Lead, S.Dak.: Seaton Publishing Co., 1975), pp. 21 and 25–27.

29. Spring, *Pioneer Years*, pp. 87 and 96.

30. *Engineering and Mining Journal*, Oct., 1935, p. 517, Apr., 1936, p. 207, June, 1937, pp. 286–91, and Sept., 1937, pp. 76–78. By December 1937 the revival was in decline (see Dec., 1937, p. 70). Michigan gold mining is found in the issue for Sept., 1937, p. 76.

31. *Engineering and Mining Journal*, June, 1937, p. 277.

32. Malcolm Ross, *Machine Age in the Hills* (New York: Macmillan, 1933), p. 42; see also pp. 40, 50, and 59 and the chapters entitled "Miners," "The People," and "Operators."

33. Lewis Mumford, *Technics and Civilization* (New York: Harcourt, Brace, 1934), p. 69; also see pp. 67–73, 74, 77, 157–58, and 170.

34. Rickard, *Man and Metals*, vol. 1, p. 23.

CHAPTER EIGHT. "A TRADITION THAT ENDURED FAR TOO LONG"

1. See, e.g., Colorado and Utah Coal Company Papers, 1955–59, Colorado Historical Society; *Congress and the Nation* (Washington, D.C.: Congressional Quarterly Service, 1969), vol. 1: 1945–64; Ropes Papers, 1946–49; and *Prospectus Leadville Lead Corporation* (Denver, Colo.: n.p., 1952).

2. "The Surface Mining Issue: A Reasoned Response," *Coal Age*, Mar., 1971, p. 92; see also W. C. Bramble, "Strip Mining: Waste or Conservation?" *American Forests*, June, 1949, p. 42; and "Strip Mining Heals Its Own Scars," *Business Week*, Nov. 13, 1965, p. 142.

3. *Northern Illinois Coal Corporation et al.* v. *Medill, Director of Mines and Minerals*, 397 Ill. 98, 72 NE 2nd 844 (1947), pp. 844–46; John Thames, ed., *Reclamation and Use of Disturbed Land in the Southwest* (Tucson: University of Arizona Press, 1977), p. 10; and Graham, "Economics of Strip Coal Mining," p. 7. Despite Pennsylvania and Illinois laws, similar legislation had been defeated in many states—Ohio, Missouri, Kentucky, and Kansas, for example. Indiana required a $25 bond per acre, which was hardly a deterrent.

4. A. E. Flowers, "Harmon Creek Goals: Profitable Stripping," *Coal Age*, May, 1955, pp. 112–13.

5. Bramble, "Strip Mining," p. 43; *Strip Mining in Kentucky*, p. 35; and "Flexibility in Stripping," *Coal Age*, Nov., 1956, p. 67. For the traditional approach see Graham, "Economics of Strip Coal Mining," p. 4; Billinger, *Pennsylvania's Coal Industry*, p. 46; "Spoil Reclamation," pp. 91 and 93; and *The Proceedings of the Rocky Mountain Coal Mining Institute* (Denver, Colo.: R. M. Coal Institute, 1942–60), which show that the western coal miners also had no interest.

6. Chase to Lyons, Sept. 13, 1952; see also Chase correspondence, 1946–52, Charles A. Chase Collection, Center of Southwest Studies, Fort Lewis College, Durango, Colorado.

7. *Engineering and Mining Journal,* Mar., 1945, p. 70, and Nov., 1947, pp. 132–35; and see also Herbert Sawin, "Dredging: An Evolving Art," *Mining World,* Jan., 1949, pp. 37–38.

8. Callahan's testimony is given in *Stream Pollution Control* (Washington, D.C.: Government Printing Office, 1947), pp. 191–93; see also pp. 201–4, 207, 271–72, 286–87, and 290.

9. Sam Dickinson, "Experiments in Propagating Plant Cover at Tailings Basins," *Mining Congress Journal,* Oct., 1972, reprint, pp. 1 and 5–6. The Erie Mining Company received a national environmental award in 1977 for its revegetation efforts.

10. Jack Van Coevering, "The Porcupines and Copper," *Nature Magazine,* Nov., 1958, pp. 482–85; and "Mining Threatens the Porcupines," *Nature Magazine,* Oct., 1958, p. 399.

11. Allen V. Kneese and Charles L. Schultze, *Pollution, Prices and Public Policy* (Washington, D.C.: Brookings Institution, 1975), pp. 2–3.

CHAPTER NINE. ENVIRONMENTAL WHIRLWIND

1. Ian G. Barbour, *Science and Secularity* (New York: Harper & Row, 1970), p. 139; see also Ian G. Barbour, ed., *Western Man and Environmental Ethics* (Menlo Park, Calif.: Addison-Wesley, 1973), pp. 1–5.

2. For an overview of the environmental movement see Petulla, *American Environmental History;* Roderick Nash, ed., *The American Environment* (Reading, Mass.: Addison-Wesley, 1976); *Quest for Quality* (Washington, D.C.: Department of the Interior, 1965), pp. 6, 41, 46, and 84; *Indivisibly One* (Washington, D.C.: Department of the Interior, 1973), p. 29; Howard Lamar, ed., *The Reader's Encyclopedia of the American West* (New York: Thomas Y. Crowell, 1977), pp. 254–56; and H. K. Richard Vietor, *Environmental Politics and the Coal Coalition* (College Station: Texas A & M University Press, 1980), pp. 5–7, 11, and 127–54.

3. Sheridan, *Hard Rock Mining,* p. 13; Arnold Miller, "The Energy Crisis as a Coal Miner Sees It," *Center Magazine,* Nov./Dec., 1973, p. 43; James Conaway, "The Last of the West: Hell, Strip It!" *Atlantic,* Sept., 1973, p. 97; Michael Frome, "Editorial," *American Forests,* Sept., 1967, p. 44, and "Conservation: The Trouble with Mining," *Field and Stream,* Dec., 1968, p. 22; and Theodore L. Harris et al., *Into Wide Worlds* (Oklahoma City, Okla.: Economy Co., 1965), pp. 93–94.

4. Quoted in David G. McCullough, "The Lonely War of a Good Angry Man," *American Heritage,* Dec., 1969, p. 98. For the history of the region see McCullough, pp. 105–6; Stuart Buck, "Coal Mining in the Kanawha Valley of West Virginia," in *Mineral Resources of the United States, 1883 and 1884* (Washington, D.C.: Government Printing Office, 1885), pp. 131–33; and Harry Caudill, *My Land Is Dying* (New York: E. P. Dutton, 1971), pp. 57–61.

5. McCullough, "The Lonely War," p. 107. For the preceding section see Frome, "Conservation," p. 22; Caudill, *My Land,* pp. 82–86; Bill Surface, *The Hollow* (New York: Coward-McCann, 1971), pp. 164, 169, and 172; and Harry M. Caudill, *Night Comes to the Cumberlands* (Boston: Little, Brown, 1963).

6. McCullough, "The Lonely War," pp. 98–101; see also Harry M. Caudill, *The Watches of the Night* (Boston: Little, Brown, 1976), pp. 35, 76–78, and 269–70.

7. Quoted in Daniel Jackson, "Strip Mining, Reclamation, and the Public," *Coal Age*, May, 1963, pp. 93–94; and see J. Clarence Davies, *The Politics of Pollution* (New York: Pegasus, 1970), p. 29.

8. Jackson, "Strip Mining," pp. 84–87, 89, and 92–93; "Responsible Strip Mining and Restoration," *Coal Age*, Jan., 1963, p. 28; Sullivan, "Voluntary Industry Program," pp. 86 and 91; and Hugh Montgomery, "Conscientious Coal Stripping," *Coal Age*, July, 1962, pp. 84 and 88.

9. McCullough, "The Lonely War," p. 107. Vietor, *Environmental Politics*, has a chapter on the fight in Pennsylvania, pp. 58–84.

10. Norman Cousins, "Fouling the Air," *Saturday Review*, Oct. 8, 1966, p. 32.

11. Ibid., p. 123.

12. *Hearings before the Subcommittee on Air and Water Pollution*, pp. 343–57 and 421.

13. Ibid., p. 321.

14. *Congress and the Nation*, vol. 2, p. 489.

15. Boyer's testimony is found in *Hearings before the Subcommittee on Air and Water Pollution*, pp. 351–57 and 421 and see also pp. 343 and 350; and *Congress and the Nation*, vol. 2, p. 489.

16. Carlin, quoted in Jackson, "Strip Mining," p. 94; and Frome, "Conservation," p. 22.

CHAPTER TEN. A VISION, A HOPE FOR THE FUTURE

1. *Mining Record*, June 30, 1971, p. 2, Oct. 6, 1971, p. 2, Mar. 29, 1972, p. 2, and July 26, 1972, p. 2. For the preceding comments see Patrick A. Moore, "The Administration of Pollution Control in British Columbia: A Focus on the Mining Industry" (Ph.D. diss., University of British Columbia, 1974), pp. 9–10; *Mining Record*, Jan. 24, 1973, p. 3; and Conaway, "Last of the West," pp. 97–98.

2. Hechler, quoted in "Coal: A $4-billion Victim of the Environmental Movement," *Forbes*, Nov. 15, 1972, p. 42; and Caudill, *Watches of the Night*, p. 270.

3. *Business Week*, Sept. 30, 1976, p. 30, and June 18, 1979, p. 152; see also the *New York Times Magazine*, Jan. 30, 1972, and the *New Republic*, Nov. 20, 1976, pp. 10–12.

4. *New York Times*, Jan. 21, 1973, p. 68. For the Yoffe episode see David Tillman, "Environmentally-Sensitive Plants Require Early Public Disclosure," *Area Development*, June, 1972, pp. 14 and 20.

5. Elburt Osborn, "Mining Industry Must Become Truly Concerned with Ecology," *Mines Magazine*, Aug., 1971, p. 117.

6. The above was summarized from *Mining Record*, Feb. 9, 1972, p. 2, Apr. 15, 1972, p. 2, Jan. 10, 1973, p. 2, and Sept. 11, 1974, p. 2; H. Rush Spedden, "Impact of Environmental Controls on Nonferrous Metals Extraction," *Mining Congress Journal*, Dec., 1970, p. 57; George Monroe, "Mining and the Environment," *Mining Congress Journal*, Sept., 1973, p. 38; *Western Resources Conference* (Golden: Colorado School of Mines, 1971), pp. 33, 34, and 97; and *Anatomy of a Mine: From Prospect to Production* (Ogden, Utah: United States Forest Service, 1977), p. 117.

7. Osborn, "Mining Industry," p. 8.

8. Sources for the preceding are: *Homestake Mining Company: Annual Report* (San Francisco, Calif.: Homestake Mining Co., 1978), p. 4; *Mining*

Record, Oct. 16, 1974, p. 4, Oct. 23, 1974, p. 5, Aug. 20, 1975, p. 1, Aug. 30, 1978, p. 9, Sept. 6, 1978, pp. 6 and 9, and Aug. 29, 1979, p. 6. The *Rocky Mountain News* (Denver), Feb. 11, 1979, p. 86, published an insightful speech by Tom Hendricks, the operator of a small mine, showing his problems. The mining industry, of course, claimed that the government had killed some mines (see David Tillman, "Environmentally-Sensitive Plants," pp. 14 and 20; and *Mining Record,* Mar. 12, 1975, p. 1, and Jan. 7, 1976, p. 1).

9. Frome, "Conservation," p. 22; see also his "Editorial," p. 3.

10. Osborn, "Mining Industry," pp. 7–9; *Mining Record,* Apr. 26, 1972, p. 2, and Feb. 14, 1979, p. 4; Freeman Bishop, "Environmentalism, Creating Crunch on Coal Industry," *Mining Congress Journal,* Feb., 1973, pp. 110–12; Ann Feeney, "Who's Getting the Shaft?" *Colorado Business,* Feb., 1978, p. 16; and *What Mining Means to Americans* (Washington, D.C.: American Mining Congress, ca. 1976), p. 15.

11. For the preceding on public relations see the *Mining Record* for the 1970s; Spedden, "Impact of Environmental Controls," p. 57; Monroe, "Mining and the Environment," p. 38; and various comments found in the *Western Resources Conference.* The *Mining Record,* June 16, 1976, p. 6, discusses the vineyard.

12. James G. Hall, vice-chairman of the Anaconda Company, quoted in *Western Resources Conference,* p. 33.

13. *What Mining Means to Americans,* p. 15; see also Tom Alexander, "A Promising Try at Environmental Detente," *Fortune,* Feb. 13, 1978, p. 94; and Monroe, "Mining and the Environment," p. 38.

14. *Mining Record,* Feb. 14, 1979, p. 4, and see also the issue for Sept. 11, 1974, p. 2; Monroe, "Mining and the Environment," p. 38; and "Anatomy of a Mine," p. 117.

15. The comments of Allan Bird are found in "Mining in the San Juans: A Look at the Future," in *Across the Great Divide* (Silverton, Colo., 1977), a privately published report of a series of town meetings in 1976.

16. *Our Environment,* p. 2; and "Anatomy of a Mine," p. 117.

17. Richard Schmidt, *Coal in America* (New York: McGraw-Hill, 1979), pp. 213–14.

18. The "Exxon Ad," *Sports Illustrated,* Oct. 16, 1978, p. 89; *Montana Copper* (Helena, Mont.: Anaconda Copper, 1979), pp. 10 and 18–19; Don Dedera, "Preserving Wyoming's Past," *Exxon USA,* no. 2 (1979), p. 5; Harry M. Conger, *Homestake Mining Company* (San Francisco, Calif.: Homestake Mining, 1979), p. 5; and *Homestake Annual Reports,* 1976–79.

19. *Our Environment* (Salt Lake City, Utah: Kennecott, ca. 1979).

20. Ian MacGregor, "Mining Needn't Be a Dirty Word," *Catalyst for Environmental Quality,* 1971(?), pp. 25–27; "Full-Scale Molybdenum Mining Reclamation Program Completed," *Mining Record,* Jan. 2, 1980, p. 8; *Comprehensive Plan for Land Reclamation and Stabilization at the Urad Mine* (Denver, Colo.: AMAX, 1974), pp. 1, 4, and 22; *Denver Post,* Mar. 3, 1981, p. 28, and Mar. 8, 1981, p. 28; *Henderson* (Denver, Colo.: AMAX, ca. 1978), pp. 13, 19, and 20; and *AMAX: Annual Report,* 1977 and 1979 (Greenwich, Conn.: AMAX, 1978 and 1980). Michael Tanzer attacks AMAX at home and abroad in *The Race for Resources: Continuing Struggles over Minerals and Fuels* (New York: Monthly Review Press, 1980), chap. 13.

21. These courses were found in the bulletins for Stanford University, Columbia University, Colorado School of Mines, and South Dakota School of

Mines and Technology; and *Mining Congress Journal* for the 1970s. The *Mining Record* also reflects the changes (see 1971–76); and the *Bibliography on Mined-Land Reclamation* lists 98 articles for 1976, as compared, for instance, with 4 in 1951.

22. Ashley A. Thornburg, "Surface Mine Reclamation in Montana," *Second Research and Applied Technology Symposium on Mined-Land Reclamation* (Washington, D.C.: National Coal Association, 1974), p. 20.

23. Alexander, "A Promising Try at Environmental Detente," p. 25; David Holm, ed., *Water Quality and Mining,* 1979 report of the Water Quality Control Division, Colorado Department of Health (Denver: Colorado Department of Health, 1979), p. 6; and Louis Newell, "Miners: Once It Was All Theirs," *San Juan Journal* (Durango, Colo.), Nov. 14, 1979, p. 4.

24. "Mount Emmons: Social and Economic Studies," Library of Western State College, Gunnison, Colo.; T. H. Watkins, "Thinking Little," *American Heritage,* Oct./Nov., 1979, pp. 38–39; Crested Butte, Gunnison, and Denver papers, 1977–79; and various AMAX studies, reviews, and reports.

25. Patricia C. Petty, "A Tale of Two Mining Towns," *Denver Post,* July 12, 1981, p. 27.

26. One of the most moving views of the threat of strip mining is found in K. Ross Toole's Introduction to his *Rape of the Great Plains.* It should be read by people on both sides of the controversy. See also the *Mining Record,* Jan. 27, 1982, p. 4; and *Western Resources Conference,* p. iii.

EPILOGUE. THE 1980s

1. *Mining Record,* June 11, 1986, p. 12; and Ronald A. Taylor and Gordon Witkin, "The Big Grab for Wild Lands," *Newsweek,* Apr. 28, 1986, pp. 68–69.

2. *Mining Record,* June 11, 1986, p. 6.

3. Ibid., June 4, 1986, p. 7.

4. *A Tradition of Leadership* (San Francisco, Calif.: Homestake Mining, 1986), p. 7.

5. *Mining Record,* Feb. 15, 1984, p. 25.

BIBLIOGRAPHY

PRIMARY SOURCES

Unpublished Materials

Acacia Gold Mining Company. Papers. Colorado Historical Society, Denver.

Bacon, Henry. Papers. Henry E. Huntington Library, San Marino, California.

Barlow, Samuel. Collection. Huntington Library, San Marino, California.

Bringhurst, Newell G. "The Mining Career of George H. Dern." Master's thesis. University of Utah, 1967.

California Mining District. Bylaws. Colorado Historical Society, Denver.

Charles S. Sprague Company. Letters. Huntington Library, San Marino, California.

Chase, Charles A. Collection. Center of Southwest Studies, Fort Lewis College, Durango, Colorado.

Clark, Henry Harmon. Papers. Montana Historical Society, Helena.

Colorado and Utah Coal Company. Papers. Colorado Historical Society, Denver.

Consolidated Virginia Mining Company. Collection. Huntington Library, San Marino, California.

Daly, George. Collection. Colorado Historical Society, Denver.

Daniell, John. Collection. Huntington Library, San Marino, California.

Dyer-Benjovsky Papers. Western Historical Collections, University of Colorado, Boulder.

Fritz, Percy. "The Mining Districts of Boulder County, Colorado." Ph.D. diss., University of Colorado, 1933.

Gaston, H. A. "The Present and Future of the Mines and Mining in Nevada." Huntington Library, San Marino, California.

Graham, Harman D. "The Economics of Strip Coal Mining with Special Reference to Knox and Fulton Counties, Illinois." Ph.D. diss., University of Illinois, 1947.

Hague, James D. Collection. Huntington Library, San Marino, California.

Harvey, Charles H. Papers. Library of Congress, Washington, D.C.

Hill, Nathaniel P. Papers, Colorado Historical Society, Denver.

Horskey, Joseph. Reminiscences. Montana Historical Society, Helena.

Janin, Charles H. Mining Papers. Huntington Library, San Marino, California.

Jones, John P. Collection. Huntington Library, San Marino, California.

Joralemon, Ira B. Collection. American Heritage Center, University of Wyoming, Laramie.

King, Clarence. Letters. Huntington Library, San Marino, California.

Livermore, Robert. Collection. American Heritage Center, University of Wyoming, Laramie.

MacMillan, Donald. "A History of the Struggle to Abate Air Pollution from Copper Smelters of the Far West, 1885–1933." Ph.D. diss., University of Montana, 1973.

Moore, Patrick A. "The Administration of Pollution Control in British Columbia: A Focus on the Mining Industry." Ph.D. diss., University of British Columbia, 1974.

"Mount Emmons: Social and Economic Studies." Library of Western State College, Gunnison, Colorado.

Muir, John. Collection. Huntington Library, San Marino, California.

New Almaden Mine. Collection. Huntington Library, San Marino, California.

Northern Belle Extension Mining Company. Papers. Huntington Library, San Marino, California.

Rockwell, John Arnold. Collection. Huntington Library, San Marino, California.

Ropes, Leverett S. Papers. Montana Historical Society, Helena.

Savage Mining Company. Collection. Huntington Library, San Marino, California.

Schurz, Carl. Papers. Library of Congress, Washington, D.C.

Shenandoah-Dives Mining Company. Collection. Center of Southwest Studies, Fort Lewis College, Durango, Colorado.

Sill, Harley. Collection. Huntington Library, San Marino, California.

Smith, Eben. Correspondence. Western History Department, Denver Public Library.

Smuggler Consolidated Mining Company. Papers. Colorado Historical Society, Denver.

Stone, Alan A. "The Vanishing Village: The Ashio Copper Mine Pollution Case, 1890–1907." Ph.D. diss., University of Washington, 1974.

Tabor, Horace. Autobiography. Bancroft Library, University of California, Berkeley.

Tamarack Mining Company. Papers. Huntington Library, San Marino, California.

United States. Bureau of Mines. Records. National Archives, Washington, D.C.

Yeatman, Pope. Collection. American Heritage Center, University of Wyoming, Laramie.

Newspapers, Journals, and Proceedings

Business Week, 1976, 1979
California Mining Journal, 1966–71
Coal Age, 1923, 1941, 1946, 1955/56, 1962/63, 1971, 1973
Colorado Miner, 1869
Daily Evening Herald (Marysville, Calif.), 1853/54
Denver Post, 1981
Elk Mountain Pilot (Crested Butte, Colo.), 1935
Engineering and Mining Journal (originally *Journal of Mining*), 1866–68, 1875–83, 1890–92, 1896/97, 1902/3, 1906–11, 1914/15, 1930–48, 1950/51
Environmental Law Reporter, 1971–78
Gold Hill (Nev.) *Daily News,* 1864, 1878
Harper's Monthly, 1850–92
Helena (Mont.) *Mining Review,* 1929
Hydraulic Press, The (North San Juan, Calif.), 1858
Mineral Industries Bulletin, 1969–79
Miner's Journal (Pottsville, Pa.), Feb. 11, 1843

Mining and Scientific Press, 1860–64, 1871, 1878–80, 1884/85, 1890–92, 1896, 1901/2, 1913, 1921
Mining Congress Journal, 1973, 1975, 1978, 1980
Mining Magazine, The (New York), 1854
Mining Record (Denver), 1971–86
Morning Union, The (Grass Valley, Nevada City, Calif.), 1934, 1936
New Reclamation Era (Washington, D.C.), 1928–30
New Republic, 1976
New York Times, various issues, twentieth century
Pit and Quarry, 1978
Poole's Index to Periodical Literature, 1802–1906
Proceedings of the Lake Superior Mining Institute, 1923
Proceedings of the Mining and Metallurgical Society of America, 1911/12, 1931–40
Proceedings of the Rocky Mountain Coal Mining Institute, 1942–60
Prospector, The (Helena, Mont.), 1904/5
Readers Guide to Periodical Literature, 1930–80
Reports of the Proceedings of the American Mining Congress, 1904, 1911, 1919, 1920, 1924
Rocky Mountain News (Denver), 1979
Silver Standard (Silver Plume, Colo.), 1888, 1894
Silverton (Colo.) *Standard*, 1980
Spirit of the Age, The (Sacramento, Calif.), 1856
Transactions of the American Institute of Mining Engineers, 1890–93, 1898–1909, 1914–18, 1921–28, 1930, 1932, 1938, 1942, 1945

Published Materials

Agricola, Georgius. *De re metallica*. Translated by Herbert Hoover and Lou Hoover. London: Mining Magazine, 1912.
Aiken, Charles S. "Farming for Gold." *Sunset*, Dec., 1909, pp. 651–56.
AMAX: Annual Report, for 1965, 1977, 1979. New York: AMAX, 1966, 1978, 1980.
American Digest. Vols. 13, 16, 34. St. Paul, Minn.: West, 1902, 1910, 1916.
Atchison v. *Peterson* (1874), 87 US (20 Wall) 507, 22 L. Ed., 414.
Atlantic and Pacific Gold and Silver Mining Company. *Prospectus of the Atlantic and Pacific Gold and Silver Mining Co.* New York: Lattimer, 1864.
Aubury, Lewis E. *Gold Dredging in California*. Sacramento, Calif.: State Printing, 1910.
Baker, G. W. *Treatment of Gold Ores in Gilpin County, Colorado*. Central City, Colo.: Herald, 1870.
Barbour, Ian G. *Science and Secularity: The Ethics of Technology*. New York: Harper & Row, 1970.
———, ed. *Western Man and Environmental Ethics*. Menlo Park, Calif.: Addison-Wesley, 1973.
Barnes, Demas. *From the Atlantic to the Pacific*. New York: Van Nostrand, 1866.
Becker, George F. *Geology of the Comstock Lode and the Washoe District*. Washington, D.C.: Government Printing Office, 1883.
Benavides, Alonso de. *The Memorial of Fray Alonso de Benavides*. Translated by Mrs. Edward Ayer. Chicago: privately printed, 1916.
Bennett, Estelline. *Old Deadwood Days*. New York: Charles Scribner's Sons, 1935.

Bird, Allan. "Mining in the San Juans: A Look at the Future." In *Across the Great Divide*. Silverton: privately published, 1977.

Bird, Isabella. *A Lady's Life in the Rocky Mountains*. Reprint. Norman: University of Oklahoma Press, 1960.

Birkinbine, John. "The American Institute of Mining Engineers and the Conservation of Natural Resources." *Transactions of the American Institute of Mining Engineers*, 1909, pp. 412–18.

Blake, Henry N. "Historical Sketch of Madison County, Montana Territory." *Contributions to the Historical Society of Montana*, 1896, pp. 76–87.

Bowen, Eli. *The Coal Regions of Pennsylvania*. Pottsville, Pa.: Carvalho, 1848.

———. *The Pictorial Sketch-Book of Pennsylvania*. Philadelphia: W. Bromwell, 1853.

Bowles, Samuel. *The Switzerland of America*. Springfield, Mass.: Bowles, 1869.

Brewer, William. *Rocky Mountain Letters, 1869*. Denver: Colorado Mountain Club, 1930.

A Brief Description of the Washoe Smelter. Anaconda, Mont.: Anaconda Copper, 1907.

Brockett, L. P. *Our Western Empire*. Philadelphia: Bradley, 1881.

Browne, J. Ross. *Mining Adventures: California and Nevada, 1863–65*. Reprint. Balboa Island, Calif.: Paisano, 1961.

———. *A Peep at Washoe*. Reprint. Balboa: Paisano, 1959.

———. *Report on the Mineral Resources of the States and Territories West of the Rocky Mountains*. Washington, D.C.: Government Printing Office, 1868.

Buck, Stuart. "Coal Mining in the Kanawha Valley of West Virginia." *Mineral Resources of the United States, 1883 and 1884*. Washington, D.C.: Government Printing Office, 1885.

Butte City Illustrated, 1890–91. Butte, Mont.: Inter Mountain, 1891.

Byrne, James K. *Argument on Motion for a Temporary Injunction*. N.p.: n.p., n.d.

Cataract and Wide West Hydraulic Gravel Mining Company. *Prospectus of the Cataract and Wide West Hydraulic Gravel Mining Co.* San Francisco, Calif.: Floto, 1876.

Cedar Creek Hydraulic Mining Company. *Report upon the Property Belonging to the Cedar Creek Hydraulic Mining Company*. N.p.: n.p., 1880.

Clark, Walter van Tilburg, ed. *The Journals of Alfred Doten, 1849–1903*. 3 vols. Reno: University of Nevada Press, 1973.

Clark, William A. "Centennial Address on the Origin, Growth and Resources of Montana." *Contributions to the Historical Society of Montana*. Helena, Mont.: State Publishing, 1896, pp. 45–60.

Clifford, Henry. *Rocks in the Road to Fortune; or The Unsound Side of Mining*. New York: Gotham Press, 1908.

"Coal, and the Coal-Mines of Pennsylvania." *Harper's Monthly*, Aug., 1857, pp. 451–69.

Colorado. *Proceedings of the Constitutional Convention . . . for the State of Colorado*. Denver, Colo.: Smith-Brooks, 1907.

"*Commonwealth* v. *Barnes & Tucker Co.*" *Environmental Law Reporter*, 1974, pp. 20545–51.

Comprehensive Plan for Land Reclamation and Stabilization at the Urad Mine. Denver, Colo. (?): AMAX, 1974.

Congdon, H. B., comp. *Mining Laws and Forms*. San Francisco, Calif.: Bancroft, 1864.

Conger, Harry M. *Homestake Mining Company.* San Francisco, Calif.: Home-stake Mining Co., 1979.

Conner, Daniel E. *Joseph Reddeford Walker and the Arizona Adventure.* Edited by Donald Berthrong. Norman: University of Oklahoma Press, 1956.

Corning, Frederick G. *Papers from the Notes of an Engineer.* New York: Scientific Publishing Co., 1889.

Coy, H. A., and H. B. Henegar. "Mining Methods of the American Zinc Co. of Tennessee." *Transactions of the American Institute of Mining Engineers,* 1918, pp. 36–47.

Crampton, Frank. *Deep Enough: A Working Stiff in the Western Mine Camps.* Denver, Colo.: Sage, 1956.

Crichton, Andrew B. "Mine-drainage Stream Pollution." *Transactions of the American Institute of Mining Engineers,* 1924, pp. 434–46.

———. "What Shall Be Done about the Growing Evil of the Pollution of Streams by Mine Drainage?" *Coal Age,* Mar. 15, 1923, pp. 447–51.

Crown King Mines Company. New York: Patteson Press, 1903.

Curtis, Joseph S. *Silver-Lead Deposits of Eureka, Nevada.* Washington, D.C.: Government Printing Office, 1884.

Daddow, Samuel H. *Coal, Iron, and Oil: or, The Practical American Miner.* Philadelphia: Lippincott, 1866.

Dahl, Arthur. "Turning Boulders into Gold." *World's Work,* Dec., 1912, pp. 214–18.

"Death Valley National Monument: Department of the Interior." *Environmental Law Reporter,* Oct., 1979, pp. 65306–7.

De Quille, Dan (pseud. of William Wright). *History of the Big Bonanza.* Hartford, Conn.: American Publishing, 1877.

Dickinson, Sam. "Experiments in Propagating Plant Cover at Tailing Basins." Reprint from *Mining Congress Journal,* Oct., 1972.

Douglas, James. "Conservation of Natural Resources." *Transactions of the American Institute of Mining Engineers,* 1909, pp. 419–31.

Durst, John. "Hydraulic Mining: A Need of State Action upon Rivers." *Californian,* Jan., 1881, pp. 9–14.

Eggleston, T. "Boston and Colorado Smelting Works." *American Institute of Mining . . . Engineers Transactions,* 1876, pp. 276–98.

Ellis, Anne. *The Life of an Ordinary Woman.* New York: Houghton Mifflin, 1929.

Ely, Richard, et al. *The Foundations of National Prosperity.* New York: Macmillan, 1917.

Emmons, Samuel. *Geology and Mining Industry of Leadville, Colorado.* Washington, D.C.: Government Printing Office, 1886.

———, and George F. Becker. *Statistics and Technology of the Precious Metals.* Washington, D.C.: Government Printing Office, 1885.

Emmons, W. H., and F. B. Laney. *Geology and Ore Deposits of the Ducktown Mining District, Tennessee.* Washington, D.C.: Government Printing Office, 1926.

F.C. *The Compleat Collier: or, The Whole Art of Sinking, Getting, and Working Coal-Mines, etc.* London: G. Conyers, 1708.

Farquhar, Francis, ed. *Up and down California in 1860–1864: The Journal of William H. Brewer.* Berkeley: University of California Press, 1966.

Featherstonhaugh, George W. *A Canoe Voyage up the Minnay Soto.* 2 vols. London: Richard Bentley, 1847.

————. *Excursion through the Slave States*. New York: Harper, 1844.

Fergus, James. "A Leaf from the Diary of James Fergus." *Contributions to the Historical Society of Montana*. Helena, Mont., 1896, vol. 2, pp. 252–54.

"Flexibility in Stripping." *Coal Age*, Nov., 1956, pp. 64–67.

Flowers, A. E. "Harmon Creek Goals: Profitable Stripping." *Coal Age*, May, 1955, pp. 108–14.

Foote, Mary H. "New Almaden: or A California Mining Camp." *Scribner's Monthly Magazine*, Feb., 1878, pp. 480–93.

Fruits of the Bonanza, The. San Francisco, Calif.: n.p., 1878.

"Full-Scale Molybdenum Mining Reclamation Program Completed." *Mining Record*, Jan. 2, 1980.

Fulton, Charles H. *Metallurgical Smoke*. Washington, D.C.: Government Printing Office, 1915.

"Galena and Its Lead Mines." *Harper's New Monthly Magazine*, May, 1866, pp. 681–96.

Galloway, John D. *Early Engineering Works Contributory to the Comstock*. Reno: University of Nevada Press, 1947.

Glazer, Sidney, ed. "A Michigan Correspondent in Colorado, 1878." *Colorado Magazine*, July, 1960, pp. 207–18.

Golden Manual: or The Royal Road to Success, The. Philadelphia: Bell, 1891.

"Gold Mining in Georgia." *Harper's New Monthly Magazine*, Sept., 1879, pp. 507–19.

Gold Valley Placer Mining Co., The. Aspen, Colo: Aspen Leader, 1893.

Gregg, Josiah. *Commerce of the Prairies*. Reprint. Norman: University of Oklahoma Press, 1954.

Gressley, Gene, ed. *Bostonians and Bullion*. Lincoln: University of Nebraska Press, 1968.

Grinnell, Joseph. *Gold Hunting in Alaska*. Chicago: Cook, 1901.

Hague, James D. "Mining Engineering and Mining Law." Reprint from *Engineering and Mining Journal*, Oct. 20, 1904.

————. *Mining Industry*. Washington, D.C.: Government Printing Office, 1870.

Hammond, John Hays. *The Autobiography of John Hays Hammond*. Reprint. New York: Arno, 1974.

Hanks, Henry. *Second Report of the State Mineralogist*. Sacramento, Calif.: State Printing, 1882.

Haywood, J. K. *Injury to Vegetation and Animal Life by Smelter Wastes*. Washington, D.C.: Government Printing Office, 1908.

————. *Injury to Vegetation by Smelter Fumes*. Washington, D.C.: Government Printing Office, 1905.

Haywood, William D. *Bill Haywood's Book: The Autobiography of William D. Haywood*. London: Martin Lawrence, n.d.

Hedburg, Eric. "The Missouri and Arkansas Zinc-Mines at the Close of 1900." *Transactions of the American Institute of Mining Engineers*, 1902, pp. 379–404.

Henrich, Carl. "The Ducktown Ore-Deposits and Treatment of Ducktown Copper-Ores." *Transactions of the American Institute of Mining Engineers* (xeroxed copy in my possession), pp. 173–245.

Hermelin, Samuel G. *Report about the Mines in the United States of America, 1783*. Translated by Amandus Johnson. Philadelphia: John Morton Memorial Museum, 1931.

Hodges, A. D. "Amalgamation at the Comstock Lode, Nevada, . . ." *Transactions of the American Institute of Mining Engineers,* 1890, 1891.

Holm, David, ed. *Water Quality and Mining.* Denver: Colorado Department of Health, Water Quality Control Division, 1979.

Homestake Mining Company: Annual Report, 1969, 1976, 1977, 1978, 1985. San Francisco, Calif.: Homestake Mining Co., 1970, 1977, 1978, 1979, 1986.

Homsher, Lola, ed. *South Pass, 1868: James Chisholm's Journal of the Wyoming Gold Rush.* Lincoln: University of Nebraska Press, 1960.

Hoover, Herbert. *Principles of Mining.* New York: Hill, 1909.

Howbert, Irving. *Memories of a Lifetime in the Pike's Peak Region.* New York: Putnam, 1925.

Hughes, Richard. *Pioneer Years in the Black Hills.* Glendale, Calif.: Arthur H. Clark, 1957.

The Humphreys Tunnel and Mining Company v. *Frank,* 46 Colo. 524, 105 P, 1093.

Hutchins, J. P. "Gold Dredging in 1905." *Engineering and Mining Journal,* Jan. 20, 1906, pp. 122–24.

———. "Tailing Disposal by Gold Dredges." *Engineering and Mining Journal,* Feb. 3, 1906, pp. 219–23.

Imboden, John D. *The Coal and Iron Resources of Virginia.* Richmond, Va.: Clemmitt & Jones, 1872.

Ingham, G. Thomas. *Digging Gold among the Rockies.* Philadelphia: Cottage Library, 1881.

Jackson, Daniel. "Strip Mining, Reclamation, and the Public." *Coal Age,* May, 1963, pp. 84–95.

Jackson, Helen Hunt. "O-Be-Joyful Creek and Poverty Gulch." *Atlantic Monthly,* Dec., 1883, pp. 753–62.

Janin, Charles. "Proposed Regulating of Gold Dredging." *Mining and Scientific Press,* Mar. 8, 1913, pp. 381–84.

Johnson, Ligon. "The History and Legal Phases of the Smoke Problem." *Transactions of the American Institute of Mining Engineers,* 1918, pp. 198–211.

Keating, William H. *Considerations upon the Art of Mining.* Philadelphia: Carey & Sons, 1821.

Keeler, Bronson C. *Leadville and Its Silver Mines.* Chicago: Perry Bros., 1879.

Kellar, Kenneth C. *Chambers Kellar: Distinguished Gentleman—Great Lawyer—Fiery Rebel.* Lead, S.Dak.: Seaton Publishing Co., 1975.

Kelley, Robert L. *Gold vs. Grain: The Hydraulic Mining Controversy in California's Sacramento Valley.* Glendale, Calif.: Arthur H. Clark, 1959.

Keyes, Winfield Scott. *Last Chance Bed-Rock Flume.* Helena, Mont.: Wilkinson & Ronan, 1868.

King, Clarence. *Mountaineering in the Sierra Nevada.* Reprint. New York: Lippincott, 1963.

Kulp, George. *Coal: Its Antiquity . . . in the Wyoming Valley.* Wilkes Barre, Pa.: Wyoming Historical & Geological Society, 1890.

Laist, Frederick. "An Address to Mining Students." *Mining and Scientific Press,* July 2, 1921, pp. 21–26.

Lake Superior Mining Institute. *Proceedings of the Lake Superior Mining Institute.* Ishpeming, Mich.: Lake Superior Mining Institute, 1923.

Leith, Charles K. "Conservation of Iron Ore." *Transactions of the American Institute of Mining Engineers,* 1914, pp. 79–83.

———. *The Mesabi Iron-Bearing District of Minnesota.* Washington, D.C.: Government Printing Office, 1903.

Leyendecker, Liston E., ed. "Young Man Gone West: George M. Pullman's Letters from the Colorado Goldfields." *Chicago History*, Winter 1978/79, pp. 208–25.

Lillard, Richard, ed. "A Literate Woman in the Mines: The Diary of Rachel Haskell." *Mississippi Valley Historical Review*, June, 1944, pp. 81–98.

Lokke, Carl. *Klondike Saga*. Minneapolis: University of Minnesota Press, 1965.

Lord, Eliot. *Comstock Mining and Miners*. Reprint. Berkeley, Calif.: Howell-North, 1959.

McClure, Alexander K. *Three Thousand Miles through the Rocky Mountains*. Philadelphia: Lippincott, 1869.

McCoy, Amasa. *Conversational Lecture on Mines and Mining in Colorado*. Chicago: International Mining & Exchange Co., 1871.

MacDonald, Bryce, and Moshe Weiss. "Impact of Environment Control Expenditures on Copper, Lead and Zinc Producers." *Mining Congress Journal*, Jan., 1978, pp. 45–50.

MacGregor, Ian. "Mining Needn't Be a Dirty Word." *Catalyst for Environmental Quality*, 1971 (?), pp. 25–27.

McKee, Lanier. *The Land of Nome*. New York: Grafton, 1902.

Marsh, George P. *The Earth as Modified by Human Action*. New York: C. Scribner's, 1885.

Mills, Enos. *The Rocky Mountain Wonderland*. Boston, Mass.: Houghton Mifflin, 1915.

Mining Act of May 10, 1872. San Francisco, Calif.: Frank Eastman, 1872.

Mining and Metallurgical Society of America. *Proceedings of the Mining and Metallurgical Society of America*. 1931–40.

Mining Debris. Marysville, Calif.: Anti-Debris Association, 1889.

Montana. *Proceedings and Debates of the Constitutional Convention*. Helena, Mont.: State Publishing, 1921.

Montana: The Most Productive Ore Center of the Inter-Mountain Region. Butte, Mont.: North American Industrial Review, 1904.

Montgomery, Hugh. "Conscientious Coal Stripping." *Coal Age*, July, 1962, pp. 84–88.

Morrison, Robert S., and Emilio de Soto. *Mining Rights on the Public Domain*. San Francisco, Calif.: Bender-Moss, 1917.

Morrison, Robert S., and Jacob Fillius. *Mining Rights in Colorado*. Denver, Colo.: Chain & Hardy, 1881.

Muir, John. *The Mountains of California*. 2 vols. New York: Houghton Mifflin, 1916.

———. *Steep Trails*. Boston, Mass.: Houghton Mifflin, 1918.

Narten, Perry F., et al. *Reclamation of Mined Lands in the Western Coal Region*. Washington, D.C.: United States Geological Survey, 1983.

National Mining and Industrial Exposition. *Programme for the First Annual Exhibition of the National Mining and Industrial Exposition*. Denver, Colo.: Tribune Publishing, 1882.

Northern Illinois Coal Corporation et al. v. Medill, Director of Mines and Minerals, 397 Ill. 98, 72 NE 2nd 844 (1947).

Osborn, Elburt. "Mining Industry Must Become Truly Concerned with Ecology." *Mines Magazine*, Aug., 1971, pp. 7–9.

Parsons, George W. *The Private Journal of George Whitwell Parsons*. Phoenix: Arizona Statewide Archival and Records Project, 1939.

Patton, Horace. *Geology and Ore Deposits of the Bonanza District*. Denver, Colo.: Eames, 1916.

The Pennsylvania Coal Company v. *Sanderson and Wife,* 113 Pa 126, 6A 453 (1886).
The People v. *Gold Run,* 66 Cal. 138.
Pinchot, Gifford. "Mining and the Forest Reserves." *Transactions of the American Institute of Mining Engineers,* 1898, pp. 339–46.
Pittsburgh and Boston Mining Co. Pittsburgh, Pa.: W. Haven, 1866.
"Pittsburgh Coal Company v. *Sanitary Water Board." Environmental Law Reporter,* 1972, pp. 20339–43.
Pliny the Elder. *The History of the World.* Translated by Philemon Holland. Carbondale: Southern Illinois University Press, 1962.
———. *Natural History.* Translated by Loyd Haberly. New York: Frederick Ungar, 1957.
Prospectus Leadville Lead Corporation. Denver, Colo. (?): n.p., 1952.
Prospectus of the Geological Survey and Report of the Gregory Gold Mining Company. New York: n.p., 1863.
Raymond, Rossiter W. *Camp and Cabin.* New York: Fords, Howard & Hulbert, 1880.
———. "Historical Sketch of Mining Law." *Mineral Resources of the United States, 1883–1884.* Washington, D.C.: Government Printing Office, 1885.
———. *Mineral Resources of the States and Territories.* 2 vols. Washington, D.C.: Government Printing Office, 1869 and 1873.
———. *Statistics of Mines and Mining.* Washington, D.C.: Government Printing Office, 1870, 1873.
"Responsible Strip Mining and Restoration." *Coal Age,* Jan., 1963, p. 28.
"Restoring Dredged Ground." *Engineering and Mining Journal,* May 8, 1909, pp. 946–47.
Rickard, Thomas A. *Across the San Juan Mountains.* New York: Engineering and Mining Journal, 1903.
———. *Interviews with Mining Engineers.* San Francisco, Calif.: Mining & Scientific Press, 1922.
———. *The Stamp Milling of Gold Ores.* New York: Scientific Publishing, 1897.
Ridler, Anne, ed. *Poems and Some Letters of James Thomson.* London: Centaur, 1963.
Rolle, Andrew D., ed. *The Road to Virginia City: The Diary of James Knox Polk Miller.* Norman: University of Oklahoma Press, 1960.
Root, Lloyd. *Report XXII of the State Mineralogist.* Sacramento: California State Printing Office, 1926.
———. *Report XXIII of the State Mineralogist.* Sacramento: California State Printing Office, 1927.
Roy, Andrew. *The Coal Mines . . . Ventilating Mines.* Cleveland, Ohio: Robison, Savage, 1876.
Rusling, James. *Across America: or The Great West and the Pacific Coast.* New York: Sheldon, 1874.
Schmidt, Richard. *Coal in America.* New York: McGraw-Hill, 1979.
Schoolcraft, Henry R. *Journal of a tour into the interior of Missouri and Arkansaw . . . .* London: W. Lewis, 1821.
———. *A View of the Lead Mines of Missouri; . . .* New York: Charles Wiley, 1819.
Slide Mines, Inc. v. *Left Hand Ditch Company et al.,* 102 Colo. 69, 77 P 2d 125.
Smelting Works: Objections to Certain Smelting Works in Populous Localities. Oakland, Calif.: n.p., 1872.
Spedden, H. Rush. "Impact of Environmental Controls on Nonferrous Metals Extraction." *Mining Congress Journal,* Dec., 1970, pp. 57–63.

"Spoil Reclamation: Assures Good Income without Leveling." *Coal Age,* July, 1946, pp. 91–94.

Stream Pollution Control. Washington, D.C.: Government Printing Office, 1947.

Stretch, Richard H. *The Laporte Gold Gravel Mines, Limited.* Glasgow: M'Corquodale, 1882.

———. *Placer Mines and Their Origin.* Seattle, Wash.: Lowman & Hanford, 1897.

———. *Report on the Cherokee Flat Blue Gravel and Spring Valley Mining and Irrigating Company's Property.* New York: Mining Record, 1879.

"Strip Mining Heals Its Own Scars." *Business Week,* Nov. 13, 1965, pp. 140–46.

"Strip Reclamation in Eastern Ohio." *Coal Age,* 1941, pp. 114–16.

Summering in Colorado. Denver, Colo.: Richards, 1874.

Taylor, Ronald A., and Gordon Witkin. "The Big Grab for Wild Lands." *Newsweek,* Apr. 28, 1986, pp. 68–69.

Tice, John. *Over the Plains, on the Mountains . . . .* St. Louis, Mo.: Industrial Age Printing, 1872.

Titus, Sara, ed. *This Is a Fine Day.* Long Beach, Calif.: Seaside Printing, 1959.

Twain, Mark. *Roughing It.* Hartford, Conn.: American Publishing, 1872.

United States. Bureau of the Census. *Abstract of the Eleventh Census: 1890.* Washington, D.C.: Government Printing Office, 1894.

United States. Senate. *Hearings before the Committee on Mines and Mining, United States Senate.* Washington, D.C.: Government Printing Office, 1918.

———. *Hearings before the Subcommittee on Air and Water Pollution.* 2 vols. Washington, D.C.: Government Printing Office, 1967.

United States Coal Commission. *Report of the United States Coal Commission.* 5 pts. Washington, D.C.: Government Printing Office, 1925.

United States National Conservation Commission. *Report of the National Conservation Commission.* 3 vols. Washington, D.C.: Government Printing Office, 1909.

"*United States* v. *Jellico Industries, Inc.*" *Environmental Reporter,* 1972, p. 20002.

Van Wagenen, T. F. *Manual of Hydraulic Mining.* Denver, Colo.: n.p., 1878.

Villard, Henry. *The Past and Present of the Pike's Peak Gold Regions.* Reprint. Princeton, N.J.: Princeton University Press, 1932.

Waldeyer, Charles. "Hydraulic Mining in California." *Mines and Mining.* Washington, D.C.: Government Printing Office, 1873, pp. 390–424.

Waldorf, John T. *A Kid on the Comstock.* Palo Alto, Calif.: American West, 1970.

Warriner, J. B. "Anthracite Stripping." *Transactions of the American Institute of Mining Engineers,* 1918, pp. 159–86.

Weatherbe, D'Arcy. *Dredging for Gold in California.* San Francisco, Calif.: Mining & Scientific Press, 1907.

Wheat, Carl, ed. *The Shirley Letters from the California Mines, 1851–1852.* New York: Alfred A. Knopf, 1970.

Whitney, Josiah D. *The Metallic Wealth of the United States described and compared with that of other countries.* Philadelphia: Lippincott, Grambo, 1854.

Wilmore et al. v. *Chain O'Mines, Inc., et al.,* 96 Colo. 319, 44 P 2d 1024.

Wilson, Eugene. *Hydraulic and Placer Mining.* New York: John Wiley & Sons, 1898.

Winchell, Horace V. "The Mesabi Iron-Range." *Transactions of the American Institute of Mining Engineers*, 1893, pp. 644–86.

Wood, J. P. *Report on Mine Tailing Pollution of Clear Creek, Clear Creek–Gilpin Counties, Colorado.* Denver, Colo.: n.p., 1935.

Woodruff v. *North Bloomfield*. Copy in Huntington Library.

Young, C. M. "Pollution of River Water in the Pittsburgh District." *American Water Works Association Journal*, May 8, 1921, pp. 201–17.

Yuba Levee Built to Protect the Farming Lands in Linda Township, Yuba County from the Hydraulic Tailings, The. San Francisco, Calif.: n.p., 1877.

SECONDARY SOURCES

Alenius, E. M. *A Brief History of the United Verde Open Pit, Jerome, Arizona.* Tucson: University of Arizona Press, 1968.

Alexander, Tom. "A Promising Try at Environmental Detente." *Fortune*, Feb. 13, 1978, pp. 94–102.

American Law of Mining, The. New York: Matthew Bender, 1979.

Barringer, Daniel, and John S. Adams. *The Law of Mines and Mining in the United States.* St. Paul, Minn.: Keefe-Davidson, 1900.

Bibliography on Mined-Land Reclamation. Washington, D.C.: United States Department of the Interior, 1979.

Billinger, Robert D. *Pennsylvania's Coal Industry.* Gettysburg: Pennsylvania Historical Association, 1954.

Bishop, Freeman. "Environmentalism, Creating Crunch on Coal Industry." *Mining Congress Journal*, Feb., 1973, pp. 110–13.

Bramble, W. C. "Strip Mining: Waste or Conservation?" *American Forests*, June, 1949, pp. 24–25 and 42–43.

Brown, Ronald C. *Hard-Rock Miners: The Intermountain West, 1860–1920.* College Station: Texas A & M University Press, 1979.

Carson, Rachel L. *Silent Spring.* Boston, Mass.: Houghton Mifflin, 1962.

Case, Earl C. *The Valley of East Tennessee: The Adjustment of Industry to Natural Environment.* Nashville, Tenn.: Department of Education, 1925.

Caudill, Harry M. *My Land Is Dying.* New York: E. P. Dutton, 1971.

———. *Night Comes to the Cumberlands.* Boston: Little, Brown, 1963.

———. *The Watches of the Night.* Boston: Little, Brown, 1976.

Charlton, Edwin A. *New Hampshire As It Is.* Claremont, N.H.: Tracy & Sanford, 1855.

"Clash along the Yellowstone: Coal vs. Moose, A." *Business Week*, June 18, 1979, p. 152.

"Coal: A $4-billion Victim of the Environmental Movement." *Forbes*, Nov. 15, 1972, pp. 32–42.

Conaway, James. "The Last of the West: Hell, Strip It!" *Atlantic*, Sept., 1973, pp. 91–103.

Congress and the Nation. Vols. 1 and 2. Washington, D.C.: Congressional Quarterly Service, 1969.

Cousins, Norman. "Fouling the Air." *Saturday Review*, Oct. 8, 1966, pp. 32 and 123.

Davies, J. Clarence. *The Politics of Pollution.* New York: Pegasus, 1970.

Dedera, Don. "Preserving Wyoming's Past." *Exxon USA*, no. 2 (1979), pp. 3–7.

"Defending the Land." *New Republic*, Nov. 20, 1976, pp. 10–12.

Dietz, Donald. "Stripmining for Western Coal: Not Necessarily Bad." *Journal of Range Management*, May, 1975, pp. 244–45.

Direct Use of Coal, The. Washington, D.C.: Government Printing Office, ca. 1979.

Eavenson, Howard. *The First Century and a Quarter of American Coal Industry.* Pittsburgh, Pa.: Waverly, 1942.

Ekirch, Arthur A., Jr. *Man and Nature in America.* New York: Columbia University Press, 1963.

Ellis, Erl. *The Gold Dredging Boats around Breckenridge, Colorado.* Boulder, Colo.: Johnson Publishing, 1967.

"EPA Is in a Bind in West Virginia, The." *Business Week*, Sept., 1976, p. 30.

EXXON ad. *Sports Illustrated*, Oct. 16, 1978, p. 89.

Feeney, Ann. "Who's Getting the Shaft?" *Colorado Business*, Feb., 1978, pp. 13–18.

Fell, James E., Jr. *Ores to Metals: The Rocky Mountain Smelting Industry.* Lincoln: University of Nebraska Press, 1980.

Frazer, Persifor. "Bibliography of Injuries to Vegetation by Furnace-Gases." *Transactions of the American Institute of Mining Engineers*, 1908, pp. 520–55.

Frome, Michael. "Conservation: The Trouble with Mining." *Field and Stream*, Dec., 1968, p. 22.

———. "Editorial." *American Forests*, Sept., 1967, pp. 3, 44, and 46.

Galperin, Si. "Against Surface Mining." *Coal Age*, Mar., 1971, p. 98.

Garraty, John A. *The New Commonwealth.* New York: Harper, 1968.

Gordon, Suzanne. *Black Mesa: The Angel of Death.* New York: John Day, 1973.

Graebner, William. *Coal-Mining Safety in the Progressive Period.* Lexington: University Press of Kentucky, 1976.

Green, Fletcher M. "Gold Mining: A Forgotten Industry of Ante-Bellum North Carolina." *North Carolina Historical Review*, Jan., 1937, pp. 1–19.

Greever, William S. *The Bonanza West.* Norman: University of Oklahoma Press, 1963.

Gunnison County, Colorado. Pitkin, Colo.: Nelson, ca. 1917.

Harris, Theodore L., et al. *Into Wide Worlds.* Oklahoma City, Okla.: Economy Co., 1965.

Hawley, James H., ed. *History of Idaho.* Vol. 1. Chicago: S. J. Clarke, 1920.

Henderson. Denver, Colo. (?): AMAX, ca. 1978.

Hopton, W. *Conversation on Mines.* Manchester, Eng.: Heywood, 1891.

Horwitz, Morton. *The Transformation of American Law, 1780–1860.* Cambridge: Harvard University Press, 1977.

Indiana Coal Producers Association. *Story of Open Cut Mining in Indiana, The.* N.p.: Indiana Coal Producers Association, 1940.

Indivisibly One. Washington, D.C.: Department of the Interior, 1973.

Jillson, Willard. *The Coal Industry in Kentucky.* Franklin, Ky.: State Journal, 1922.

Josephson, Matthew. *The Robber Barons.* New York: Harcourt, 1962.

Kentucky. Department of Natural Resources. *Strip Mining in Kentucky.* Lexington: Kentucky Department of Natural Resources, 1965.

Kneese, Allen V., and Charles L. Schultze. *Pollution, Prices, and Public Policy.* Washington, D.C.: Brookings Institution, 1975.

Lake, James A. *Law and Mineral Wealth: The Legal Profile of the Wisconsin Mining Industry.* Madison: University of Wisconsin Press, 1962.

Lamar, Howard, ed. *Reader's Encyclopedia of the American West*. New York: Thomas Y. Crowell, 1977.

Lieder, Paul R., et al., eds. *British Poetry and Prose*. Vol. 1. Boston, Mass.: Houghton Mifflin, 1950.

Lindley, Curtis H. *A Treatise on the American Law Relating to Mines and Mineral Lands*. 2 vols. San Francisco, Calif.: Bancroft-Whitney, 1903.

Lingenfelter, Richard E. *The Hardrock Miners*. Berkeley: University of California Press, 1974.

Liroff, Richard A. *A National Policy for the Environment: NEPA and Its Aftermath*. Bloomington: Indiana University Press, 1976.

Livesay, Harold C., and Glenn Porter. "William Savery and the Wonderful Parsons Smoke-Eating Machine." *Delaware History*, Apr., 1971, pp. 161–76.

McCarthy, G. Michael. *Hour of Trial*. Norman: University of Oklahoma Press, 1977.

McCullough, David G. "The Lonely War of a Good Angry Man." *American Heritage*, Dec., 1969, pp. 97–113.

MacDonald, George. *Poetical Works of George MacDonald*. 2 vols. London: Chatto & Windus, 1893.

McDowell, Edwin. "The Shootout over Western Coal." *Wall Street Journal*, June 21, 1974, p. 10.

Malone, Michael P., ed. *Historians and the American West*. Lincoln: University of Nebraska Press, 1983.

———. "Midas of the West: The Incredible Career of William Andrews Clark." *Montana*, Autumn 1983, pp. 2–17.

Marcosson, Isaac F. *Anaconda*. New York: Dodd, Mead, 1957.

Marks, Geoffrey, and William K. Beatty. *The Story of Medicine in America*. New York: Charles Scribner's, 1973.

Merchant, Carolyn. *The Death of Nature*. San Francisco, Calif.: Harper & Row, 1980.

Miller, Arnold. "The Energy Crisis as a Coal Miner Sees It." *Center Magazine*, Nov./Dec., 1973, pp. 35–45.

"Mining Threatens the Porcupines." *Nature Magazine*, Oct., 1958, p. 399.

Modern Mining and Milling Practice. New York: Engineering and Mining Journal, ca. 1940.

Monroe, George. "Mining and the Environment." *Mining Congress Journal*, Sept., 1973, pp. 32–38.

Montana Copper. Helena, Mont. (?): Anaconda Copper, 1979.

Moore, Elwood. *Coal: Its Properties . . . Distribution*. New York: John Wiley, 1922.

Mumford, Lewis. *Technics and Civilization*. New York: Harcourt, Brace, 1934.

Nash, Roderick, ed. *The American Environment*. Reading, Mass.: Addison-Wesley, 1976.

———. *Wilderness and the American Mind*. New Haven, Conn.: Yale University Press, 1973.

Newell, Louis. "Miners: Once It Was All Theirs." *San Juan Journal* (Durango, Colo.), Nov. 14, 1979, p. 4.

New Ideas in Coal Mining. New York: Coal Age, 1917.

Our Environment. Salt Lake City, Utah: Kennecott, ca. 1979.

Our Environment . . . Doing about It. Philadelphia: Westmoreland Coal, ca. 1978.

Paul, Rodman. *Mining Frontiers of the Far West, 1848–1880.* New York: Holt, Rinehart & Winston, 1963.

Peele, Robert. *Mining Engineers' Handbook.* New York: Wiley, 1918.

Petty, Patricia C. "A Tale of Two Mining Towns." *Denver Post,* July 12, 1981.

Petulla, Joseph M. *American Environmental History.* San Francisco, Calif.: Boyd & Fraser, 1977.

Potter, David M. *People of Plenty.* Chicago: University of Chicago Press, 1954.

Powell, John J. *Nevada: The Land of Silver.* San Francisco, Calif.: Bacon, 1876.

Quest for Quality. Washington, D.C.: Department of the Interior, 1965.

Rickard, Thomas A. *A History of American Mining.* New York: McGraw-Hill, 1932.

———. *Man and Metals.* 2 vols. Reprint. New York: Arno, 1974.

Ross, Malcolm. *Machine Age in the Hills.* New York: Macmillan, 1933.

Sawin, Herbert. "Dredging: An Evolving Art." *Mining World,* Jan., 1949, pp. 37–39.

Service, Robert. *Ballads of a Cheechako.* Toronto: William Briggs, 1909.

Shamel, Charles. *Mining, Mineral and Geological Law.* New York: Hill, 1907.

Sheridan, David. *Hard Rock Mining on the Public Land.* Washington, D.C.: Government Printing Office, 1977.

Spence, Clark. "Golden Age of Dredging: The Development of an Industry and Its Environmental Impact." *Western Historical Quarterly,* Oct., 1980, pp. 401–14.

———. *Mining Engineers and the American West.* New Haven, Conn.: Yale University Press, 1970.

Successful Operating Ideas for Mine-Mill and Smelter. New York: Engineering and Mining Journal, 1936.

Sullivan, G. D. "A Voluntary Industry Program for Mined-Land Conservation." *Illinois Mining Institute Proceedings,* 1963, pp. 85–94.

Surface, Bill. *The Hollow.* New York: Coward-McCann, 1971.

"Surface Mining Issue: A Reasoned Response, The." *Coal Age,* Mar., 1971, pp. 92–95.

Tanzer, Michael. *The Race for Resources: Continuing Struggles over Minerals and Fuels.* New York: Monthly Review Press, 1980.

Thames, John, ed. *Reclamation and Use of Disturbed Land in the Southwest.* Tucson: University of Arizona Press, 1977.

Thornburg, Ashley A. "Surface Mine Reclamation in Montana." *Second Research and Applied Technology Symposium on Mined-Land Reclamation.* Washington, D.C.: National Coal Association, 1974.

Tillman, David. "Environmentally-Sensitive Plants Require Early Public Disclosure." *Area Development,* June, 1972, pp. 14 and 20.

Toole, K. Ross. *The Rape of the Great Plains: Northwest America, Cattle and Coal.* New York: Atlantic Monthly, 1976.

United States Forest Service. *Anatomy of a Mine: From Prospect to Production.* Ogden, Utah: United States Forest Service, 1977.

Van Coevering, Jack. "The Porcupines and Copper." *Nature Magazine,* Nov., 1958, pp. 482–85.

Van Hise, Charles R. *The Conservation of Natural Resources in the United States.* New York: Macmillan, 1910.

Vietor, Richard. *Environmental Politics and the Coal Coalition.* College Station: Texas A & M University Press, 1980.

Wall, Joseph. *Andrew Carnegie.* New York: Oxford University Press, 1970.

Watkins, T. H. "Thinking Little." *American Heritage,* Oct./Nov., 1979, pp. 38–39.

Western Resources Conference. Golden: Colorado School of Mines, 1971.

What Mining Means to Americans. Washington, D.C.: American Mining Congress, ca. 1976.

What Mining Means to You. Cleveland, Ohio: Pickands Mather, ca. 1978.

Wiebe, Robert. *Businessmen and Reform: A Study of the Progressive Movement.* Reprint. Quadrangle Books, 1968.

Wiley, Farida A., ed. *Theodore Roosevelt's America.* New York: Doubleday, 1962.

Woodruff, Seth D. *Methods of Working Coal and Metal Mines.* Vol. 3. New York: Pergamon, 1966.

Wyman, Mark. *Hard-Rock Epic.* Berkeley: University of California Press, 1979.

Young, Lewis H. "Public Reputation of the Mining Industry." *Mining Congress Journal,* Jan., 1972, pp. 37–40.

Young, Otis E. *Western Mining.* Norman: University of Oklahoma Press, 1970.

INDEX

Abbott, Emma, 76
Abdnor, Joseph, 146
Agricola, Georgius, 27, 121
Agriculture: opposes mining, 117–19.
  See also California; Hydraulic mining
Alabama, 120, 141
Alaska: gold rush in, 17; coal lands in,
  90; dredging in, 91
Albright, Horace, 122
AMAX, 166; environmental program of,
  157; at Crested Butte, Colo., 159–60,
  163
Anaconda, Mont., 79, 165; and pollu-
  tion, 95–96
Anaconda Mining Co., 156; and pollu-
  tion controversy, 95–96; closes
  smelter, 165. *See also* Butte, Mont.
Animals: mining's impact on, 15
Appalachia: mining's impact on, 140,
  141, 143, 150
Aubury, Lewis, 93
Auraria, Ga., 15, 120
Austin, Nev., 55
Australia: dredging in, 91, 93

Baker, G. W., 50
Bannack, Mont., 29, 38
Barbour, Ian G., 137
Barnes, Demas, 55
Bartlesville, Okla., 152
Bennett, Estelline, 44
Berkeley Pit, Mont., 76
Bird, Allan, 155
Bird, Isabella, 61
Birmingham, Ala., 120
Bituminous Coal Research Laboratory,
  145
Black Hawk, Colo., 94, 139; pollution in,
  11–12
Bodie, Calif., 16
Booming, 7–8, 59
Bowles, Samuel, 9
Boyer, James, 146
Breckenridge, Colo., 9
Brewer, William, 11; visits Buckskin Joe,
  21
Brier Patch Mine, Lumpkin, Ga., 73

Brockett, Linus, 6
Browne, J. Ross, 136; on pollution, 11;
  on waste, 16; on placering, 29; and
  environmental concern, 54; and con-
  servation, 64–65; ideas of, 84
Browning, Robert, 124
Bureau of Mines, U.S., 89–90, 122
Burgettstown, Pa., 128
Butler, Charles, 117–18
Butte, Mont.: smoke pollution in, 11,
  75–80, 94–95; and benefits of smelter
  smoke, 45–46

California: gold rush in, 1; hydraulic
  mining in, 7; and John Muir, 8–9;
  hydraulic fight in, 67–73; smoke pollu-
  tion in, 74–75, 182 n. 37; dredging
  fight in, 91–94; of the 1930s, 109
Callahan, Donald, 131
Callbreath, J. F., 90
Caribou, Colo., 55
Carlin, R. S., 145, 147
Carnegie, Andrew, 52, 88; on exhaus-
  tion of minerals, 83
Carter, Bernard T., 140
Case, Earl, 98
Cats, 76
Caudill, Harry, 136, 142, 150
Central City, Colo., 8; bad water in,
  9–10; mining's impact on, 61
Channing, J. Parke, 98
Chase, Charles: on environmental
  awareness, 118, 129–31
Chinese miners, 73, 92
Chisholm, James, 44
Clappe, Louise Amelia. *See* Dame
  Shirley
Clark, Henry H., 6, 28
Clark, Joseph, 115
Clark, William A.: on mining people,
  29–30; on mining's benefits to Butte,
  Mont., 45; defends mining, 82
Clemens, Samuel. *See* Twain, Mark
Clifford, Henry, 91
Coal mining: and pollution, 101–2;
  damage to, 123; defended, 144. *See
  also* Appalachia; Pennsylvania
Colby, William, 122

Colorado: gold rush in, 1; stream pollution in, 116–18, 138, 139. *See also* Black Hawk, Colo.; Central City, Colo.; Leadville, Colo.; Silverton, Colo.
Colorado Fuel and Iron Co., 88
Compleat Collier, The, 27
Comstock silver rush, 1. *See also* Nevada; Virginia City, Nev.; Wright, William
Connecticut, 46
Conservation, 57; mining efforts toward, 64–65; and fear of mineral exhaustion, 81–82; mining's views on, 83–84; mining supports, 85–86; Woodrow Wilson on, 89, 90. *See also* Environment
Corning, Frederick, 31; on life of a mine, 59
Couch, Thomas, 77
Courts, 63; support mining, 47–50; and water law, 50
Cousins, Norman, 144–45
Coxe, Eckley B., 62
Crampton, Frank, 88
Creede, Colo., 117
Crested Butte, Colo., 159–60, 163
Crichton, Andrew, 114
Crowell, John, 164

Daddow, Samuel, 59
Dahlonega, Ga., 5–6, 14
Daly, George, 34
Dame Shirley (pseud. of Louise Amelia Clappe), 39; on littering, 15–16; on noise, 18; on mining life, 32–33
Day, Harry, 105
Dempsey, Stanley, 164
Denver: smoke pollution in, 12, 100
De Quille, Dan. *See* Wright, William
Dern, George, 99
Dickinson, Sam, 132–33
Donne, John, 26
Dorrence, Charles, 114
Doten, Alfred, 44
Douglas, James, 91
Dredging: efficiency of, 59; and pollution, 91–93; promotion of, 108; protested, 131; remains of, 138
Ducktown, Tenn.: pollution in, 11, 96–98, 99

East Helena, Mont., 112–13
Eisenhower, Dwight D., 134
Ekirch, Arthur A., xi
Ellis, Anne, 44
Ely, Richard, 85
Ely, Nev., 160

Emmons, Samuel, 58
England: smelter pollution in, 74, 77
Environment: definition of, 3; reasons for ignoring, 40–41, 52; concern for, 54–56; and reformers, 60–61, 62, 66; and dredging, 93; waning interest in, 107–8; rising interest in, 125, 133–35; issue of, in 1960s, 136–37, 147; impact of 1970s on, 149, 155, 156; and AMAX, 157
Environmental Protection Agency, 136–37, 164
Errol, N.H., 151
Eveleth, Minn., 87
Exxon, 156

Featherstonhaugh, George: visits Missouri, 5, Georgia, 5–6, North Carolina, 6, Wisconsin, 20
Fergus, James, 38
Fish: mining's impact on, 14–15
Florida, 142
Foote, Mary Hallock: as poet, 4; on quicksilver mining, 8
Forests: mining's impact on, 12–13. *See also* Pollution; Raymond, Rossiter
Franklin County Coal Operators Association (Ky.), 89
Frome, Mike, 153
Frontier: capitalist, xii; role of, in mining, 1–4, 21–22, 24; impact of end of, 81, 105

Galena, Ill., 10
Garnett, Louis, 72
Georgia, 120; placer mining in, 5–6; water pollution in, 10; hydraulic mining in, 73; protests pollution, 97, 98; mining controversy in, 142
Germany: smelter pollution in, 74, 77
Goldfield, Nev., 88
Government, 63–64. *See also* United States Government; *and individual states*
Graham, William, 28
Gregg, Josiah, 5
Grinnell, Joseph, 17

Hague, James D., 39, 45; on mining engineers, 38
Hamilton, Colo., 15
Hammond, John Hays, 82; on exhaustion of resources, 83; on conservation, 89; and fumes committee, 96; on coal, 109
Hanks, Henry, 59

Hard-rock mining, 8, 146–47. *See also* Mining
Harrison, Benjamin: on forests, 55–56
Hart, Gary, 170
Hartke, Vance, xi
Harvey, Charles, 9, 12
Haywood, Bill, 79
Hazard, Ky., 141
Hechler, Ken, 150
Helena, Mont., 59
Hendricks, Tom, 187 n. 8
Henrich, Carl, 11
Hermelin, Samuel, 27
Hewitt, Abram S., 64
Hill, Nathaniel, 28; is shocked by waste, 16; and appreciation of scenery, 42
Hillman, James, 128
History: its impact on mining, xii, 4, 24, 103–4, 168, 169
Hittell, John, 67
Hodges, A. D., 35
Homestake Mining Co., 57, 119, 156, 165
Hoover, Herbert, 88
Houghton, Mich., 100
Howbert, Irving, 15
Hughes, Richard, 28, 119
Hutchins, J. P., 92
Hydraulic mining: impact of, 6–7; controversy about, 67–73; demise of, 108–9. *See also* California; Mining

Illinois: receives mining's blessings, 33; and coal mining, 34; and strip mining, 110, 112, 126–28, 152
Imboden, John D., 33
Indiana, 36, 102; Sullivan County, 101; strip mining in, 109–10, 184 n. 3
Indiana Coal Producers Association, 110, 111
Indian Bar, Calif., 15, 16
Iowa, 167

Jackson, Helen Hunt, 155; on mining's values, 60–61
Jamestown, N.C., 6
Janin, Charles, 92
Japan: copper pollution in, 80
Jeremiah, 54
Jerome, Ariz., 108
Johnson, Ligon, 102
Johnson, Lyndon B., 141
Jones, John P., 42

Kansas, 119; strip mining in, 152
Keating, William, 33
Kellar, Chambers, 119

Kellar, Kenneth, 119
Kennecott Minerals Co., 156
Kentucky, 140; strip mining in, 110, 112, 120–21, 129; Appalachia, 141, 142, 143; reclamation in, 154
Kentucky Reclamation Association, 129
Keyes, Winfield Scott: on placer waste, 59; on hydraulic mining, 67–68
King, Clarence, 169; on mining fever, 35; in praise of mining, 36–37; on nature, 62
Knoxville, Tenn., 108

Laissez faire, 61, 63–64, 113, 147–48
Laist, Frederick, 112
Lake Superior Mining Institute, 107
Land: and profit motive, xi, xii, 5; attitude toward, 66; stewardship of, 169. *See also* Conservation; Environment
Leadville, Colo., 11, 31
Lee, Joseph, 143
Leith, Charles, 85–86
Lindgren, Waldemar, 84
Lingle, Benson, 144
Livermore, Robert, 103
Lord, Eliot: on wood consumption, 13; on shareholders, 35; on waste, 46
Lovilia, Iowa, 167

McClure, Alexander, 10
McCoy, Amasa, 43
MacGregor, Ian, 157
Mackenzie, John, 11
Magnuson, Harry F., 165
Malone, Michael, xii
Marsh, Benjamin, 15
Marsh, George P.: and mining disturbance, 177 n. 8
Marysville, Calif., 31, 51; hydraulic problems in, 68, 70, 72
Mather, Stephen T., 122
Mathewson, Edward, 125
Merchant, Carolyn, 165
Mesabi Range (Minn.), 103; mining modernized in, 86–88
Michigan, 103; copper in, 34, 100; gold in, 120; Porcupine Park, 133–34
Miller, Arnold, 140
Miller, James, 38
Milling: and waste, 46; and smoke, 58, 94–96, 97–99, 100–101, 140; and pollution, 74–75; in Butte, Mont., 75–79; complaints against, 182 n. 37
Mills, Enos A., 81–82
Milton, John, 26
Mineral Point, Wis., 20

Minerals: fears of exhaustion of, 82–84, 158–59, 163

Miners: treatment of, 18; definition of, 30; hard life of, 32; coal, 33; Chinese, 73, 92; strikes by, 90; image of, 91; denounced, 137

Mining: significance of, 2, 3, 25–26, 168, 169, 170; booming, 7–8; wastefulness of, 15–18, 20; transitory nature of, 19–20; attacks on, 26–27; future of, 31–32; glamorized, 32–34; investors in, 35–36; pioneer mystique of, 39–40; and appreciation of land, 42–44; and pollution as advantage, 45–46; placer, 49–50; defense of, 50–51, 131–34, 143–44; and small owners vs. corporations, 56–57, 73; and waste, 58–59, 65; and technological change, 59; values of, 60–61; and reclamation, 63, 93–94, 110–12; hydraulic, 67–74; defends pollution, 79–80, 82; on conservation, 85–86, 89; corporation dominance of, 88; changes image, 90; and dredging, 91–93; and automobile, 103; in 1920s, 108; in depression era, 108–9; and stream pollution, 113–19; impact of, on international market, 123; is hurt by tourism, 123; as the "good life," 126; and national security, 132; attacked, 140–42; and tourism, 139; collapse of defense of, 145–46; 1970s defense of, 149–50, 151–52, 153–56; changed attitude toward, 158, 159; impact of 1970s on, 161; in 1980s, 163, 165; shares guilt for environmental damage, 168–69. See also Conservation; History; Pollution

Mining communities, 19. See also individual communities

Mining engineers, 35; training of, 37–38, 58; advice to, 88; and environment, 107, 152, 158

Mining law: state, 23, 47; district, 23–24; United States, 47; damnum absque injuria, 49, 58. See also individual cases

Minnesota, 151; Mesabi Range in, 36, 86–88, 103; and reclamation, 132–33

Missouri: lead mines in, 5; roads in, 14; lead mining in, 119

Monroe, Ga., 154

Montana, 2, 44; placer mining in, 6. See also Anaconda, Mont.; Butte, Mont.; Virginia City, Mont.

Montgomery, Hugh, 144

Moore, Elwood, 107

Muir, John, 81; on mining, 8–9, 21; forest plan of, 56

Mumford, Lewis, 121

Murphy's Camp, Calif., 29

National Conservation Commission: report of, 83–84

National Mining and Industrial Exposition, 31

Nevada: Comstock, 1, 11–12; Muir describes, 8; Ely, 160

New Almaden Mine, 8

New Deal, 113–14, 119, 121–22

New Hampshire, 31, 151

New Jersey, 27, 100

New Mexico: Spanish mining in, 5

New York, N.Y., 100, 101

New Zealand: dredging in, 91–92, 93; coal in, 102

North Carolina, 28, 97; placer mining in, 6

Oakland, Calif., 74–75, 77

Ohio, 58; Division of Forestry, 93–94; strip mining in, 112

Oklahoma, 119, 152

Oregon: stream pollution in, 118–19

Osborn, Elburt, 151, 152

Palmer, Charles, 78

Park City, Utah, 99

Parsons, George, 32

Parsons, John: his "smoke eating machine," 101

Peele, Robert, 108

Pennsylvania, 127; coal in, 6; water pollution in, 10; and lost barges, 16; and steam shovels, 36; and Sanderson case, 48–49; and pollution, 60, 102–3, 114–16; coal, 110, 139; strip mining in, 112, 126; reclamation in, 128–29

Pennsylvania Coal Company v. Sanderson and Wife, 48–49

People, The, v. Gold Run, 179n. 12

Perkins, Henry C., 72

Petty, Patricia, 160

Pike's Peak rush, 1

Pinchot, Gifford: on forests, 56, 57

Pliny the Elder, 26

Pogo (comic strip character), quoted, xi

Pollution: water, 9–11, 57, 70–73, 102–3, 113–16; air, 11–12; impact of, on birds, animals, 14–15; littering, 15–16; natural, 49–50; smoke, 58, 74–75, 94–99, 100–101, 102, 140; visual, 59–61; in Butte, Mont., 75–80; by dredging, 91–93

Porcupine Mountains State Park, 133–34

Potter, David, xii

Pottsville, Pa., 29, 31
Progressive Era, 84, 90
Prospectors, 30, 140
Prunes (cartoon character), 149–50
Pullman, George, 18

Quality of life, 134–35, 160–61; in California, 69–70. *See also* Conservation; Environment
Quigley, Jim, 145

Raymond, Rossiter, 136; on booming, 7–8; is concerned about waste, 13, 46; on ditches, 14; and mining education, 38; on timber, 45, 55; on waste, 62; on laissez faire, 63–64
Reagan, Ronald, 164
Reclamation: by mining, 93–94, 110–12, 128–29, 154; on Urad project, 166; at Star Coal Mine, 167; in Midwest, 167
Rickard, T. A.: evaluates mine, xi; on hunting, 15; defends mining, 27–28; on water utilization, 57; on history, 122
Rico, Colo., 62
Roads: impact of, 13–14
Robart, Herbert, 77
Rockefeller, John D., 52, 88
Rock Springs, Wyo., 160
Rockwell, John, 34
Roosevelt, Franklin D., 113
Roosevelt, Theodore, 81; on conservation, 82, 83
Ross, Malcolm, 120–21
Roy, Andrew, 58
Rusling, James, 8, 31; describes miners, 32; on reclamation, 63

Salt Lake City, Utah, 98–99
Sanderson, Eliza, 48, 49
Sanderson, J. Gardiner, 48–49
San Francisco, Calif., 100
Sargeant, F. E., 45
Schmidt, Richard, 156
Schoolcraft, Henry Rowe: visits Missouri, 5; on pollution, 11; on roads, 14; on botanical changes, 57
Scranton, Pa., 102, 109
Service, Robert, 91
Shirley. *See* Dame Shirley
Sierra Club, 146, 149
Silver Plume, Colo., 63
Silverton, Colo., 15, 118, 129
Smelting: and pollution, 11–12; and waste, 16, 21; and noise, 18. *See also* Pollution

South Dakota: stream pollution in, 119
South Pass, Wyo., 138
"Spaceship Earthers," 154–55
Spenser, Edmund, 26
Sprague, Charles, 88
Star Coal Mine (Iowa), 167
Streams: mining's impact on, 9–11. *See also* Pollution; Water
Stretch, Richard, 65, 72
Strip mining: impact of, 109–11, 120–21, 129; protest about, 126–28, 142; in Appalachia, 141; defended, 143–44. *See also* Mining
Sugar Loaf District (Colo.), 23–24
Sullivan County, Ind., 101–2
Symms, Steve, 164

Tabor, Horace, 31
Technology: impact of, on nineteenth-century mining, 6–8, 17–18; impact of, on miners, 19; American advances in, 36–37. *See also* Mining
Tennessee: copper pollution in, 96–98
Texas, 152
Thomson, James, 61
Tice, John, 16; on timber loss, 55; on waste 58
Timber: waste of, 55, 62; in national forests, 55–56; protection of, 62; exhaustion of, 81; impact of pollution on, 96, 97. *See also* Conservation; Raymond, Rossiter
Toole, K. Ross, 66
Trivoli, Ill., 152
Turner, J. E., 109, 111
Twain, Mark, 10; on noise, 18; and mining fever, 28; and Tahoe fire, 43

Udall, Stewart L., 146
United States, Bureau of Mines, 89–90, 122
United States Government: aids mining, 46–47; mining opposes, 84; involvement of, in mining, 89–90; impact of World War I on, 105; and New Deal, 113–14; impact of World War II on, 124–25; and uranium, 125; as mining's partner, 132; its involvement with mining, 136–37, 145–46; regulations of, 146, 150, 152; and oil shale, 158–59; changes in policy of, 164, 165
Urad Mine (Colo.), 157, 166
Uranium mining: federal role in, 125
Utah, 156; and smoke pollution, 98–99

Van Hise, Charles, 85
Vegetation: impact of mining on, 57–58

Virginia, 33; Walton Mine in, 34
Virginia City, Mont., 6, 38–39
Virginia City, Nev., 28, 30, 57; and
    water pollution, 11; Mark Twain on,
    18; mining dumps in, 59

Waldorf, John, 46
Warriner J. B., 109, 110
Water: and stream pollution, 113–19. See
    also California; Colorado; Hydraulic
    mining; Pennsylvania
Water law, 50, 57
Watt, James, 164, 165
Weatherbe, D'Arcy, 93
Weible, L. E., 168
Wells, Bulkeley, 84
Wells, David, 52
West Virginia, 141; coal in, 102; strip
    mining in, 112, 120–21, 150
Whitney, Josiah, 55
Wilkes-Barre, Pa., 102

Williams, Henry, 78
Wilson, Eugene, 73–74
Wilson, James, 153
Wilson, Woodrow, 89, 90
Wisconsin, 47
Woodruff, Edward, 69, 71
Woodruff v. North Bloomfield, et al., 69–73
World War I, 105, 107
World War II, 124–25
Wright, William: his concern about
    timbering, 12, 13; on quicksilver
    waste, 16; on noise, 18; on mining
    dumps, 59
W. W. Wilmore, et al. v. Chain O'Mines,
    Inc., et al., 117–18
Wyoming, 65, 160; South Pass, 138;
    strip mining in, 152–53

Yeatman, Pope, 34
Yoffe, Franklin, 151
Young, C. M., 115